PENGUIN BOOKS

EPICS OF EVERYDAY LIFE

Susan Richards trained as a journalist before completing her doctorate on Aleksandr Solzhenitsyn. She has produced four films for David Puttnam and lives in London with her husband, the director and writer Roger Graef.

SUSAN RICHARDS

EPICS OF
EVERYDAY LIFE

*Encounters in a
Changing Russia*

PENGUIN BOOKS

PENGUIN BOOKS
Published by the Penguin Group
Viking Penguin, a division of Penguin Books USA Inc.,
375 Hudson Street, New York, New York 10014, U.S.A.
Penguin Books Ltd, 27 Wrights Lane,
London W8 5TZ, England
Penguin Books Australia Ltd, Ringwood,
Victoria, Australia
Penguin Books Canada Ltd, 10 Alcorn Avenue, Suite 300,
Toronto, Ontario, Canada M4V 3B2
Penguin Books (N.Z.) Ltd, 182–190 Wairau Road,
Auckland 10, New Zealand

Penguin Books Ltd, Registered Offices:
Harmondsworth, Middlesex, England

First published in Great Britain by Penguin Books Ltd 1990
First published in the United States of America by
Viking Penguin, a division of Penguin Books USA Inc., 1991
Published in Penguin Books 1992

1 3 5 7 9 10 8 6 4 2

THE LIBRARY OF CONGRESS HAS CATALOGUED THE HARDCOVER AS FOLLOWS:
Richards, Susan, 1950–
Epics of everyday life: encounters in a changing Russia/Susan
Richards.
p. cm.
ISBN 0–670–82743–6 (hc.)
ISBN 0 14 01.6929 6 (pbk.)
1. Russian S.F.S.R.—Description and travel. 2. Azerbaijan
S.S.R.—Description and travel. 3. Richards, Susan, 1950– —
Journeys—Russian S.F.S.R. 4. Richards, Susan, 1950– —Journeys—
Azerbaijan S.S.R. 5. Soviet Union—Politics and government—1985–
I. Title.
DK510.29.R53 1991
947.085'4—dc20 90–50578

Printed in the United States of America

To Roger, for all his love and support

Contents

Acknowledgements

The support system behind this book was unfailing. Roger Graef, my husband and most valued critic, carried the family during my absences. My parents gave me the curiosity to explore. My agent Toby Eady believed in me. From Peter Carson, my editor, I gained the confidence to write in my own voice. Celina Fox corrected the proofs with meticulous care. But it was my Russian family, Elena, Grisha and Ira, whose adoption of me, a stranger from abroad, changed this book and my life. I owe my deep thanks to all of them.

Prologue

Occasionally, a political event has the power to affect us, as did the assassination of President Kennedy, with the force of personal tragedy. The radio was on at the other end of the house and when the news came on, I could hear little except that it was about Russia. But the sepulchral tone of the announcer's voice was unmistakable. It meant death. Gorbachev must have been assassinated. My knees gave way.

It was not long before I found out that Gorbachev was still alive. But it was time enough to appreciate the catastrophe that would have overtaken Russia at that point if the news had been true. It was also time enough to appreciate my own reaction: I had unfinished business with the Soviet Union.

My involvement with Russia went back a long way. I had begun to learn Russian at school, because of Dostoevsky. His novels hinted at an extraordinary world, barely comprehensible in English, in which feeling and thought were not divorced as they were in my culture, but possessed people like a fever. I wanted to understand the language in which such passions made sense. I became fascinated by the struggle that is played out in the pages of Russian history and literature between the tradition of control and the impulse towards freedom. Through writing a doctorate about Solzhenitsyn, I followed this struggle as it was reflected in his own writing. I found two voices, one creative and one didactic, at war through the pages of his prose. I was also dragged through the experience central to the old Soviet economy by Solzhenitsyn's brilliant history of the camps, which he compiled in his head while he was still a prisoner. All this had left me with an exile's ambiguous love for Russia and a feeling of complicity in its future. These were emotions too complicated for the ideological force field of the Cold War. At a time when to have any contact with decent Russians was to risk harming them, my response had been to have none at all.

In retrospect, my response to the news that I heard that day does not seem to have been such an overreaction. A Soviet newspaper had published a trenchant Stalinist letter written by some Leningrad teacher. That was all. But the announcer's funereal tone had been appropriate. The teacher's name, Nina Andreevna, is now known from end to end of the Soviet Union. Her letter had precipitated a political crisis. Within the coded conventions of the Soviet press, its appearance had declared an imminent right-wing coup. We may never know the details, but we do know that it took *Pravda* twenty days to denounce the letter as 'a manifesto of the anti-*perestroika* forces'. During those days, a struggle was going on in which Ligachev and the right appear to have had the upper hand.

Gorbachev's 'reprieve' prompted me to write this book. I felt that I had to do something. The country's history was at a turning-point and the will of the West to help was circumscribed by our ignorance. The Russians, the colonial force holding together the Soviet Union, were for us as they had been for the Marquis de Custine in 1839, 'a half savage people who have been regimented without being civilized'. I wanted to understand things that no journalist or diplomat could tell me. I wanted to spend my time with people who had lived within the experience of totalitarianism and who, as a result of an initiative from above, were having to emerge from that security into a world of uncertainty.

What was it like to come to terms with the fact that you had succumbed to what Pasternak called 'the tyranny of the glittering phrase'? What was it like to experience the return of a lost history? What was it like to have to learn to think for yourself? 'In the West you talk about things as if you were looking down on them,' a young Russian had said to me on his first trip to the West: 'Our perspective is from the middle, or maybe from underneath.' That was what I wanted to explore, the perspective of people whom totalitarianism had deprived of any overview.

I made four journeys to the Soviet Union between the autumn of 1988 and the summer of 1990. The first two short visits were never intended to be part of this book. They were meant to give me answers to two questions: how was I going to travel and how I was going to meet people? I knew that I did not want to spend my time in hotels. I also knew that no Western contacts could help me reach the people I wanted to meet. I went with no address book and no idea as to how I would proceed. But from my first day on it became clear that I had already embarked upon a journey that was to rely on the generosity of strangers.

I chose to travel as if all that I knew about the country had been learned in a previous and unreliable existence. In this I followed the advice of Nikolai Gogol, who wrote in a letter to his closest friend and benefactor Count A. P. Tolstoy:

This is how you should make your voyage: first of all get out of your head all your opinions on Russia, whatever they may be: repudiate the conclusions that you have already drawn; present yourself knowing exactly nothing and travel as though in a new land hitherto unknown to you. In the same way that a Russian traveller arriving in some celebrated European city hurries to see all its antiquities and famous sites, in the same way, with even greater curiosity, after you have arrived in the chief town of a district or province, strive to get to know the sights. They are not in architectural works and antiquities but in people. I swear to you that a man is worth being

xiii

considered with greater curiosity than a factory or a ruin. Only endeavour to look for him with a drop of brotherly love and you will not be able to tear yourself away from him, he will appear so interesting to you.

I

MOSCOW
Autumn

Homo Sovieticus from L'vov

There are blanks and blanks. There is the way that a form is blank, before it has been filled out. There are blanks where something has been withdrawn, like a picture from the wall. On Moscow's Kalinin Prospect that sunny autumn day, the faces were blank like that. The life was withdrawn; nothing was left but arrangements of stolid Slavic features. Fifteen years ago, when I was last here, people had looked similarly impenetrable. Why had I imagined it would be different now?

Kalinin Prospect had been conceived in the thirties as the triumphal way into Red Square for demonstrations of massed enthusiasm. Hundreds of eighteenth-century houses had been demolished to make way for it. On an ordinary day it was a grim sight, enthusiasm's antithesis. The statues ranged along the pediment of the Lenin Library were wrapped up against winter. So too, despite the warm autumn sunshine, were the pedestrians with their shuttered faces and their silence. All I could hear was the sound of their feet. I walked on. A group of officers passed by chatting. They cut an ominous dash, with their polished boots, tailored breeches and their air of being the only ones at ease. With every step I became more daunted by the innocence of my undertaking. Or was it arrogance that had induced me to think that I could come here with no plan and no contacts, trusting that my journey would make itself?

I hurried down Kalinin Prospect towards Arbat Street, which had become Moscow's advertisement for change. Last time I had been here, it had been just another street. I had no memory of it, but I recognized it at once. With its modern street lamps, its artists with their easels, its cafés and video shops, it looked for a moment like a pedestrian precinct in Düsseldorf or Bonn. Everywhere there were well-dressed, smiling people. They turned out to be foreigners. I walked on.

Further down, the street was thronged. Here, the crowd was Soviet, but they looked different from the people in Kalinin Prospect. No better dressed, their faces were alive with excitement. What about? They did not look as if they had come to buy. Indeed, except for a straggle of pictures in hectic acrylic shades, there was little for sale. These people were promenading. But unlike the early evening promenaders in a small Italian town or on Gogol's Nevsky Prospect, these men were not pursuing a glimpse of a Grecian nose, or a foot in a bewitching shoe. This crowd was looking for something else.

I allowed myself to be carried along with it. Ahead, a man with a cracked voice was singing a song by the poet Bulat Okudzhava: 'Oh Arbat, my Arbat, you are my fatherland . . .' The early nineteenth-century streets of the district which were now being smartened up had for a long time housed the city's artists and poets. Some of the names of the little streets on either side of the road – Old Stables Lane, Carpenters' Lane – recalled the time when Ivan the Terrible had cleared the area to house his royal servants here. Its wooden buildings, which had become fashionable in the eighteenth century, had been burned down in the fire started by Napoleon's soldiers in 1812. We passed an elegant building in which Pushkin had briefly lived after his unfortunate marriage to Natalya Goncharova. It was she who caused him to fight his fatal duel.

Along with the crowd, I paused to listen to the singer with the cracked voice. He stood in front of a bank of theatre posters advertising a theatre group from Kiev. A young man in a felt hat came round offering to sell me a ticket to one of their shows. Why not? There was an awkward moment while I tried to make myself understood. On my arrival, I had

4

developed tonsillitis. The body plays cruelly with our fears. Mine was that this language would not come to life when I needed it. I had studied it years ago as if it were ancient Greek, feeling the political barrier to be as final as death. Barely audibly I asked the man for a ticket to the Bulgakov play in a few days' time. Misunderstanding my whisper he said: 'Don't be frightened. It's all right to do Bulgakov now . . .' We were interrupted by the singer, who had come up to listen: 'Why go to the Bulgakov?' He sounded annoyed. 'The Vysotsky's much more important.' Vysotsky had been Russia's Bob Dylan, the people's conscience during the Brezhnev era. He was dead and, not understanding how alive he still was none the less, I did not feel like seeing a play about him: 'How are things in Kiev, then?' I asked, stalling. 'Do you mean Chernobyl'?' the singer's face lit up. 'We went in there and played for fifty-five days, right after the reactor went up. That's what did in my voice.' I changed my mind and walked away with a ticket for the Vysotsky performance that night.

Further on, a group of students were heckling two men standing on crates. A large handwritten board read: DO YOU WANT SUCCESS IN LOVE AND WORK? DO YOU WANT YOUR PROBLEMS SOLVED? THEN COME TO THE PSYCHIATRIST'S CHAIR. WE CAN DO IT FOR ONLY FIVE ROUBLES. Five roubles is a lot of money in Russia. It did not seem to be an appealing offer. The two men looked like villains. The speaker was burly with a pitted face and the Russian equivalent of a cockney accent. 'It's now or never, the chance you've been waiting for – not you squinty, you need a different kind of treatment – step on up now.' In this badly dressed country, he was conspicuous for his well-cut overcoat. Meanwhile, his weasel-faced companion was scrutinizing the audience with suspicious eyes. 'I know your way of straightening people out!' shouted a boy with glasses and a studious face. 'Take a look at that one. See what swotting did for him,' the burly man continued: 'He'd be better off with us. Come on up!' There were

5

no volunteers. Eventually, a girl with a snub nose standing by me muttered: 'All right, why not? What harm can it do?' Ignoring her boy-friend's protestations, she gave her money to the weasel-faced man and climbed on to the box. But before her therapy could begin, he had spotted something in the crowd, muttered a word to his companion and the two men were off, running down the Arbat at full pelt with their board under their arm. No one seemed surprised except me. The students wandered off and the girl was helped down from the box by her friend.

'What was that all about?' I asked the girl. She shrugged her shoulders. 'I expect they're *Lyuberi*.' *Lyuberi* were young thugs who took their name from a suburb of Moscow. They saw themselves as moral vigilantes with a mission to clean up the decadent youth of the capital. They had a reputation for doing this violently. Before the girl could go on, her boy-friend butted in. He was a short man in his mid-twenties, and his face, which should have been good-looking in a conventional way, was vaguely repellent. As he spoke, his shock of dark hair quivered with outraged energy: 'They're an evil lot. Did you see how they turned tail when I spoke to them?' I laughed, thinking that he was being funny. He was serious. I looked at the girl, but she avoided my eye. He spoke with such conviction that he almost made me believe what he said. Beaming with satisfaction, the young man clicked his heels in a gesture of mock formality and introduced himself as Victor and his friend as Irina.

Victor gripped my arm, as if to make sure that I would not make off like the *Lyuberi* and we proceeded down the Arbat. He moved with an exaggerated, springy gait, clamping his feet down on the street as if his shoes alone were preventing him from becoming airborne. As he launched into an enthusiastic endorsement of *perestroika*, damning the machinations of the conservatives, I could hear the pleasure it gave him to listen to the sound of his own voice. 'Look how intellectually independent I am!' his performance seemed to declare. Some things had not changed. Victor was not showing off, he was testing a new script. He was a Party member of a kind that I remembered.

Victor went on to question me about England. It was hard work to make my whisper audible to the two of them and I was not sorry when he started to tell Irina about London himself. He had never left the Soviet Union or met a foreigner before but, as he explained, 'I know these things because I read a lot.' He did indeed know facts. But the image he conjured up of my home town was swathed in Dickensian fog and riddled with lung disease. It was not all dark in Victor's Britain though. Run by a Boadicea, as strong as she was beautiful, it was defended by a 'militaristic organization for boys', which turned out to be the Boy Scouts.

Victor broke off, his attention caught by something across the street. Bounding in that direction, he pointed to a row of pictures displayed against the wall of a house. They were executed in lurid slashes of orange and black and belonged to that homogenized style of kitsch which can be found all over the world from the railings of Bayswater to Bangkok. 'Do you have paintings like these in Britain?' he asked, though it was not really a question. Victor knew that these pictures were unique to his culture. Yes, it was Victor's smugness that made his clean-cut face so unattractive. I admitted that we too had pictures like this. He looked surprised. So kitsch grew also under conditions of capitalism? Recovering his poise, he turned to me with the *gravitas* of one connoisseur consulting another. 'Which, in your opinion, are the best?' Not wanting to hurt his feelings, I said something non-committal and changed the subject. I recognized the conditioning. Over the decades, the Soviet people had been whipped forward with the slogan, 'We shall catch up with and overtake America ...' It was to have happened in 1965, and again in 1980. Now, with the economy in tatters, it was poignant to hear the rhetoric of rivalry being applied to Arbat's *kitsch*.

Irina was describing to me the rigours of being a trainee

trapeze artist when Victor butted in, pursuing his cultural train of thought. 'Which is the best gallery, in your opinion – your National Gallery, or our own Tretyakov or Hermitage galleries?' His tone was casual, but his unflinching gaze said something else: I was not going to be able to get out of this one so easily. Ah yes, having understood my reaction to the kitsch canvases as élitist in a capitalist way, he had chosen his cultural ground more carefully this time. 'Pictures are not warheads, you know,' I whispered, irritated, before returning to my conversation, 'that we need to compare our relative arsenals.'

Oddly enough, Victor's conversation improved after that, as if, as in an electronic game, he had been moved on from Beginners to Advanced. Victor's problem was not stupidity. He had recognized that my refusal to enter the lists with him was a sign of sophistication on my part. But he had no idea how to handle my reactions. However strange Victor might be for me, I was evidently far stranger for him.

Victor turned out to know Moscow as little as I did. A historian from L'vov in the western Ukraine, he was here for a conference. He had only met Irina the night before, at the Ukrainian House of Friendship. 'It's the equivalent of the Ukrainian Embassy in Moscow, you know,' he explained. I didn't respond to the ludicrous assumption behind this remark. Victor was describing a poem, written in Ukrainian, which he had read out at the House of Friendship the night before: 'It's about Prince Vladimir of Kiev, who brought Christianity to this country, in 988. I must admit, it went down well.' The success of his performance seemed to have fused in his memory with the golden age of Kiev. Bounding down the street, Victor delivered a grandiloquent passage in praise of the princedom of Kiev. Although as a poet he overestimated himself, as a historian his pride was to some extent justified. Before the Mongol invasion in 1240, this wealthy state, which had marked the north-eastern boundary of Christendom, had embraced Moscow in its rule.

Victor's national pride had its endearing side, but as he went on and on about the reclamation of Ukrainian history I found myself longing to escape. Mercifully, I had soon to set off for the Vysotsky play. As we reached a Metro station I tried to interrupt his flow. '. . . You see, Susan, my future as a historian depends on Gorbachev's survival. Without *perestroika* . . .' 'Victor, I'm afraid that I must go . . .' '. . . My thesis is about an ancient tribe in the west of what is now the Ukraine —' 'I'm sorry, Victor, I really must —' '. . . They aren't Slav, but up until now no one has been able to say that . . .' 'Look, Victor I —' 'What! You're going! Ah, of course.' He stopped and thought for a moment. 'In that case, we'll accompany you part of the way. There's something I must show you.'

Our short journey ended, appropriately enough, at the 'Kiev' Metro station. Victor was just reaching the climax of another story in which, as a student, he had contradicted the teacher's account of an episode in Brezhnev's life. 'You see, I'd found this book published before he was General Secretary which showed that he hadn't been there at all at the time . . .' There were echoes of an ancient ritual in this account by the young aspirant to power of how he had holed the hagiography of the old leader. 'I stood there in front of them all and read out the passage!'

We came out into an arched hallway between two Metro tracks. It was decorated with colourful narrative mosaics. 'This', Victor gestured to them expansively, raising himself on the balls of his feet to increase his height, 'is the history of the Ukrainian people . . .' I caught him as he launched off on his illustrated account: 'Victor, I'm afraid I'll be late . . .' 'It won't take me five minutes . . .' 'I'm sorry . . .' 'Well, let me just show you this.' He led me to a mosaic entitled *The Struggle for Soviet Power in the Ukraine*: 'Here you see the heroic victory of the Bolsheviks over the Germans and Denikin's Whites in their task of unifying the Ukraine and Russia.' In the mosaic, a group of worried-looking soldiers were looking through binoculars at something out of frame. 'Between the Russian and Ukrainian people, there has always been friendship. While you are here, you are bound to meet people who will tell you otherwise. But don't believe a word of it.'

After the nationalist ring of his earlier conversations, this was a change of tune. It was as if, at the news that I was going, he had panicked at the freedom with which he had expressed himself to a foreigner and cast around for the Stalinist mosaics as an emergency antidote. A train was drawing in: 'Victor, I really have got to dash . . .' 'Let me just show you one more thing . . .' I leapt on to the train.

I had my own idea as to why the soldiers in the mural were looking worried. But my lack of a voice had restrained me from challenging him. On the train, I reflected on the history of the Ukraine that was not depicted in the mosaics of the Moscow Metro. After Bogdan Khmelnitsky had thrown out the Polish overlords in the seventeenth century, he had rashly asked for Russian help in establishing an independent Ukraine. The Russians had been keeping out the Poles ever since. There had been no support for the Bolshevik Party before the Revolution. It was regarded not as internationalist, but as Russian. Lenin had been obliged to win over the Ukraine, subsequently, by granting the country the cultural autonomy which had for so long been denied. But it lasted only ten years.

As the train rattled out towards the suburbs, I wondered why I had been seized by such an urgent need to get away from Victor. He had managed, I suppose, to illustrate my own worst fears for *perestroika*. His country was emerging from a historic attempt to insulate itself from reality. With no memory and no terms of reference outside the Soviet experience, he was the perfect product of that system, 'homo Sovieticus'. He was excited by the idea of *perestroika*, restructuring. But from his starting-point what could it mean except a little more latitude to be the way he already was?

10

The Chernobyl' Effect

Somewhere beyond the edge of my map I got off the Metro. There were no street signs and no one had heard of the Diamond Theatre. An elderly man with medals on his chest refused even to look at me when I asked him the way. He walked past bristling with hostility. It would take me time to become accustomed to the reaction of people like this, who had lived the best part of their lives under Stalin.

Eventually, I found a bus whose number had been written on the theatre poster. A young woman with long hair elaborately arranged around her head like a bolt of cloth, told me where to get off. The broad thoroughfare was badly lit and the office blocks were dark. It was an unpromising site for an evening's entertainment. Only one man at the bus stop knew the whereabouts of the theatre and he was drunk. Unsteadily, he led me down a side street to an incongruous building wedged between slabs of housing. Could this be the Diamond Theatre? It bore no name. Its white Corinthian columns were cast from concrete. High in the air, an outsize digital clock twitched forward second by second, scattering seconds into the night. I was late. My drunken guide bowed courteously and was swallowed up by the dark.

The building turned out to be a Soviet community centre, a House of Culture, as they are splendidly named. In the theatre, which was surprisingly large, the stage was dominated by a blown-up photograph of Vysotsky's brooding face. The actors from Kiev were entertaining the rapt audience to a highly

11

choreographed performance full of music. The show was set in the antechamber of death, where a foul-mouthed Charon was admitting newcomers on to his ferry. One by one, a series of young casualties arrived. There was a pretty schoolgirl, who had thrown herself from a tenth-storey window when she found that she was pregnant. 'I was dancing with this boy in my class. We'd never really talked. We weren't interested in the same things. Then he walked me home. There was no one in. There often wasn't. My father had left and my mother, well . . . I didn't want to let him in. But he was so persistent . . . Next day at school he never even looked at me . . .'

The problems were familiar. But here they had not been talked about. The mood in the young audience was cathartic. There was the conscript killed in the Afghan war. 'What good was my death? What good did the war do to anyone?' cried the soldier and I recognized the cracked voice of the singer on the Arbat that afternoon. A sigh passed through the audience like the wind through poplar trees. 'No! No! You've got it all wrong!' raged an old man, shaking his fist at the stage. He walked out, muttering.

When the lights came up, I found that I was sitting next to the girl with the festooned hair who had helped me on the bus. Her face was bathed in tears. 'I was so anxious about you going off with that drunkard that I jumped off the bus and followed you,' she explained. 'I didn't mean to stay. But I'm so glad I did! It is quite something to be taught what is going on in one's own neighbourhood by a foreigner!'

I too had been captured by the show. It had been driven by an energy that seemed in tune with the pace of history. The actors whom I had met in the Arbat asked me to join them for a drink. Surrounded by heaps of discarded costumes, we sat around the table in their dressing-room and ate cake while Prokofiev and Glinka looked down at us from photographs on the walls. After the pace of the show, the room seemed unnaturally still.

A boy with a peasant face played a wandering tune on the violin. 'That's Igor. He plays five instruments and doesn't read music. I found him in a lorry depot, on his way to becoming a drunk. None of them are trained. I'd have to spend too much time unteaching them,' said the man with the cracked voice, Volodya, who had written and directed the play. His slightly Mongol features seemed too small for a man of his size. As he sat at the table, relaxed, his expression was one of faint surprise, as if he had not expected his life to turn out like this. Volodya's brother took up his guitar and together the brothers sang.

Early next morning I was back on the steps of the Diamond House of Culture. The actors had asked me if I would like to join them, at 9 a.m. sharp, for their Saturday round of the Moscow markets. A battered bus stood empty but there was no sign of life. I went up to the dressing-room. The door was closed. I opened it a crack. From the dark came the smell of sleep and hair. Figures were beginning to materialize from hammocks, from the floor and from beds strung together out of chairs. So this was the men's dormitory. One by one, the girls turned up. The actors sang themselves to life as they pulled their Ukrainian costumes over as many clothes as possible. The men wore black hats, tunics and baggy red trousers. The women capped their red-and-white costumes with flowered head-dresses.

The battered bus carried us out of Moscow for miles through a landscape of towering concrete tenements. Two-thirds of the Soviet population were housed in structures like these. Between the blocks, nothing but rough grass grew. The bus drew up by an expanse of asphalt over which hung plastic pennants; it was surrounded by tower blocks. The place did not resemble any market I had ever seen. But I knew we had arrived because of a plywood archway on which the word 'Market' was written in folksy letters. The space was defined on two sides by a string of tatty huts. Dwarfed by the tower blocks, they looked like children's toys laid out for a forgotten game. The gloom of the place was accentuated by the faded touches of paint in primary colours that decorated the gateway and huts. When the actors had been talking the night before, the words 'market' and 'dancing' had evoked images of colour, abundance and movement. But this, it was explained to me, was the land of the *limitchiki*, workers who had been given limited rights of residence in the capital to do the jobs no Muscovite would touch.

Dressed in their absurd costumes, the players set off through the puddles with their instruments, playing their way round the market square before mounting a bandstand with a tattered awning. The day was raw and cold. They eased into a routine of Ukrainian songs and jokes. The sound system mangled their voices, making them rasp like a badly opened tin. Volodya winced and ran off to look for the sound operator. Briefly, the sound recovered and their voices floated upwards, perfectly reproduced, before the sound degenerated once more. Volodya strode back, furious: 'He just shrugged his shoulders. I yelled at him and he deigned to touch a knob. Men like that are a metaphor for the system. He's got his job. It's secure, though it doesn't pay much. And he doesn't give a damn.'

It hardly mattered. The poorly dressed shoppers who were picking their way between the puddles were taking no notice of the performance. With hunched shoulders they queued for Chinese cotton shirts at one chalet, for onions at another. Judging from their expressions, the players might have been sent as another obstacle in the path of survival. The dislike was mutual. 'Look at them. Wretched, aren't they? They live in limbo, these *limitchiki*, belonging to neither town nor country.' Volodya spoke as though they had betrayed the countryside by leaving it.

He had returned from negotiating with the girl from the district executive committee which was employing them. He had failed to get her signature on their agreement. 'By rights we shouldn't perform until it's signed. She's left the paperwork in her office. She says she'll come to the show with it on Monday.

14

But who knows? Sometimes they do and sometimes they don't.'

The rain came down and the players continued to respond with professional gaiety to each other's jokes. After last night's performance, I did not like to ask what they were doing, acting out this mundane routine. But Volodya seemed to guess what I was thinking. 'This act keeps us alive. We have no subsidy of any kind.' He turned out to be a refugee from the conventional theatre. 'I hated it. I loathed the plays and what they did with them. So I left and went to this factory in Kiev and persuaded them to take me on as a director. They'd never done anything like that before. It was a miracle that we got anything done. Imagine driving a heavy goods vehicle all day and acting *Hamlet* in the evening. And did those boys drink! They wouldn't lift a hand without it. Our "theatre" was in what they call the Red Corner in the factory. Every factory has one. It's the place where people go to eat their food and hang out. Most of them had never seen theatre before, and I was a pretty odd person to introduce them to it. They would sit there and gape at us.'

After a while, he had asked a park in Kiev if they would take on his troupe as entertainers. 'The park's a sort of Soviet Disneyland. They used to hire the occasional juggler to entertain people, or a husband-and-wife team of crooners. They said they'd be happy to take two or three people on, but no more. I persuaded them to give all ten of us a trial and we went down all right. People came back for more. We struck a deal that in return for this sort of thing,' he nodded his head towards the bandstand, where his troupe was on its last song, 'they'd give us a place to work.'

I soon began to understand why Volodya had fled from the established theatre. There was little in the repertoire of even the most celebrated theatres in Moscow that winter and spring that was untouched by institutional inertia. Each Soviet theatre had its own company and, as no one could be fired, each had accrued a bloated backlist of actors too ancient or incompetent to contribute creatively. Only the talented moved on. Volodya's ingenuity in devising a way of running a theatre independently in the unreformed Ukraine owed nothing to *perestroika*. He had simply exploited the latitude in the system. It was a vital Soviet skill.

Their performance over, the players scrambled down, blue with cold. No one clapped. A fat man ran up the steps, strung up a teddy bear from the awning and announced it as the first prize in a talent contest. A crowd collected from nowhere and two boys with sloping shoulders started to sing, out of tune. The actors bought hunks of flesh from an open grill and vented their feelings on the meat:

'Did you see that survey they did which showed that even cats won't eat the sausage now?'

'How do you explain to animals that they're living under socialism?'

'Perhaps I could resell mine to the *limitchiki*?'

The bus did not break down until it was on its way back to the Diamond House of Culture after the second market. Here, by contrast, the players had been enthusiastically received. The reason was simple. The shoppers were visibly more prosperous. Among the people who had crowded round after the performance had been a young policeman, who had wrung the hand of the handsome clown Sasha, saying: 'Where are you from? My people come from near L'vov. And guess what? My grandad joined up with the Fascists! No one forced him to. He spent the entire war fighting us, the Soviets!' The policeman had seemed positively proud of his grandfather: 'How are things there?' 'Nothing much has changed,' Sasha had replied. 'But here,' the policeman had spread his arms wide, 'it's a different place! Pray God it stays like this!' 'It's man, not God, that you've got to watch . . . ' I had put in, unwisely. 'Are you from the Baltic states?' 'No, I'm from London.' 'Come off it, you're Estonian!'

16

'Well, actually . . .' 'If you say you're a Londoner, tell me where Piccadilly Circus is?' 'Just up the road from Buckingham Palace.' The policeman had changed colour and melted into the crowd. 'Three years ago, that poor fellow would have lost his job for saying what he just did!' Sasha had chuckled as we walked to the bus.

So the policeman's grandfather had been one of the two or three hundred thousand Soviet citizens fighting on Hitler's side. If he had joined up voluntarily he would not have been one of General Vlasov's men. Those had been starving Soviet prisoners of war whom Stalin's refusal to sign the Red Cross convention had driven to fight for the enemy. He must have joined up with the SS Galicia division when the Germans invaded the Ukraine at the beginning of the war. Their aim had been to free the Ukraine of Bolshevism. Up until now, Soviet history had breathed not a word about them.

The bus had been taking a short cut across a waste land between some tower blocks. It had stopped to let off one of the actors. Sasha, clowning still, had refused to sit down after finding the date 1932 stamped on the antimacassar of his seat. 'Ooh, I wouldn't trust a seat like that!' He stood in the aisle and, after a low drum roll, entertained us to a falsetto rendering of Pushkin's poem: 'I remember the wonderful moment. You appeared before me like a fleeting vision . . .'

Since we had met in the Arbat yesterday, I had been wanting to ask Volodya about Chernobyl'. What had he been doing there after the reactor went up? 'Well, we'd been out there, in Pripyat', playing for three weeks just before the accident. Vitaly, my brother, Eva and I, are the only ones left now who were out there. You've met Eva, haven't you?' He jerked his head towards the seat behind where his teenage girl-friend was removing her head-dress. 'Pripyat''s the new town where the Chernobyl' workers used to live. We'd had a wonderful reception. They were our friends. So the week the reactor went up we worked up this show. It was beautiful in Kiev that week. The

17

blossom was out. But the city was empty. Everyone was fleeing, but we went back in. What else could we do?' Volodya frowned crossly to cover his emotion: 'I wouldn't have missed those days for anything in the world. Yes, I do feel the effects. It's not just my voice. It's slowed me down. But they were the happiest days of my life.

'I understand now why people love war. It's got nothing to do with the fighting. Out there, we were all on the same side, and we were all equals. Even now, we stick together. The general in command is my friend. He calls me, an actor, "*ty*".' ('*Ty*' is the intimate form of 'you'.) 'You can have no idea what that means in a country like this. Chernobyl' was our crucible. It changed my life. It made me understand what I had to do.'

The actor for whom we had been waiting climbed back into the bus. The driver started the engine, or tried to. Nothing happened. He tried once more. Nothing. No one seemed surprised. I was briefly annoyed, because I would be late for my next meeting. I had not yet learned Russian time. After various attempts to coax the engine to life, Sasha and Volodya got out to gaze at the engine with the driver. Eva curled up and went to sleep. In her coloured costume, she looked like a crumpled doll. Sasha's wife, a big girl who had given up a job as a theatre critic to join the company, turned round on the seat in front and said with a grin, 'Don't worry. This is normality. The exception is when the bus works.'

18

A Damaged Man

I heard about the exhibition on its last day. It was the central event in a 'week of conscience' that had been declared by Memorial, the unofficial group which planned to erect a monument to the victims of revolutionary justice. It was being held in the Palace of Culture attached to the great Electrofactory in the city centre.

The weather had changed. It was bitterly cold as I crossed the square towards the imposing white building with a classical front. A queue wrapped its way round the building. I arrived at the end of it at the same time as a dour man who said: 'It'll be two hours.' Having mastered this very Soviet skill, he was right to the minute. On the side street where we waited, the crude proletarian temple to culture stood opposite an eighteenth-century variation on the classical theme. Rusting metal containers blocked the elegant yellow-and-white façade with its crumbling plasterwork. A carved dovecot on a pole leaned over the road at an improbable angle.

Behind me, a man with a country accent muttered that it was time Stalin was removed from Red Square. Another man, with a cultivated voice, jumped at him: 'Oh, leave him alone! We bury him and we dig him up, bury him and dig him up.' In 1953, Stalin had been embalmed and laid beside Lenin. Eight years later, they moved him to the Kremlin wall. 'Let's leave him there and spit on him. There are more important things to be getting on with.' 'Like Kuropaty . . .' the first man responded eagerly. He was referring to the mass graves near Minsk which

19

had just been excavated. The blindfolded victims had been shot two at a time to save on bullets. Much of the evidence was removed in the 1940s, but what remains shows that 100,000 people died there.

I turned to look at the first speaker. His rough face, at once peasant and Mongol, was alive with excitement as he referred to recent articles about the buried past. The educated man interrupted him again to continue his own train of thought. His face was as cold as his voice. 'It's high time we faced up to the fact that the roots of the whole thing go far deeper than Stalin.' He was condescending, as though he knew he should not be wasting his opinions on this company.

'But there are still people out there who don't believe it happened at all, you know,' broke in a housewife dressed in brown. The conversation had flared up like a fire in dry leaves. 'Personally, I think that's why they let Adamovich do the Kuropaty article,' the first speaker responded. 'It was one place where they could actually show the bones being dug up and photograph them. No one could say they'd invented that . . .' He was off again, citing articles that had appeared recently which had implied that the Terror was a giant fiction. The condescending man and his bookish neighbour winced at his unsophisticated judgements. But he knew more than all of them.

'It's time we did something,' a middle-aged blonde interrupted him. She spoke with resolve. 'What do you mean?' he asked, surprised. 'It's time we stopped talking and got on with it.' 'You tell me what to do and I'll do it,' he sulked as though she had criticized him personally. 'We should join the Popular Front. At least they're doing something. We must get out on the streets.' 'What's this if it's not getting out on the streets?' the bookish man defused the moment. At that moment, his wife returned from shopping and all eyes turned on an oblong purchase wrapped in brown paper which she transferred to her husband's bag. The woman in brown tried to find out what it was. They were not telling her.

After an hour, we were edging round to the front of the building. The condescending man went off shopping, leaving his wife in the queue. No sooner was he out of earshot than she picked up the conversation again. Russian women often seemed to find their tongues once their husbands disappeared, I was to find. 'I know it's only a passive protest, but at least I don't vote.' 'What good is that? You must vote.' The talkative man was shocked. 'Do you mean to say that you don't vote at all?' asked a Mongol with a weathered face and long white beard who looked as if he had just arrived in Moscow on horseback. 'Well, no, I couldn't do that. I go down there and drop in an empty slip of paper. What else can I do?' Attendance at the polling booths is strictly monitored. 'At some point the vote will become so low', she continued, 'that they'll have to do something.' 'Do you honestly think it makes any difference to them whether they get fifty per cent or five per cent?' the bookish man said bitterly. 'Who is ever going to know but them?'

Inside the foyer people were filing past a prison wheelbarrow and throwing their money on to the pile. Behind the barrow was a huge map of the Soviet Union, on which the names of the camps were printed. Over the last few days, many more had been added in chalk. As I went past two men were rubbing out each other's chalk marks and squabbling over the exact location of a camp in the far north. 'How could I be wrong? I spent five years there . . .' an aggrieved voice followed us up the stairs.

At the top, there was a long line of backs. Row upon row of people were gazing in silence at a twenty-foot-high wall which had been erected. From top to bottom, the wall was covered in a patchwork of photographs and documents. The atmosphere in the crowd was not one of mourning but of relief so deep that it felt almost like gaiety. It would be a long time before I could get close enough to see the wall properly. But I was in no hurry. No finished monument that Memorial could erect would have

21

the power of this collage of faces and fates. At last Solzhenitsyn's fellow countrymen were picking up the task of historical archaeology which he had set himself in camp. His *Gulag
Archipelago* had been composed on scraps of paper which he
had memorized before destroying them. By dint of repeating it
to himself all day, every day, he had held the entire work in his
head.

My neighbour asked the woman in front if she would take
off her woolly hat so that we could see. I found myself gazing at
a black-and-white picture of two plump adults in thirties clothes
and a tubby girl with an enormous bow in her hair. 'Father, I
did not betray you! Anyone who ended up in Gor'kij and who
knows about burial places there, ring 133-15-75.' The Kalina
family next to it had three boards, each with its own photograph
and official documents of sentence and rehabilitation. A car-
nation and black ribbon adorned that of father, whose impeccably
groomed appearance marked him as a figure from a lost world.
Mother and daughter had survived camp. The accomplishments
of a bourgeois upbringing had stood them in good stead.
Mother was now employed making soft toys and daughter
painted boxes. To the right hung pictures of an abandoned
watch-tower and railway line. 'I built this track leading nowhere.
A dead track, it buried thousands. It was built by *Zeks*. It led to
the Kareky Gates. I, one of the victims of the Stalin era, appeal
to you, the people, to ensure that nothing like it should happen
again. May the memory live in your hearts and awaken your
consciences. Iyevleva Valentina, 1949–52.'

In front of the wall of memory stood a young man with a
card around his neck that read: 'Georgiy Fokovich Nichiporenko. Seventeen years inside. Ten under Stalin. Seven now. Put
away in '81 for daring to remind people that he was in a camp
under Stalin. He got seven years and five of exile.' Nichiporenko
was still serving out his exile. People were ignoring the young
man's board. It was as if they could not bear to be reminded
that the camps were not quite a thing of the past.

I walked through to the next room. A child had painted a picture of the Terror in the shape of a dragon with a fiery mouth wrapped round a house. In front of it a woman stood talking to no one in particular. Around her neck was a board bearing her prison number, 'Shch 270'. 'We were just numbers in MinLag INTA. If they wanted to know our identity, we had to turn our back to show them. I got to know Mendeleev's widow there . . .'

'Were you tortured in camp?' asked a short man standing by me. He had shiny jet-black hair, close-set eyes and a nose like a rat's. 'That isn't necessary, you know,' put in a man with a pedagogical air. 'But I say it is, absolutely necessary,' insisted the ratlike man. The schoolteacher winced and walked away. 'They used to shut us up in a concrete cell as a punishment. It was so dark I couldn't even see what I was eating. That would last for nine days and nights.' 'Is that all?' 'It was enough,' replied the woman with dignity. The woman seemed upset, so I tried to deflect the questioner by asking him if he had been in camp himself. 'No, only mental hospital and only for a few months. But it was enough to ruin my life . . .'

At that moment, as he was poised to pour out his story, the double doors by us opened and we were swamped by an exodus from the building. I allowed myself to be carried downstairs with the crowd, away from this unattractive man. But half-way down he was there again 'I didn't have time to tell you my story.' He went on without a pause, hissing in my ear. His breath was rank. 'I wasn't put away for anything political. I was only twenty. No, I was done for wanting a job! Our precious constitution is meant to guarantee us a job. But in those days it was difficult. Unless you had connections you hadn't a hope.' He had paused on the landing. The picture behind him on the wall showed a stone fist poised to crush a figure that had fallen to its knees.

'You know this Party machine of ours which dogs our every step? Well, it's supposed to be able to help us with things like getting jobs, so I used to go along to central Party headquarters in Kalinin Prospect and ask for one. I used to go a lot. In fact I went every day for a month and a half. There was a group of us. Then one day, when we were down there, this official bloke said to me: "I might be able to help you. Just step this way." I thought: "Hm, things are looking up." "Go down the corridor and through the double doors and you'll be met by someone," he said. Well, I was. I was grabbed by two men in plain clothes, carried out by a back door into a van and taken to the mental hospital. They gave me one chance to phone home, but by ill luck my aunt was out. Later, they told my family that I'd said I didn't want to be in touch.' He gave a grim chuckle. 'Then they stuck a needle into my bum and I lost consciousness. They did that every day for the next two and a half months. I was in a general ward. Most of them were in a far worse state than I was.'

We were standing in the foyer, where the organizers were shepherding out visitors with a politeness that showed they had nothing to do with officialdom. Memorial had some private function starting. I joined the queue for my coat. But the rat-faced man put his hand on my sleeve: 'There's no need to go. You stick with Oleg. Come along.' He seemed bent on finishing his story within the building, as though it offered him sanctuary. He led me into an annexe, which the organizers were using as their base. One long wall was covered with lists, columns of typed names, stretching from floor to ceiling. They were lists of victims, arranged alphabetically. 'That was only the beginning. Soon after I got my call-up for the Army. They turned me down on the grounds that I had been in mental hospital. Well, to be exact, they didn't even turn me down. They treated me as if I was trying to evade conscription.'

A bearded man asked us politely to leave. Oleg crossed his arms, planted his feet wide and lowered his head. 'I won't move.' His mood was belligerent. I could imagine him standing like this outside Party headquarters in Kalinin Prospect. Charm could never have been his strong suit. The bearded man shrugged and went away. 'That's the way you have to deal with them!' Oleg hissed in my ear triumphantly. Standing with his back to the wall of names, he went on: 'The punishment for dodging conscription is that you are given a white passport instead of the usual red one you're given when you pass out of the Army. That little red book is the key to the future. Without it, armed only with my book of shame, I couldn't get a job at all. They had forbidden me to work! Instead they put me on a state pension. Since then I have done nothing at all.' He paused and looked at me craftily. 'Sounds all right, doesn't it? But do you know how much that pension gives me to live on? Forty roubles a month.' Forty roubles a month was half the minimum wage. I must have looked doubtful, for Oleg hauled out his white book from an inner pocket and showed me the sum written in it. 'It's not a life,' he said. 'It's an existence.'

Once again the bearded man, who had been hovering round, told us it was time to leave. I headed for the door. As I rounded the corner I could see that Oleg had turned his back on the bearded man and was standing with his shoulders bowed, like a horse in the rain. 'I too am a victim,' he was whining. Embarrassed, I hurried away. But before I had advanced more than a few steps, a familiar conspiratorial voice behind me said: 'Don't you worry! I can handle this!' He put his nose in my ear and added: 'I don't know if you've ever been told this, but it was the Jews who were responsible for the Revolution. All the revolutionaries were Jewish!' I averted my face from the foul blast of breath. 'I have to whisper as I think the man who is trying to get us out is Jewish. It wasn't the Russian people at all. They had nothing to do with the Revolution! The Jews had had a hard time before the Revolution and they wanted to punish the Russians! Does anyone tell you these things in the West?'

Oleg's explanation of the Revolution convinced me that the man was mad. But his delusion, I was soon to discover, was not of his own creation. It was by chance that I found, a few days later, that I had been handed a *samizdat* paper written on this very theme. It was the Popular Front's refutation of a paper circulated by the powerful and clandestine Russian nationalist organization, Pamyat'. Eighty per cent of the People's Commissars in the Revolution, the Pamyat' circular maintained, had been Jewish. The Popular Front paper showed how this figure had been arrived at, by dint of rearranging dates and changing the nationalities of various commissars. The actual percentage, though high, was half that. Also among the papers was a synopsis of a *samizdat* book which Pamyat' had issued. It contained a warning about a Zionist–Masonic conspiracy to take over the world by the year 2000. At its heart lay an organization with a hierarchy of 100 steps, at the top of which sat Satan himself. Perhaps after all, Oleg would have been better protected from such insanity inside the walls of the mental asylum.

To retrieve my coat I had rejoined the queue. Oleg, whose head came up to my shoulder, kept up the monologue in my ear, trying to persuade me to stay: 'Don't you see I've won? You're free to stay as long as you like!' As I put on my coat and made for the door, my route was intercepted by a robust old man, even shorter than Oleg: 'Forgive me for interrupting,' he began with a bow, 'but there are one or two misconceptions which I would be grateful if you could clear up on your return to the West.' He spoke as if he were making a formal representation, as between ambassadors. The two little men took me by the arm and guided me back to the annexe.

'You must tell them not to interfere with us,' the old man pronounced. 'And not to lure us in the direction of democracy! Autocracy is the only path for us! Every time you interfere with Russian history, it goes wrong for us. Your intervention in the aftermath of the First World War was disastrous. The Revolution would never have happened if only you had left us alone. And now you're all for this so-called democratization. We don't want your materialistic way of life!' The indignant little man was bouncing up and down and wagging his finger at me. As I started to respond, he interrupted me to ask in a furtive undertone: 'By the way, what do you think of Pamyat'? It's a bit suspect, don't you think? Riddled with *provocateurs*?' Incautiously, I agreed. 'It also seems to be extremely anti-Semitic,' I added. The old man screwed up his face like a pink rosebud. 'No,' he declared. 'No.' He glanced over his shoulder, where the bearded man, Oleg's supposed Jew, was now listening with interest: 'Absolutely not. Absolutely not.' He kept on shaking his head and repeating over and over like a mechanical doll: 'Absolutely not.'

So that was it. I had fallen into his trap. 'And another thing,' he said, pulling himself back into his ambassadorial role: 'You must stop them supporting the sectarian churches – Baptists, Uniates and that lot. Only the Orthodox Church will do for Russia! I know, because I've suffered for it. When I came out of camp in the fifties, I was persecuted by the Baptists! I mean it literally! I used to think that all Christians were on the same side. But they're not. They locked me up and bullied me, trying to get me to fall in with them! They're vicious! We must free ourselves from them! And it's all the fault of the West! You keep on sending all this literature and crates of Bibles! You think you're helping! You're not, you're destroying everything!' I tried to speak, but the old man, standing on the tips of his toes now, kept interrupting me in a shrill voice: 'It's your fault, it's all the fault of the West!'

I had had enough: 'Yes, yes, I admit it! It's all our fault! Isn't it remarkable that in your history there is always someone else to blame? And what about all these murdered men and women?' I pointed at the lists that ran from top to bottom of the wall. 'I suppose they're our fault too?' Oleg's suspected Jew smiled sympathetically from a distance while the old man plucked at my sleeve: 'Don't take offence.' Oleg plucked at the other sleeve as he whispered in my ear: 'Take no notice. He's a damaged man. On the contrary, it all depends on the West. Without the West, nothing can happen. It's only because Reagan was so insistent on human rights that Gorbachev gave way. But you know' – there was no avoiding the sour gust as he moved closer in – 'though I couldn't have had this conversation with you two years ago, remember that everything else is the same. It's only the fear that has gone.'

Tying the Broken Thread

The next morning was sunny and warm. I wandered down to the Arbat to find Sergei, the man in the felt hat who had sold me the theatre ticket, still in the same place. This time he was accompanied by Volodya's brother Vitaly, who was singing to the guitar. As we stood talking, a sturdy young woman in trousers came up to Sergei and said: 'Hello. Remember me? Olya?' The gap between her teeth yawned as she gave him a radiant smile. Sergei, who looked like a ladies' man, went blank. 'From Magadan. You must remember . . .' 'Ah, Magadan . . .' Sergei gazed at her in disbelief. Magadan is thousands of miles from Moscow, at the farthest end of Siberia, beyond which there is only emptiness. People here say 'Magadan' in the way that we say 'Timbuctoo' to mean the end of the world.

Sergei did know Magadan, he admitted. He had spent nine years there. He had been a young member of the Party, with everything in front of him, when he had knocked the hat off the head of an Important Person in a fight one night in Kiev. Before the case ever came to court, he had fled to Magadan. Olya worked as a construction worker there. Together they had acted in amateur theatrical productions. Those years, when Sergei had got into all kinds of trouble, now seemed like a story from someone else's life.

The Arbat, the Arbat would be the place that would bring these two together in a city of eight million people. Olya had come straight off her flight from Magadan. Sergei, in from Kiev, put in time here every day. For Muscovites, the Arbat might be nothing but a floor show. But for people from out of town, from places where change had brought nothing good so far, the Arbat was a magnet. This was where they came to keep their hope alive.

The promise of the Arbat was self-fulfilling. The atmosphere was so volatile that excitement would spin itself out of the air. As we stood there, an old woman shouted at Vitaly out of a window: 'Stop making that din! There are people trying to live here!' Immediately, Vitaly's music found defenders and a shouting match began. The issue was not his singing, but the clamour of change. As we stood there, I took out an exhibition catalogue to show it to Sergei and Olya. In a moment, a knot of people were pressing round us, like fishes biting at a handful of bread. Only those at the front could see the catalogue. The rest had no idea why they had stopped. But momentarily, the action was here. From the back of the crowd, a tall young man with a shaven head, seeing that I was a foreigner, shouted out: 'Don't believe a word they say! It's all a con! Why do you think I look like this? They put me in gaol for being at a peaceful demonstration!' There was more shouting, someone tugged at the catalogue and as suddenly as the crowd had materialized, it dissolved again.

We were joined by Volodya, who stood about looking pre-occupied while we talked. He was wearing a cheap suit in which he looked ill at ease. 'Are you doing anything? Would you like to come and visit Vysotsky's grave?' he asked me, his broken voice sounding slightly uncertain. We made our way through the faded grandeur of the nineteenth-century streets that lie behind the Stalinist thoroughfares. I saw the gate by the Patriarch's Ponds where Anna had dropped the fateful bottle of sunflower oil, precipitating the bizarre events that surrounded the Devil's visit to Moscow. They may have happened in Bulgakov's novel *Master and Margarita*, but they did not seem any stranger than the reality which the city had seen this century. Round the corner from the Patriarch's Ponds we skirted the high yellow wall of Beria's house, Stalin's satanic chief of secret police. It was there that he had taken the girls whom he regularly abducted off the streets. Many were never seen again.

Volodya strode along looking hunted. He wore a knapsack on his back and kept his hands stuffed in his trouser pockets. When he took them out I saw that his left hand was covered in tattoos. The words 'Adventurer' and 'Love' were written across the back in English. He did not know any other words of English. As we walked, a well-dressed young man made his way unsteadily towards Volodya across the pavement. When he came close, we could see that his expensive cardigan was covered in spittle and that his eyes were glazed over. 'Gimme some money, my friend. I need a bottle,' he said to Volodya in a voice drowned in alcohol. The man, who was not in the least derelict, was so far gone that it was remarkable that he still had control of his tongue and limbs. This was drunkenness of a high order, the search for oblivion. 'Why have you got yourself in such a state then, brother? You've messed up your nice jersey.' Volodya straightened out the man's shirt and cardigan. His tone was as indulgent as if he had been speaking to a child. He slipped the man, who looked much richer than he did, some money and we walked on.

I was to become familiar with this tone. The tolerance of drunks in Russia is special. It consists of more than understanding. There is something closer to envy at their escape. 'A drunk here doesn't just go up to anyone, you know,' Volodya remarked as we left the young man behind. He did not seem displeased at having been thus picked out. 'He'd just be put away. Somehow he can tell that I'm a potential drunk like him. Not that I'll ever become one,' he added hastily. 'I've given up drink. There's too much to be done. But I know all about it and he can see that.'

At that moment a pale grey-blue van pulled up at the nearby traffic lights. 'That's a "raven",' Volodya said. The word is slang for a prison van. 'Do you see the two air vents on top? They're raised, which means there are prisoners inside. The front one's for the guards' compartment. I've been in one. In fact, if I hadn't been to prison, I'd probably never have got the theatre going.' He talked with the same headlong urgency that had distinguished his show. 'Shall I tell you what happened? One day I was walking down the street with a friend. We'd had a glass, but we weren't drunk, just happy. My friend had a guitar and we were singing. They nicked us, put us inside for five days.

'They used to take us out to work every day. Me and my friend had to move bricks from one place to another at this police station. We had a guard watching us, but he soon got bored and started looking in the other direction. So we legged it. Not into town, where they'd have expected us to go, but back into the police station. After all, I am a director. It's my business to think of these things. We'd been quite tidily dressed when they arrested us. So we just walked down the corridor and out into the street. They caught up with us in the end, of course, but only after two and a half months. This time they weren't taking any chances. They put me in a basement cell and wouldn't let me go out to work. They were convinced that I'd escape. They were right, actually.

'I was in a cell with forty others. They were a good lot, drinkers mostly, none of them real crooks. Well, there was one thief, but he was fine because he was on his own. We used to play a lot of dice. You make the dice out of bread. No one had anything to bet with. We won and lost fabulous sums and forgave each other the debts. I wouldn't have missed that experience. You get close to people at times like that. During the day, I would be the only one left in the cell. I spent the time trying to remember all the poetry I had ever learned. And I thought . . . When I got out, they'd given my part to someone else. So I left and started the theatre.'

The incident with the drunk had set Volodya going. Most of

his stories involved drink. But they were not casual anecdotes. He seemed to be using this occasion of talking to someone who knew nothing about him, to make sense of something to himself: 'I spend my life trying to be free. I lost my passport a couple of years ago. It's meant to be impossible to live without one, but it isn't. In my own way I'm quite an important person, a director with my own theatre. So I can get away with it. It happened one day after the kids had been playing me up, drinking and fooling around. I was in a state. We'd just been paid so I bought myself four bottles of cognac. I went to my father's grave and got plastered. When I came to it was about four in the morning. They'd taken my passport and the rest of my money. There was just one remaining bottle in the bag. So I drank that too.' In the way Volodya talked, there was a discrepancy. Well into his thirties, he was a man driven by ambition for his theatre. Yet the stories he told were those of a young man who needed to prove that he could live outside the rules.

'It's hard work staying free, not getting tied down by the rules,' he went on. 'People think I'm not scared, but I am. All the time. I just make a lot of noise. But I go on and do whatever it is that scares me. Even so, I've sobered down a lot. Look at this suit. I thought I might see you today so I put it on in your honour. I loathe it. But what can you do?' We were walking up the pathway to the old walled cemetery of Vagankovskoye. It was a Sunday and there were people everywhere, carrying flowers. 'It's funny, my talking to you like this. Usually I just don't have time to stop and think. I love my life. But I suppose I'm lonely. I used to have close friends when I was young. I'd do anything in the world for my actors. I belong to them, really. But I wouldn't confide in them.'

A small crowd was gathered round Vysotsky's elaborate grave by the entrance to the cemetery. It was piled high with flowers. Before dying at the age of forty-three, Vysotsky had lived his life with something of the recklessness that had characterized Volodya's descriptions of his own life. While he added his flowers and stood, with his head bowed, as if in church, my mind went back to a story he had been telling me on the way, about an old friend whom he had just visited. 'He's become very respectable and thinks I'm a bit of a hooligan. He translates best-sellers. But the funny thing is when I last saw him, which was a while ago now, he was scared stiff. The night before he had got blind drunk, rung up the American Embassy and told them that he had these important documents to give them. Can you imagine? I may get drunk from time to time, but I'd never do a thing like that! It had the most terrible consequences. Not that anything actually happened to him. But he spent the next six months in a cold sweat, leaping at every knock on the door, convinced that people were following him. So much for respectability.' That recklessness, so clearly a response to the constraints of life under totalitarianism, was also a very Slavic trait.

We walked along the wooded pathways between the old graves of the cemetery. It was here that 1,500 people had been buried in a mass grave in 1896, after the catastrophe that occurred during the celebrations for the coronation of Nicholas II. In this country where good and bad intentions so often seem to have the same effects, they had been killed in the crush to receive gifts that were being distributed. We came to the grave of the poet Sergei Yesenin, whose fortune, even in death, was just about to change. A Soviet newspaper was soon to announce that, far from having committed suicide in 1925, Yesenin had been murdered.

Volodya stopped. 'Look at that,' he said, pointing at a grave with a large stone cross on top. 'V. A. Gavrilov, died 1834. Who was he then? Nobody in particular. But there he lies, just as he did 150 years ago. It may seem normal to you, but for us it's a miracle for anything like that to have survived all these years intact. We've lost our past, you see. There are very few people who know anything about their families further back than their grandfathers. It's only recently that I've started to take my own past seriously. I'm beginning to try and knit the pieces together. But it's already too late.

'Take my father, for instance. We lived together until just before he died two years ago. But he never spoke about the past. While he was alive, I knew almost nothing about him. Then all these people turned up to his funeral whom I had never met before, although they lived in Kiev. Some of them were relations. I still don't know why we didn't ever see them. They told me all I know about him. He came from the poorest of poor peasant families in the Ukraine. He was one of eight children. All of them died of illness or famine except for him and a sister. People were living off human flesh. Once, when he was on a train, two men tried to kill him for food. He was standing smoking on the platform between two carriages. It was open on either side. One man came from the carriage on one side. The second man came from the other side. In the fight, one man fell off the train. The other got away.' That must have been the famine that Stalin contrived in 1932 to break the resistance of the Ukrainian peasantry to collectivization. Five million people had been starved to death.

'Somehow he got to Kiev and joined the Navy and the Party. Then it all started to happen for him. Officers were going down like flies.' In 1937, after the Terror had cut swathes through the rest of the population, it turned on its own, the Party and the armed forces. 'But he was all right. He wasn't an officer and he came from a background with nothing "irregular" about it. He did well in the war and was quickly promoted to fill the empty officer ranks.

'He owed everything to Stalin. We grew up with this portrait of Stalin on the wall at home. Only the other day, Vitaly, who still lives in the flat with his wife, asked my mother to take it down. She agreed. But a few days later, it was back there again. Not that my mother's got particularly strong opinions about politics. She just inherited hers.'

Volodya had been born the year Stalin had died. Brought up in a background with no 'irregularities', as he had put it, in the continuous present that is totalitarianism's medium of control, it was no wonder that drink had been the puerile substitute for a rebellion for which he had lacked not the spirit, but the concepts. Had *perestroika* come a few years later, I guessed, it would have been too late for Volodya. He would soon have become a drunkard. But there was something about him which made me certain that the process that was beginning in him was one that would go on. As he had said earlier, apropos his drinking: 'I am a maximalist. Whatever I do, I do to the bitter end.

'We all used to live together in that flat,' Volodya went on; 'me and my wife, as well as Vitaly and his wife and my parents. We had two rooms. It was quite a strain. I didn't like my Dad's style, and we used to shout at each other a lot. But not about politics, because there were no politics.' Volodya looked round the peaceful wooded scene as if he were looking for something and stretched out his tattooed hands. His hunted look had gone and he looked happy: 'History is what is happening every day now, and what we learn about our lost past. History is only beginning now!'

'Is that really true? What about Khrushchev's secret speech and the twentieth Party conference? It's not as though you knew nothing,' I said, referring to Khrushchev's revelations about Stalin in 1956, and the political thaw that followed. 'Yes, but that was all so partial that it didn't change anything. We'd got so used to the idea that everything that went wrong was always someone's fault. People never gave up believing.' 'But what about the things that you could see around you? Life wasn't that rosy.' 'No. But we had nothing to compare our lives with.' I persisted: 'But not everyone around you can have led the charmed life that your father did.' 'I know it sounds incredible now, but we all said to ourselves that what was happening immediately around us might be awful, but that

36

over there, elsewhere, it was all right. You see, people so wanted to believe.'

Yes, the long-term effect of that desire to believe, in a regime where people and information had been heavily policed, had been to ensure that what we call 'society' had been unable to cohere. It had been fragmented into millions of isolated cells, consisting of single people or tiny groups who shared information among themselves. The fear might now have gone, but, as my rat-faced companion at the exhibition had said, nothing else had changed. The country might now be alive with information, with people getting up at six in the morning to queue for five or six newspapers a day, but those same people had been formed over decades by the other experience. Every day now brought its own reminder of this for me. Only the day before a young man and his wife who, in order to work in Moscow, were forced to live hundreds of miles away from both their children, had asked me, really expecting that I might have an answer that could be framed in these terms: 'Susan, who is to blame?' Imprinted as it was in people's minds, it was a question that would haunt the country for a long time.

'History is only beginning now!' Volodya had said, and his words stirred a memory. When I got home, I looked through the letters of Peter Chaadaev, little known in the West, whose writing set the agenda for Russian intellectuals in the nineteenth century. 'We live in the narrowest of presents,' he wrote in 1836, 'without past and without future, in the midst of a flat calm. Nations live but by the mighty impressions which past centuries have left in their minds and by contact with other people. But we Russians have in our hearts none of the lessons which have preceded our existence. Each one of us must once again tie the broken thread in the family.' Chaadaev's words, which caused him to be banned from writing for the rest of his life, seemed to describe just what Volodya was trying to do.

Chaadaev's Russia had been living with the crisis of identity engendered by Peter the Great's monumental attempt to make his country European. Reading the letter again, I was struck by the warning contained in it. It seemed equally appropriate today: 'Our memories go no further back than yesterday. We walk through time so singly that, as we advance, the past escapes us for ever. This is a natural result of a culture based wholly on borrowing and imitation.' At this juncture too, the alternative to totalitarianism had to be more than an imitation of the West.

The Gift for Intimacy

The address of the Moscow flat read cryptically: Timiryazev-skaya, 15-103-350. It had been accompanied by instructions which, delivered over the telephone, sounded like a route map for the blind: 'Get out of the last carriage of the Metro at Dinamo. Turn left and left again out of the station. Take a 94 bus (but check that it is not an express). Get out at the second stop; walk left for two hundred yards then turn right down the path. At the second block, take the third staircase.'

At first, I had not taken such instructions nearly seriously enough. I had assumed that once I had got off the bus, I would have few problems. After all, knowing the address, if I could not find it, I could always ask. This approach contained two fallacies. The first was that other residents would be able to help. More often than not, the only block whose number they knew would be their own. This would not be as good an orientation point as it sounded, as the tower blocks were rarely numbered logically. Only a Westerner would have expected Block 15 to stand anywhere near Block 14 or 16. In addition, the number of the block would often have fallen off or be obscured by trees.

Once I had found the right block, the next problem would be the staircase number. Each of these huge residential blocks had many entrances. Sometimes the numbers of the flats leading off a staircase entrance would not be written above the door. Then I would end up trying to guess which staircase the flat was on. That meant I would have to get inside the main door to the staircase in order to look at the numbers on the post-boxes inside.

Next would come the problem of the door code. Sometimes, my host would forget to give me the three-digit code that opened the door. Or, overwhelmed by instructions, I would have written it down wrong. I would then be obliged to make a minute examination of the graffiti around the door until I found the number written in tiny letters by someone who had anticipated my plight. It was almost always there, but sometimes it was difficult to find. If I failed to find it, I would be reduced to loitering awkwardly until someone came in or went out. Sometimes this would be a child, who would direct a look of scorn at me before landing a precisely aimed kick at the door which would spring open with no code. If I then found that I had guessed the wrong staircase, I would have to repeat the entire procedure at the next door staircase.

That evening, I did not know anything about the woman who had given me just such instructions as to how to reach her flat. My visit had its origin back in London, where I had lent money to a Soviet film director. I lent it not out of generosity, but out of superstition, against some future kindness that someone quite different would therefore show to me in Russia. I never expected to see the money again. When I arrived in Moscow, I rang the Moscow number which the director from the provinces had given me. But I did so anticipating one of those Soviet voices whose tone of indifference would, I knew, lead me to apologize and replace the receiver. Instead, there was a cry of recognition: 'Ah, we were giving up on you! How soon can you come round?'

The voice belonged to a small, smiling, middle-aged woman. Behind her head I caught sight of the same photograph of the bearded Vysotsky which had hung over the stage at the Diamond House of Culture the other night. It was a striking picture, strong and sorrowful, and it made me feel as if I had come to a familiar place. I told the woman that I had just been

40

taken to visit Vysotsky's grave. 'Yes, isn't it vulgar? He would have hated it,' my hostess commented.

The warm flat, as neat as a ship's cabin and lined with books, was a haven after the bleakness of the hotel and the Moscow streets. 'Poor man. I was so sorry for him. He minded so much that he was never allowed to sing in public. Night after night he had to sing in the houses of the very people who refused him permission to play publicly,' she went on, placing a plate of steaming food in front of me. 'I tried to help him in the only way I could. I tried to get an evening performance organized through Cinema House, which is where I work.' Vysotsky's profession had been acting, not singing. He had been famous for his film parts. 'The woman in charge of the bookings said "Nyel'zya! Impossible!" Then finally she asked to see him. He came in like a little boy. "Well, what do you want to do?" "I thought I'd have a few film clips and some songs, a bit of Shakespeare and some Mayakovsky . . ." "Nye nado Shakespeare, don't bother with Shakespeare . . ."'

The difference between *nyel'zya* and *nye nado* is helpful for the understanding of power in the Soviet Union. *Nyel'zya* expresses prohibition. *Nye nado* means nothing definite. It is a warning, but whatever the tone in which it is expressed, it is lined with threat. *Nye nado* is the power that has kept people in place, defining as it does the area of danger, imaginary or otherwise, in a state where there is no rule of law. *Nye nado* is rocking the boat.

Elena removed my plate and brought us both cups of tea before going on with her story: 'So the woman from Cinema House said: "Let me hear a song." And he sung for her, this man whose voice all Russia loved and listened to secretly; he sung like a little boy wanting to get into the choir. I died of embarrassment and shame. She interrupted him: "That'll do."' As she imitated the woman, Elena's face became like a rubber stamp. 'Underneath it all I think she was as charmed by him as everyone else. It wasn't that he was so good-looking. He was a slip of a man, so thin and weak, poor dear. But when he looked at you with those clear eyes of his . . . well . . . He had a real actor's charisma . . .' Elena sighed.

'Anyway, the evening was on. It was to be in Tallinn. A huge auditorium. Of course, it was sold out in minutes. And as the day grew closer, he would ring up every day and say, "Is it still all right?" He just couldn't believe it. Then, just a few days before the concert, the woman called me in: "You've got to call it off. The General Secretary of the Estonian Communist Party says so." "But everything's organized," I said, "I can't call it off. I know, let me ring him up." It's not that I'm in the habit of ringing up General Secretaries every day, but what else could I do? "I forbid you to. Anyway, he's away at his *dacha* and he is not to be disturbed. The matter's closed." Well, I rang him up anyway, at his office, at his *dacha*, everywhere. No answer anywhere. What could I do? I dreaded telling Vysotsky. In the end I rang him. I'd said nothing but "Volodya". But he knew, he knew at once. He'd been expecting it. Then he started comforting me. Can you imagine that? So ridiculous. But that's the way he was.' A tear rolled down her face. 'Anyway, some time later he got to meet Mme Furtseva, who was Minister of Culture then. She was all over him. And when he told her the story of the concert she said: "It's a scandal. There's nothing anywhere that says you can't play official concerts, I promise you." Nothing official, that is. Only that quiet *nye nado* that was so characteristic of the Brezhnev era. It went round and it was enough. Poor thing.'

I was to get to know Elena well over the next winter and spring. She did not talk about herself that evening, but that was characteristic. Her story about Vysotsky said more about the way she lived her life than anything she could have told me about herself. For thirty years she had worked for Cinema House. Her job, which involved arranging for directors and screen-writers to go and talk about their new films all over the Soviet Union, was badly paid and humble. But throughout the

42

Brezhnev years it had given her the opportunity to help film-makers whose talent and independence of spirit doomed them to sterile obscurity. She could not get their films made, but she could help them stay alive by getting them bookings to show their existing films. Elena was one of the countless thousands in small, official positions who had kept the spirit of the country alive through the dark years. The child of passionate Communist parents killed by the Germans in occupied Brest in the war, she had early developed a view of power in her society. It was best to keep out of its way: 'I remember my mother, who was not an emotional woman, coming home one day in tears. I thought something was wrong, but no. They'd let her into the Party! As a little girl, of course I wanted all that too. I used to dream of being a lawyer and Party member, of serving the cause until death or glory! After my parents were taken and after my grandmother died, when I was fourteen and had neither money nor food, the only thing that kept me going through the war was the thought of how marvellous it would be when it was all over and everyone would think we were so brave, the way we'd held on, when there was no food, nothing. And we'd be able to tell them how we resisted the Germans. But, of course, that's not the way it turned out. After the war, I changed my mind about the Party. When no one would give me a job of any kind in Leningrad, simply because, as a child, I'd lived in occupied territory. Honestly! We were tarred as traitors! When they asked me if I'd like to join the Party I said to them: "What has your Party ever done for me, or for anyone?" I was bitter. But then I had nothing to lose. I knew what I was giving up. Money, a good job and all that. But I knew that, whatever else, I didn't want power.'

Elena went on to play me tapes of Vysotsky's songs on her ancient tape-recorder while I followed the text in her *samizdat* book. Now that I could understand the words, his power was no mystery. I listened to early ballads in which, with an actor's ability to possess another's soul, he sang the song of the gangster betrayed by his best friend; he sang of jealousy paid for with a knife in the heart; of the lonely man befriended by the bottle. I listened to the complex poetry of his later music, the songs of a man torn between heaven and hell. I began to understand how right they had been to fear him. Not as a politician but as an artist, he gave voice to the most dispossessed of all the dispossessed in this country, to ordinary people, that proletariat in whose name the Revolution had been fought. So it was that, having learned nothing about Vysotsky from visiting his grave, the same evening I fell under the spell of his racked voice.

After we had listened to the songs together, Elena and I did not feel like strangers any more. We had enjoyed ourselves so much that we both forgot the purpose of my visit. I did come again to collect the money. But it was just an excuse to see her again. It was on that second occasion that Elena asked me if I would like to come and live in her flat, and use it as the point of departure for my travels in the spring. I ought to have been surprised. In this desperately overcrowded capital, whose population of eight million was continually being swamped by fresh waves of illegal arrivals; where people were sleeping rough all year round at the railway stations; where people would pay thousands of roubles for arranged marriages that would win them residence, it was a miracle to be offered a home in this way by a stranger. Where the allotted space per person in Moscow was seven square metres, Elena, who had until recently lived in two rooms with her daughter and difficult mother-in-law, lived in luxury. She had two rooms to herself. Unhesitatingly, I accepted her invitation. I would return as her guest in the spring.

Those first days in Moscow were touched with magic for me. It was as if the obdurate surface of the Soviet capital which I had found so daunting on my arrival was fissured with invisible cracks. If I was lucky enough to stand in the right place or say the right thing, it seemed, a crack would open up and I would find myself in a different world. There had to be, I felt, some correlation between those blank faces in Kalinin Prospect and the gift for intimacy of these people. It was as if the giving or the withholding of charm was, in a totalitarian society, essentially a political act. It involved a person's integrity. Smiles were not to be given as we give them in the West, carelessly, profligately. 'Have a nice day!' 'Mind how you go!' The Kiev theatre group had accepted me because I liked what they were trying to do. Elena had opened up her heart and her home at Vysotsky's name.

A Very Pure Man

'If in countries where machines abound, wood and metal seem to have a soul, under despotism men seem to be of wood.'

Marquis de Custine, *Journals*, 1839

Moscow still looked like a city at war. It was as if all the information had been hidden, to baffle the enemy. I spent the morning trying, as I walked, to discover where a particular film was playing. Posters giving details of the week's films did exist, but that morning they eluded me. The news-stands, in the brief period between their opening in the morning and their closing for lunch, sold nothing helpful. The weekly entertainment guide for Moscow could, I was told, be bought only on subscription.

The longer I walked, the more enraged I became at the contempt of those with information and power for those without, a contempt demonstrated in every detail of Soviet life. Then my eye was caught by a banner, ten foot high, bearing the device: SOVIET MAN MUST REMEMBER HIS RIGHT TO LEISURE. Presumably it had not been thought ideological enough to require removal when the city had been swept of slogans recently. What a mysterious Revolution it had been that had resulted in the suppression of so many layers of information down to the merely useful and their substitution by words that had neither meaning nor function. The result was that, even at the most mundane level, information seemed to be valued in inverse proportion to its availability. If a good film was on, a Muscovite did not need a poster to tell him about it. He would know where it was playing. But to be a foreigner or a provincial in this city was to be surrounded by trivial mystifications.

I would never have known about the Belov exhibition had I not just come from London, where I had been talking to one of its instigators. In Moscow, there was no publicity. Yet the queue stretched for forty yards along the pavement on Tverskoi Boulevard. Between the lines of traffic ran the broad green boulevard. For an hour I queued, watching while a phalanx of massive women advanced down the gardens in the autumn sunshine. They were lifting begonias. Their progress was slow, but continual. Mine was not. The longer I stood in the queue, the further I was from the head of it. As we retreated steadily away from the entrance, I realized that I would not see the exhibition that day unless I too jumped the queue. To invoke my status as a foreigner as a reason for special treatment gave me no pleasure. As I pushed past the hostile crowd, I became one of the millions of people that morning who, where demand exceeded supply, found a reason for being treated differently.

Pyotr Belov did not appear to have been outstanding as a theatre designer. He had painted the pictures now being exhibited in the last two years of his life, after his retirement following a heart attack. Icons to a lost history, they were remarkable for the way they turned the propagandist style of socialist art against the regime. I gazed at a picture of Stalin's arm, unmistakable with its khaki tunic and pipe, sweeping across a snowy table, crushing millions of little figures. The mood in the crowded rooms was charged. One middle-aged woman wept openly. A noisy group of people was gathered around a picture in which two crows standing on a frozen river scavenged among the litter. Under the ice, a mass of faces were trapped: 'Look there's Vysotsky. But who's that? Looks a bit like

47

Gorky . . .' 'Don't be silly. Gorky – a victim!' The face was Tarkovsky's. An old man, his chest covered in medals, gazed at the picture, lost in thought.

From the exhibition, I made my way out of Moscow. I had been invited to supper by the girl who had followed me to the theatre the other night, concerned at my safety with a drunken man. Bella was waiting for me on the street when I came out of the Metro. She greeted me as if we were old friends. She was a beautiful girl, with long fair hair looped back from a high-cheekboned face. Anywhere in the world people passing would have turned their heads to look at her. But in this drab street the careworn figures did not give her a second glance.

We walked away from the road, along a well-trodden path between straggling trees. Yellow autumn leaves caught the light. After the desolate landscape where the Kiev actors had played, the lighted windows of the low utilitarian blocks behind the trees – *khrushchovtsi* as they were called, after the period of their construction – looked inviting from the path.

Bella's husband Andrei and two small boys greeted us at the door to the flat. Andrei had an expressionless face and stiff manners. He could not have been much more than thirty, but his stolid bearing made him look older. Their father's funereal demeanour did not inhibit the boys, who careered round the two low-ceilinged rooms. Andrei was an ingenious handyman, and his efforts had disguised the mean proportions of the rooms. As I took off my boots, I noticed long strips of elaborately carved wood on the back of the front door. This carving, Bella boasted, was her husband's special hobby. The lettering was so ornate that I only deciphered the first two lines with help: TO LIVE WITHOUT WOMEN IS BORING. TO LIVE WITH A FOOL IS EVEN MORE BORING. A WISE MAN LISTENS WHEN A FOOL SPEAKS. Despite the interesting ambiguity of this last phrase, I was puzzled that Bella's husband should have expended such effort on immortalizing these homilies. Maybe it was a joke. But Andrei's face did not inspire me to laugh.

I put on the slippers which Bella offered me. *Tufli* – the very word for slippers has a comfortable ring. *Tufli* are never new and never the right size. The ritual of giving *tufli* to guests when they enter your home is one of a people who have a gift for intimacy. However little you know your hosts and however smartly dressed you may have been when you arrived, it is hard not to feel at home when your costume ends in an old pair of your host's slippers.

Bella settled us in the sitting-room, which Andrei had cunningly partitioned off from their double bed. 'Now you two will have a lot to talk about. Andrei has been studying English and he has read such a lot about your country! But he's never had the chance to talk to anyone.' Bella ruffled his hair and retired to the kitchen.

'How long have you been studying English?' I asked Andrei slowly in my own language, aware now why I had been asked to supper. An even more guarded look than usual came over Andrei's face. He laughed non-committally, as though I had made a witty remark which he could not quite catch. I tried again, more slowly still. 'Your wife Bella is a beautiful woman.' His brows knitted and he glowered at me. He understood nothing. After a few more unsuccessful attempts on my part, during which he glared at me, an awful suspicion came to me: this man thought I was teasing him by speaking gibberish. I gave up and turned my attention to the boys, who were hurling themselves around the room. As a father, Andrei came to life and we played energetic games until Bella brought in the supper.

Over supper, Andrei asked me whether I had seen anything interesting in Moscow. Still under the spell of the Belov exhibition, I fumbled for the catalogue in my large bag and, in the course of finding it, brought out a package which someone had asked me to bring from England. 'What's this?' Bella asked. I explained that they were flea collars for dogs. Husband and wife subjected the transparent bands to a minute examination.

49

Andrei regarded the collars as a capitalist swindle. 'But Andrei, people wouldn't continue to buy them if they didn't work,' I explained. That the power of science should have been harnessed to such a trivial end seemed extraordinary to them.

But the Belov catalogue, which I handed to Andrei, changed the mood of the room. Andrei's face closed up like a sea anemone. 'Very interesting,' he commented in a tight voice, after flicking through it. He handed it back without showing it to Bella. An uncomfortable silence followed. I decided to make no more initiatives.

My family turned out to be as safe a topic of conversation as any. But even here there were difficulties. Andrei's attachment to the word turned out to be literal. 'Do you have any pets?' he asked, presumably inspired by having met someone who went around with a supply of flea collars in their bag. 'We have a cat.' 'Is it black?' 'Well, no, more tortoiseshell.' 'That's a pity. Black cats have more biorhythms than other animals.' I could think of no good reply to make to this.

'Is it true', he went on, 'that the English love their pets more than their children?' I laughed. But the sight of his wooden face made me realize that the question had been meant seriously. 'Well, of course, it's not literally true, but the joke is often made about us because we are extremely fond of animals,' I explained carefully this time. I was beginning to be aware that, before he and I could communicate in any language, a number of basic assumptions would have to be established. That the English were people too was clearly one of them.

The delicious food which Bella had prepared softened the awkwardness of our meal. Bella, who had been talkative as we walked to the flat, said barely a word in Andrei's company. She confined her role to keeping us well supplied with affection and food. The conversation creaked on until Andrei happened to remark that the English were the most sentimental people in the world. Coming from a Russian, the remark was too much.

I could not resist asking him how he had arrived at this conclusion. 'Well, I've got this book . . .' He jumped up from the table, pulled a book out of the shelf and leafed through until he reached a page in which lines had been neatly underscored in red pen. He handed it to me. The double page contained a list of aphorisms about different nationalities: 'Never trust a Frenchman with money or your wife.' 'The Germans are famous for their industry.' 'The English are a cold people.' Phrases, round and blank as eggs. The day had been replete with such phrases: 'Soviet man must remember his right to leisure.' 'A wise man listens when a fool speaks.' I looked at Andrei's suspicious face and seemed to see through to his mind. It was neatly fitted out with phrases like an apothecary's shop with jars. There were phrases for every eventuality: phrases as missiles, phrases to lean on, phrases to be taken for comfort when the night was long. He had been lobbing them at me ever since I had arrived, as though he might manage to hold me at bay if he could only find the right one.

Underlined in ink or carved in wood, Andrei's phrases had a reassuring solidity. But once, when we were talking about *perestroika*, I caught a glimpse of something more authentic. 'How can I be sure that in ten years' time we won't be rubbishing the present leadership the way that we have all the others?' There was anguish behind the question. As long as it remained in the power of leaders to give meaning to language and to take it away, there was no answer to it.

Luckily, whatever her husband's suspicions of me, Bella had decided that she and I were going to be friends. When Andrei was out of the room, she invited me to come to the Sandunov Baths with her next day. As I was leaving, she pressed on me a series of cuttings that she had been collecting from her local paper. They were from a regular column which described bizarre and violent crimes that had been committed in Moscow during the week. It had been a recent development, I knew, to publish crime statistics and stories in the press. Several times in the course of the evening she had mentioned the column. Her fascination with it intrigued me. Brought up in a society in which crime was meant to have withered away in the absence of the class struggle, she had evidently been shocked to discover that what had withered away was not the crime but the information about it. Her husband, however, was more shocked at her behaviour. As I was putting on my coat, I heard him muttering to her: 'Bella, sometimes I wonder which side you are on!'

The evening had reminded me that, for all the recent developments, I was still the enemy. When Andrei had asked me how it was that I came to know Russian, I had had a curious response when I mentioned that I had studied at Oxford. 'But Oxford does not take women,' he had checkmated me. I did attempt to explain that his information was out of date. But from the look on his face, I knew that he felt he had caught me out at last.

The *beaux-arts* building that houses the Sandunov Baths is tucked up a narrow alley-way near the city centre. From the outside, it looked to be in a terrible state. The walls were buckling and damp. Inside, we passed through a cosy, Dantean torture chamber, where a line of thirties' thrones with drier-helmets attached looked like electric chairs. A talkative crone in backless slippers was finishing off another who looked as if she had just had her hair dipped in black ink. A woman sat wearing a green swimming cap through which chunks of bleached hair escaped. Above her head on the wall a plaque announced that the salon had won a prize in 1988 from the Moscow Association of Hairdressers.

It did not take Bella long to wipe away the lingering animosity I felt towards her husband. As she smeared my back with Byelorussian honey in the sweltering heat of the steamroom, I realized that this was the perfect antidote to conversation with the unhappy Andrei. In this female haven intimacy developed like a jungle flower. I was struck by the contrast between these famous old Russian baths and the newly fashionable saunas in the West. There elegant women swathed in towels moved between one contraption and the next, intent on the lonely business of beauty. The faded grandeur of these rooms, on the other hand, held promise of comfort and forgiveness.

When I could bear the heat of the steam-room no longer, we rushed out into the wash-room next door, clad only in the woolly hats which Bella had brought from home. It appeared that there were no such things as bath-hats to be bought in Moscow now. The wash-room was large and tiled, with low marble counters round each side. In front of one an ample woman stood naked, kneading her friend's tired flesh. A mother lathered her small child as if she were beating white of egg. Next to her, a woman with sumptuous stomachs and breasts was gouging a knife into the dead skin on her heel. We headed for the pool and, after a swim, retired to the outer room, the *pribanya*, where we had left our clothes.

Here, other women were relaxing on rows of double-sided high-backed upholstered seats. On to them were fixed lamps covered in green-tasselled silk scarves. Louche murals of puttis on clouds covered the plum-coloured ceiling, whose cornice someone had lovingly picked out with a pot of gold paint. Except that we were now all demurely clad in white cotton robes which fastened up the back, the room looked like a *fin de siècle* bordello. Two aged attendants slopped around in flip-flops, muttering endearments over us like spells.

'The baths mean a lot to women,' said Bella as she produced, from her bag rose-hip tea for my sore throat, apples and chocolate. 'It feels like home to us. Traditionally, this is the place where we begin and end our lives. Women used to come to the baths to give birth. The heat is easing, and the pine-scented steam disinfects. Brides used to come here, too, the day before they were married. And when people died, it was in the baths that the women washed the bodies down.'

As Bella sat there, her long pale neck revealed by the beret into which her hair was bundled, I admired her northern beauty and unaffected charm. What on earth did she see in the ponderous Andrei, I wondered. As though I had spoken out loud, she started to talk of him, lovingly, but defensively. She told me how they had met and of their dreams of rearing a large family. It was a rare dream in this country where women, denied contraceptives, were prepared to subject themselves to multiple abortions in filthy conditions in order to limit the size of their families to one child.

'What I love about Andrei is that he could never do a mean thing. He is a totally honest man. We've known each other now for nine years, and I keep on discovering new things about him that I love.' Andrei was technical manager of a factory which made prefabricated building sections. 'But what he really wants to do is to work for the Party. He's been in the Party since he was seventeen. I'm sure he'll be offered something soon. He's a good worker. And he's been putting himself through all these courses in the evening. He never stops. He's done one on telecommunications, and one on engineering. And of course, he did English too . . .' Bella paused, but I made no comment. What could I say? That he and I had been unable to communicate? 'Now he's applied for a course at the International Trade Institute, which could take him abroad. The competition is fearsome. They only take two candidates from each region. But his English will stand him in good stead. Oh, by the way, I had a message for you.' She looked serious all of a sudden: 'About that flea collar. Andrei wanted you to know the Russian cure: you soak the dog in vodka, then sprinkle brick dust all over it.' She paused and looked at my puzzled face. 'Do you want to know why? The fleas get drunk, beat each other up with the bricks, and out they fall!' The joke was the more successful in that I would never have guessed that Andrei had a sense of humour.

'Look, I'm sorry he was so odd the other night. He does get these . . . funny ideas.' She paused, as though wondering how much she should say. 'He hasn't met a foreigner before. I know I haven't either, but it's not the same for me because I'm not that interested in politics. He's going through a terrible time at the moment. He's a very pure man. He believed everything. He's that kind of person. We did read Solzhenitsyn and we thought, well, it's only one man, perhaps he's a bit . . . Andrei used to listen to the Voice of America occasionally too. And now it turns out that it wasn't all disinformation, that the Voice of America, the voice of the enemy, was telling the truth! Now it's all there, in our own Soviet newspapers! What really took the wind out of him was the news of the Kuropaty massacre in Byelorussia. You know, where they shot people two at a time, to economize on bullets? After that, what's he to do?

'It turns out that we can't believe in Gorbachev either. You see, three years ago, Gorbachev said that a person should only hold one post at a time. Well, now he's taken over the Premiership as well as the post of General Secretary. As Andrei says, how can we have any faith in anything he ever says again? It's terrible. He's a believer, you see.' She paused. 'Sometimes I look at him lying in bed in the morning and I don't know how he's going to get up.' She was silent. 'The trouble is, I have no idea what he's going to believe in next.'

Just a Phrase

'I, who have consumed so much that I can no longer remember how much and in what order, I am the soberest man alive.'

Venedikt Yerofeev

To say that the monumental statues which punctuate Moscow's squares and boulevards are its meeting-places would be to say something neutral. Their role is wildly partisan. Through the city's statuary, Muscovites define themselves. Each site has its own force field, attracting people or keeping them at bay. They are points of seismic weakness in the impassive surface of the capital through which the emotions of the city find their outlet.

That autumn, no one would have dreamed of suggesting an assignation by Dzerzhinsky, the first Soviet Chief of Secret Police, who stands in the shadow of the Lyubyanka Prison. The first Soviet poet laureate, Mayakovsky, was also not attracting a soul, despite the quality of his poetry. But across the square from the Bolshoi, Sverdlov, the first Soviet head of state, remained a popular, though conservative, meeting-place. He died early enough, in 1919. More significantly, the nineteenth-century victory monument in Nogina Square provided a gathering-point for Russian nationalists because it happened to be the only remaining monument with a cross on it. Sometimes, the adoption of a monument by a particular group had about it an element of whimsy. The young were said to have chosen as their rallying point the statue of Gogol in Kropotkinskaya Square for no better reason than that he had shoulder-length hair.

But by far the most popular meeting-place was Pushkin's monument in Gor'kij Street. Here Pushkin looked out over the traffic with fastidious sorrow on his delicate, slightly Negroid face. 'Long shall I be dear to the people . . . for having sung of Freedom in this harsh age of mine,' he wrote. One hundred and fifty years later, to make a meeting 'at Pushkin's' was still to identify in a humble way with the aspiration towards freedom. The site of political demonstrations of old, the monument had always been 'hot' since its unveiling in 1880. Tolstoy refused to turn up at the ceremony because he was afraid that the crowd would favour Dostoevsky over him. Perhaps he was wise to stay away. A woman was crushed to death that day in the throng around his rival.

That morning, I was waiting there for Volodya to turn up with a friend of his. She was going to take us to visit a poet who, being still alive, remained without honour in his own country. It was too early in the day for strong eruptions of emotion, even at this volcanic site. The Indian-summer sun had returned to warm those of us who sat on the curved wooden benches round the statue. 'Babyo lyoto,' commented my neighbour on the bench disgustedly. In Russian, the phrase for this kind of weather means literally 'women's summer'. As a phrase it manages to be wonderfully expressive of the contemptuous attitude of Russian men for women.

Here and there, a little quiet trading was going on. A man with a length of white net curtain in a bag was making a deal with a cautious housewife. She did not trust that the material was all in one piece. Deeply embarrassed, he was forced to take it out and unroll it like a Turkish pedlar, before her eyes. No one except me appeared to take any notice. As usual, there was a woman selling standardized, scentless red carnations. They seemed to be the only flowers whose sale was permitted on the streets of the capital. I kept being given them, which was kind, except that I was conceiving a dislike of these unnatural blooms. They were an eternal reminder of the reduction of choice I saw all around me. They even refused to behave like ordinary flowers. They would not die, but lived on way beyond their time, like Lenin in his mausoleum.

Eventually, keeping Russian time, Volodya arrived without his friend. She was on her way, he said. Volodya seemed in a hurry to say something before she arrived: 'You know what we were talking about last time? I hope you didn't get the impression that I'm against the Soviet regime, because I'm not. The ideals of the Revolution are wonderful. You couldn't improve on them. It's just the execution that was not so hot.' He paused, and changed tack slightly, 'Besides, it's not going to change. It's we who have got to change it. That's the challenge. It's no answer just to get out. That's why I get so cross with the Jews. And all those wretched dissidents. I hate dissidents.' He spoke with venom: 'How can you just turn your country down like that? It's so negative. It's not that I don't respect Christianity . . .' For him the connection of ideas was clear. The concept of patriotism and that of Orthodoxy had been intimately bound up ever since the country had fallen to the Mongols in the thirteenth century: 'But it's become a sort of fashion, you know. It's different when it's real. But for half of them, it's a sort of fair-weather protest. They won't be there when the churches are closed down.'

Just then, the splendid figure of a woman came to stand in front of us. Balanced on high white heels, her ample body cased in clinging black clothes, she looked like a ripe plum on a stalk. Her heavily made-up face framed by peroxide hair was still pretty but looked extremely tough. This was Anna. She and Volodya were old friends. The two of them were drama students together in Kiev. Afterwards, ignoring the constraints of the permit system, devised to prevent the free movement of people within the Soviet Union, she had set off for the capital. If you had money or connections, that was an easy thing to do. She had had nothing. But, through sheer determination, she had worked her way through to become the lead actress in a theatre.

As we travelled out of town, Anna spoke phlegmatically of the experience: 'For a year I couldn't get a job of any kind, because I had no residence permit. I had no friends here. I lived on the money I had raised by selling off my possessions in Kiev. When I finally managed to get a job in a theatre, they couldn't pay me, because I had no permit. It was a miserable existence. I was at the theatre from dawn until ten o'clock at night. I couldn't even get out to the shops to buy food. And no one talked to me. They didn't talk to each other nicely, but to me they didn't talk at all, because I was an outsider. Once I started getting the lead roles, they all became charming, of course . . .'

Anna's friend Yerofeev, whom we were going to visit, was a Russian phenomenon. Ever since he had been expelled from Moscow University for refusing to attend military classes, he had lived his life without documents and with no fixed abode. While earning his living as a cable-layer, lorry-driver, librarian, bottle collector and builder's labourer, he had travelled from one end of the Soviet Union to the other consuming every alcoholic substance he could lay his hands on. In a country where writers must belong to the Writers' Union, Yerofeev was not a member and, in the third year of *glasnost*, had never been published in his own country. Yet it was said of his prose poem *From Moscow to Pyetushki* that it was the great Russian novel of the second half of the twentieth century. Volodya and Anna had taken part in the only public reading of the poem. It was otherwise known only from the copies, lovingly typed, that had been passed from hand to hand. Volodya spoke of him with awe. Anna, who knew him well, had a more complicated attitude which I could not yet fathom. 'We're going to read something new. It's a sort of collage of quotations from Lenin culled from the new edition of the Complete Works. I must warn you, Volodya, it won't be the Lenin you know.' She laughed. 'You mean he just takes quotations out of context? You can't do that. It's not fair.' She was confident: 'You wait and see.'

I was aware that Yerofeev had cancer. But nothing Anna had said prepared me for the sight of the writer in bed. He lay like the fallen statue of a medieval knight. Even now, white as stone and clotted from illness and drink, his face had traces of chivalric beauty. He cannot have been much more than fifty, though his hair had gone white. The cancer, that disease that seemed to plan its moves with a dreadful intelligence, had eaten away his throat, which was covered by a piece of white gauze. His vocal chords had gone and he could speak only by digging a battery-powered microphone into his throat. The high-pitched monotone which it amplified was like a parody of an Orthodox chant, for Yerofeev spoke in a stream of blasphemy. Galya, his wife, who looked tired beyond the point of vanity, suggested that we retire to the living-room to wait for him.

The warm, light living-room reeked of poverty and neglect. A large white cotton brassière sat on the ancient typewriter. Yellowing papers were strewn over the flat surfaces. In the middle of this dereliction, a wildly carved black piano stood incongruous against one wall. Galya brought in a handful of small green apples, a few sweets and pistachios. We contributed a bottle of vodka which, with prohibition still in force and the hard-currency shops not open, I had obtained with difficulty that morning. From Galya's face I could see that, however welcome it might be to Yerofeev, this was a present she could have managed without.

Yerofeev's entrance was dramatic. He walked very upright, though with difficulty. With a white silk scarf at his throat and his hair arranged, the knight was back on his pedestal. It was for Anna that he had made the effort. The moment she had walked into his room, he had rallied. He must have been dazzlingly handsome before the ravages of drink and sickness. For the first time I saw his eyes. They were brightest blue and they sparkled like a child's. But every now and then, when he did not like something that was going on in his entourage, they turned an ice-cold blast on the offending party.

Anna started to read from Yerofeev's only copy of *My Leniniana*, a series of quotes from Lenin's works, seasoned with sharp asides from the author: . . . 'To Comrade Fedorov, Chairman of the Nizhniy Novgorod Provincial Executive Committee: "It is evident that a rebellion by White Guards is in the offing. Use all your might to begin a mass terror right away, shoot and cart off hundreds of prostitutes who have been ruining the soldiers through drink, and former officers etc." 9 August 1918.' Yerofeev's editorial note continued: 'It is not quite clear who should be killed. Is it the prostitutes who have been ruining the soldiers and former officers with drink? Or the prostitutes who have been ruining the soldiers and, separately, the former officers? And who should be shot and who should be carted off? Or should they be carted off after they have been shot? And what does "etc." mean? . . . "Be a model of ruthlessness," Lenin concluded.' The cavalier attitude to violence that hung behind the phrase 'begin a mass terror' sounded pornographic coming from the mouth of the object of Soviet idolatry. He was still, at that juncture, unassailable.

The atmosphere in the room while Anna read was complicated. Yerofeev was creased with silent laughter. Volodya sat in a trance. Galya kept shaking her head. Disapproval came off her in waves. The cause, which was not at first obvious, turned out to be Anna's style of reading. Finally she could contain herself no longer. She grabbed the pages off Anna and started to read herself. This was the only sign of jealousy she allowed herself for the way Yerofeev fawned on his voluptuous visitor. It was Galya who had given Yerofeev a home. She had taken him in from where he lay, drunk on the staircase outside her flat. He had never left and in due course she had given up her work as a microbiologist to look after him.

'Lenin to Comrade Krestinskii: "The brochure has been printed on paper that is too luxurious. It is in my opinion necessary to prosecute, throw out of their jobs and arrest, those responsible for this waste of luxurious paper and printing resources." 2 September 1920.'

Yerofeev had been looking at me with his cold blue eyes. He interrupted the reading to say to the rest of the table: 'She doesn't understand a word, does she?' Then, to Volodya: 'They're all the same, these tourists . . .' and off he spun into a male world of blue jokes around the only English phrase he knew, 'Who is who', whose sound in Russian is rich with filthy promise. As a mark of his favour, Yerofeev indicated that he wished Volodya to read: '. . . "If after a Soviet book has come out, it is not in the library, it is important that you (and we) know with absolute certainty who to imprison for this." Lenin to Comrade Litkens, 17 May 1921.'

Yerofeev was right about one thing. I was not enjoying myself. But he had misread the cause. The reactions going on around this dying man were too intimate for me to feel anything but an intruder on the scene. Galya's rivalry with Anna may have had sexual overtones. But in this country whose lasting monuments are its writers, the real competition was to be the vehicle for Yerofeev's words. Volodya was soon relieved of the manuscript by Anna. If Galya had more rights than Anna, Anna certainly felt she had more than Volodya.

There was another, stronger reason for my discomfort. I was hearing Yerofeev's work of demolition with Volodya's ears. Politically, he was an innocent. Coming from anyone but Yerofeev, he would have dismissed these damning excerpts. As Galya continued to read, I glanced at Volodya. He looked bereft. His face had lost its assurance and black ice was forming in his eyes.

'Lenin to Kiselev's Commission: "Tell the Scientific Institute for the Study of Nutrition that in three months' time they must present their findings, precisely and in full, concerning their success in converting sawdust into sugar."'

This instruction of Lenin's recalled the utopian hysteria of those days, when the laws of scientific socialism seemed about to prevail over those of nature. It was to be a tenacious delusion. By the late forties the pseudo-geneticist Lysenko had attained a position of such eminence that he could dictate that maize be sown above the permafrost line. 'Good stuff,' continued Yerofeev's editorial note: 'I picture to myself the faces of Anatolii Lunacharsky's People's Commission on Enlightenment when he received the following telegram from his leader: "I advise you to bury all theatres." November 1921.'

Galya, whose frown had been deepening, seized the pages off Anna for the final section, in which Yerofeev caught Lenin handing the baton to Stalin: 'Lenin to Comrade Unschlict: "It is not, by now, imperative that the revolutionary tribunals should be heard in public. Strengthen their composition with your people, strengthen all links with the VChK [the Cheka, the All-Russian Extraordinary Commission for Combating Counter-Revolution, Sabotage and Speculation]; their repressive powers should be both reinforced and speeded up. Talk to Stalin. Show him this letter." 31 January 1922.'

We sat in silence. At some point in the reading, the mood which, led by Yerofeev's silent laughter, had been one of hilarity, had turned like the weather. The light had gone out of Yerofeev's eyes and he sat crumpled in his chair. He had gone, leaving his body behind. Galya left the room for a moment and Anna made a quick move to fill up Yerofeev's glass and get it down him before his wife returned. It had no effect. Vodka was obviously not what he needed. Yerofeev was the only one who knew. After all, he was the master of the Russian cocktail tailored for every mood, as his writing made clear: 'There are only two ways of staving off the imminence of these dark forces. The first is not to drink Canaan Balsam and the second is to drink the cocktail Spirit of Geneva instead. Spirit of Geneva has no drop of nobility, but it does have a bouquet . . . I have nothing but contempt for people who make Spirit of Geneva by adding Lily of the Valley eau-de-Cologne to foot deodorant! Here's the correct recipe: White Lilac eau-de-Cologne 50 grams. Foot deodorant 50 grams. Zhigulev beer 200 grams. Hair spray 150 grams . . .'

Volodya looked as if he could have done with some of it too. In a hoarse voice, he asked Galya: 'So how far back did it start to go wrong, then?' This inquiring man had never doubted that the origins of the Terror might lie further back than Stalin. 'It started to go wrong, of course,' Galya pronounced, 'when they persecuted the Church.' 'Why then? Why not when Lenin started bumping people off?' Volodya asked. 'Every nation has its own religion and the religion is an essential part of the country's nature. So once you persecute the Church, you persecute the whole nation.' 'But there are lots of different religions in the world with lots of different beliefs, and some people aren't religious at all. So how can you talk about the Church as though it is an essential part of human nature like that?' Volodya asked, with the logic of one who has been untouched by the pull of religion.

I looked to see how Yerofeev related to his wife's conviction. He did not give the impression of being a religious man. But Yerofeev was past reacting. He remained slumped in his chair like a corpse. Later, I learned that among his drinking companions he had in fact been an unlikely carrier of the idea of God. 'Look at America,' Galya continued. 'There, the President finishes every speech by saying "God Bless America".' 'But that's just a phrase.' Volodya had not surrendered. 'He's not a religious man . . .' Galya pounced: 'What do you mean "just a phrase"?'

A Beautiful Idea

That autumn, politics had not yet begun in the Soviet Union. There were two groups organizing in the big cities, the Democratic Union and the Popular Front. Though the existence of both was still unofficial, the Popular Front had more room for manoeuvre. The Democratic Union was Western in its orientation, favouring a multi-party system and the complete dismantlement of socialism. Organizationally, though they were highly effective in their distribution of literature, they did not command large-scale support and were severely harassed by the police. The Popular Front, on the other hand, was socialist in its orientation and, though it too was still harassed by the police, it was not without its supporters in power. Its membership in Russia, five months after its inception, was 80,000, one-quarter of whom were Party members. The Popular Front expected discontent with rising prices and with the nascent cooperative movement to result in a surge of support for them. It had the confidence of a mass organization in waiting.

I had been given the address of a Popular Front meeting which was taking place that night. It took me a long time to find the right place. By the time I arrived, the meeting had been under way for some time. Behind the last door that I tried in the long passage of blank doors was a room crammed with people and heavy with the smell and heat of bodies. It looked like a classroom, except for the thin pink curtains in artificial silk hanging at the windows, which added a bizarre touch to the austerity.

A dapper young man in a leather jacket, black shirt and stringy red tie was standing on the podium addressing the shabbily dressed and mostly male audience. Behind the speaker loomed a six-foot head of Lenin in white plaster. 'Without world revolution, of course, it was bound to fail . . .' he was saying. 'The First World War, following the Treaty of Versailles, which exacted an impossible price from Germany, left the two countries in exactly the same position. We were two countries without capital. It is hardly surprising that subsequent developments in the two countries were similar . . .' The young man expelled his words into the room with a precise movement of his lips, as if he were blowing smoke rings. He paused and a patronizing little smile came over his neat-featured face.

I had missed his speech. The audience was asking questions. The room was full of types who might have stepped out of Dostoevsky's novel *The Devils*. To my right sat a fat man in a badly made pin-striped suit. He might have been a revolutionary caricature of a capitalist. Next to him a working man sat poised, with his large hands on his knees, as Samson might have just before he brought the temple down. In front of me, a man was reading a report in English and Japanese on future market trends.

'Surely the economy cannot be regenerated without a massive growth in cooperatives?' asked a man who looked like a student. The speaker smiled his condescending smile: 'That road leads back to capitalism.'

'In what respect was ours a socialist Revolution?' a skinny young man inquired. 'Wasn't it just a bureaucratic revolution?' A balding worker shouted at him: 'Young man, how old are you?' 'Twenty-two.' 'Then sit down and shut up.' The audience roared with laughter.

'Why are you so convinced', asked the student's neighbour, picking up the theme again, 'that decentralization of the economy would lead back to capitalism?'

'I know it for a fact. If individuals are allowed to accumulate capital or if we get it from capitalist countries, we will have to expropriate it sooner or later.' The mutinous murmur in the audience was beginning to grow.

'What makes you so sure that our proletariat, in its present state of development, would know how to use the expropriated capital?' As the murmur rose, I could not make out his answer, but the tone was dismissive.

'Am I right in thinking', the man studying future market trends raised his head from the page, 'that, according to you, only another world war can resolve the problem of excess capital in one part of the world and lack of it in another?'

'Yes, indeed. And from our own experience of socialism in one country it is quite clear that the only way in which Soviet socialism can be brought about is through the world revolution that will follow it.'

As a sad-eyed Armenian mounted the platform, to talk about the plight of his country, I slipped out of the room. I could only bear such information in small doses. I was unable to shake off the feeling of gloom that oppressed me. Even as the country steeled itself to come to terms with the price it had paid for the realization of a beautiful idea, there were those who were working on a world strategy which would allow Russia another stab at getting the Revolution right.

That autumn, Russians were reeling under the impact of the return of a lost history. I thought about the quasi-religious attitude to the word that had characterized this twentieth-century empire stretching from Germany to Japan. This had led to an attempt to manage reality by controlling the information about it. Coming from a tiny island whose history had been chiefly distinguished by its maritime traditions and its prag-matism, I could not help speculating on the part played by geography in the mentality which had resulted. The vast land mass of Russia had won its first access to a southern sea only two hundred years ago. For most of its previous history, it had been locked in on itself by forests, attached by the lightest of threads to the experience of the rest of the world. Did this not go some way towards explaining the extraordinary attitude to ideas that had long prevailed in this country? Their bright beauty seemed capable of possessing Russians in a way that was not cerebral, but almost demonic, or divine. There was in half-educated Russians an almost fairy-tale inability to grasp the difference between categories of reality.

Those attending the Popular Front meeting had not been keen on the programme for world revolution outlined to them. But they had not laughed the man with the condescending smile off the stage. I found myself fearing that, if the Russians became desperate enough, this characteristic could lead them to seek comfort once again in the beauty of another idea.

Just then, as I was coming out of the Metro, I was stopped by a spry old man whose weather-beaten face declared that he had never worked behind a desk in his life. He must have been well over eighty. He was beaming from ear to ear: 'What are you doing walking along like that with two foxtails hanging round your neck?' He had a strong country accent, and he was bursting with good humour. 'You look as if you've just come back from a day's hunting.' I laughed. 'How about us getting married then?' he suggested, his eyes twinkling, though he was quite sober. I explained that I already had one husband. 'Well, divorce him. Divorce him at once. We'd make a good couple, you and I.' We shook hands, and I walked on feeling reconciled to the Russians.

II

MOSCOW
Spring

The Looking-Glass Economy

'"Why do you tell me, my dear fellow, that my estate is in a
bad way?" says the landowner to his agent. "I know that,
my dear fellow, without your telling me ... Let me not
know it. Then I shall be happy."'

Nikolai Gogol, *Dead Souls*

I came back to Moscow a few months later to find the city deep
under powdery snow. Benevolently, it had airbrushed out the
city's mess, lending it a fairy-tale quality. As I came back to
Elena's flat where I was now living, a woman was beating three
carpets on the untrodden snow between the trees. They made
dramatic splashes of colour: one red, one blue, one brown.
Excited by the snow, her dog bounded round barking, looking
for someone against whom to defend her. A cat sat blinking in
the small window that opened in the double glazing, poised
between heat and cold.

On the door to our staircase hung an official poster giving
information about the candidates who were running for election
to the new Soviet parliament in three weeks' time. Information
was perhaps not the word. Their pictures made the three look
like clones, as did their biographies. All three were born in
either 1937 or 1938. All were Party members and none of them
had any political programme. In England, the newspapers had
been full of the election. Here, no one even mentioned it.

It might have been ten years since I was here last. A different mood had settled on the city. People had lost hope in the possibility of change. On my last visit, the momentum generated by the revelations of the past bore people up. There was an implicit promise that, once the past had been returned, the present too would change and people's energies would be released. With that hope gone, the mood was dark. I found my friends overwhelmed by the problems of their daily lives.

As for me, I would be woken morning after morning on the pull-out bed in Elena's tiny second room by a torrent of angry words through the wall in the next-door flat. They came from an old woman whom I had never seen. But I knew what she looked like. She was fat, with her hair scraped back in a bun and a face mapped with lines of disappointment. I could not hear what she was saying. But the tone was always the same. It was low and vengeful, as she visited punishment on her silent companion for all that had gone wrong with her life. I would strain to make out the words. It seemed to me, in my sleepiness, that she was the voice of all the things that I could not understand in the world around me.

Coming to live here had been a shock. I loved being with Elena, but I had not been prepared for the sudden change of perspective. I felt as if, like Alice, I had shrunk. The ordinary things of life loomed around me in unfathomable shapes. The present had turned out to be far more obscure to me than the past. I did not understand what was going on around me. Why? I was not ignorant of the country's history, and I knew Russian. How was it that nothing I knew about the economy had prepared me to understand how life here worked?

Partly this was because our experience in the West told us that we could make observations and generalize on the basis of those observations. That is how we made sense of the world around us. Here, you could not do that. The generalizations were the problem. They were like the old ideological lies, preventing me from seeing how little I really understood.

Reality, having been uncharted for so long, had escaped to a realm beyond analysis or generality. It had broken up into tiny dots, like the surface of an Impressionist picture.

Why, I asked myself, had the work of Sovietologists not managed to convey to me the surreal nature of this world? So isolated had the country been that even the least sycophantic of Sovietologists had, in the past, been obliged to analyse the successes and failures of the Soviet economy in terms partly defined by official versions of reality. There had been Russian writers, like Sinyavsky, Voinovich and Zinoviev, who might have cushioned the shock that I experienced. But I had not understood enough to take the fantastical element of their style as a literal description, rather than a stylistic approach.

Making sense of nothing around me, I realized that I had to start with the details of life which mystified me. It was a hard discipline. The generalizations would keep crawling back, longing to be said, each looking as seductive as the prostitutes in the Mezhdunarodnaya Hotel.

Each mystification was trivial enough. But cumulatively, they were disturbing. On television, for instance, I kept seeing advertisements for products which, I was assured, had never been in the shops. What was the point of the advertisements? When I arrived, I had tried to join the well-attended swimming pool near Elena's flat. As people walked in around me, the woman in charge told me calmly that it was closed and always would be. To whom was it not closed, I asked? She did not answer. The other day, I was offered 110 roubles in exchange for a 100-rouble note. Why? Elena was talking to a friend of hers on the telephone who had just come out of hospital. She had been seriously ill, and had waited a year for a hospital bed. From the conversation it was clear that, whatever had happened, the doctors were pleased. It had been successful. I assumed an operation. When she put the telephone down, Elena explained that her friend had had no operation or treatment. She had just been 'successfully' diagnosed. The doctors proposed to take no further action. Her case was closed. If she wanted to be treated, she would have to go back to the end of the queue and wait for another year. How was that possible? People were not good at explaining these little absurdities. They laughed and said, 'What do you expect?'

I got to know our neighbourhood. There was the nearby market, with its overpriced vegetables and crowded second-hand-clothes store that smelled of sweat. There were the shops, high-ceilinged, concrete boxes, officiated by matrons in white overalls, called 'Products' and 'Goods'. Their rudimentary style carried a strong, underlying message: the little that we have, they seemed to say, we share with you. But the food they sold bore little relation to what I ate in people's flats.

The surface of the city, I began to realize, was a mask. What it hid, I did not know. To seize on any strand and to follow it was likely to end in absurdity. One day, for instance, I was passing a grimy reach of plate glass in a street not far from the flat. Behind it a single twist of pink net decorated the emptiness, announcing to all prospective shoppers that there was no point in entering. None the less, a stream of people were making their way inside. Intrigued, I followed. Inside, a glass counter displayed the usual array of plastic combs, hairbands and soap-dishes. But behind the counter was arranged a splendid display of scent and make-up. A notice stipulated that these goods could only be bought for vouchers. Worth five roubles each, these were obtainable in return for: ten kilograms of *mukulatura* (which I deduced must be waste paper); ten kilograms of polymers; three kilograms of old rags; ten kilograms of black scrap metal or two kilograms of coloured metal. That meant a generous bottle of scent cost sixty kilograms of waste paper.

Everyone, I discovered, was collecting *mukulatura*. In his class at school, the son of a friend had reached the target of a tonne of waste paper. I was impressed by all this evidence of recycling. 'It's nothing now to what it was like a few years ago when it all began,' Elena's son-in-law Grisha explained to me.

'Then we were all rushing round like mad things collecting *mukulatura*. Offices miraculously emptied of paper – old files were quite suddenly gone, copies of letters which you had only written yesterday – they were all traded in by somebody.' 'The point is', interrupted a friend of Elena's, 'that everyone who collected a certain amount of waste paper could cash it in for a good book not on general release . . .' 'Good book, my foot!' interrupted Grisha: 'It got to the ridiculous point where people were collecting good books and trading them in for a coupon with which to buy a new bit of pulp fiction!'

The Soviet Union was well known to be suffering from a paper shortage. Because of it, there had been an abortive move earlier in the year to cut the circulation of the country's most popular radical magazines. Why, I wondered, with so much recycling going on, should there be a shortage of paper, especially in a country of forests and water? 'What do you expect?' people would say, bored by my question. Eventually I did get an explanation from a Soviet journalist who had investigated the shortage himself. There were two problems. First, the pulping plants, all built to the same faulty design and all ripe for closure, were poisoning the rivers. Second, although the country was geared up for paper collection, they lacked the technology to recycle it, he said. 'That cannot be true,' I objected, 'or there would be no reason for collecting it.' 'How like a foreigner you sound!' he smiled. 'Once it has been collected it sits and rots in huge mountains.' I chose to imagine that he had been pulling my leg.

After a conversation with a woman who had a doctorate in Marxist dialectics, I finally gave up trying to find out the ultimate fate of the *mukulatura*. Having confirmed, as others had, what the journalist had told me, she offered the following explanation: 'Just because we collect paper, that is no reason why we should recycle it. What you do not understand is that the process of collection and that of recycling bear no relation to one another. The process of collection is considered complete in itself.'

Whatever the truth about the Soviet recycling of *mukulatura*, the point was that no one believed it was happening. They were living in an economy in which it made perfect sense to organize a system of collection superior to any in the West, and then to leave the waste paper to rot. It was not just that, as the scholar of Marxism had pointed out, the economy did not require the two processes to be related. People did not believe in recycling because, to put it at its most basic, what went into the economy was not coming out. Once demand had been dispensed with as a concept, there was no real need for anything to add up any more. I was shaken in those first few weeks by the revelation that this economy was not just irremediably inefficient, as we seemed to think in the West. It was not delivering the goods at all, or at least not in the way intended by the system.

People did, of course, still earn money, feed and clothe themselves. But on the whole, they did so by some bizarre mechanism of cheating the system. If you were Somebody, this cheating was legal, though clandestine. It meant that, while seeming to live under the same meagre conditions as everyone else, you had your every need serviced by special closed institutions: shops, clinics, saunas, holiday retreats and indeed swimming pools, like the one to which I had innocently turned up and asked admittance. Of this world I came to know little at first hand, although I was fascinated to find myself in a city full of unmarked doors, all closed, leading to another world, that of the shops, clinics and saunas which 'did not exist'. But it was not the world of the Somebodies that really interested me.

If you were not Somebody, the ways in which you might cheat the system were infinite. The only people I met who clearly did not cheat were those who loved their jobs, like my friend and hostess Elena, who worked at Cinema House, and her son-in-law Grisha, who was a journalist. Because people in one way or another were mostly on the fiddle, they were reluctant to talk about how they managed. The economy that worked was subterranean, amenable neither to description nor, therefore, to reform. It consisted of a series of microscopic cells which, in a parody of revolutionary political tactics, were safe from control or infiltration because each cell knew nothing of the others. Beyond their own lives, or those of their friends, people knew little about how 'the system' worked. It was absurd not because it did not make sense, but because it was unknowable.

Occasionally I met someone who was prepared to describe exactly how they made the economy work for them. There was the prosperous ceramic engineer, whose official income was below the average wage. The bulk of his income, that is to say nearly twice his regular salary, came from ghosting the work of rich students at the university. Through his efforts, 'his' students could pass out from the university entirely innocent of the subject which they had been studying. He also had other ways of making his life comfortable. By volunteering to go and work on full pay at a collective farm twice a year, in June and September, which he enjoyed, he earned himself an extra month's paid holiday. This he would use on his third job, taking Soviet tourists on expeditions in the mountains.

About one thing everyone tacitly agreed. It was not done to talk about it. This was illustrated by a scandal that was on everyone's lips when I arrived. It concerned a man who had made three million roubles, quite legally, last year, selling minerals to Korea. Since he could not be paid in foreign currency, the Koreans had given him computers instead. His offer to pay the 90,000 roubles he now owed in tax had caused a sensation. In the furore, his subsidiary companies had been closed down and the bank had refused to handle his money. The wave of public indignation was predictable, but it was not principally because of the wealth he had accumulated and not the most significant aspect of the story. The point was that ninety-five per cent of people questioned in a newspaper survey believed, not that he should not have had the money, but that he should not have admitted to having it.

77

Glasnost filled the pages of the newspapers with the confessions of KGB officers and the exposure of the Terror and of decades of ideological lies. But, coinciding as it did with the final collapse of the economy, the obsession with secrecy had not disappeared, it had just been privatized. Gently, people tried to dissuade me from bothering with a level of inquiry which they appeared to find too trivial to be of the slightest interest. My questions, I was given to understand, were boring. Although they would have fiercely resisted the suggestion, I concluded that people had put voluntary limits on their own curiosity as they wished to do on mine. The hidden irony of *perestroika* was that most people would actively have worked to frustrate any reform radical enough to threaten the complex houses of cards which they had built to supply their own needs. Who could blame them? Apart from those houses of cards, they had nothing.

None of this, of course, was evident to me. It was all as hidden as the mess of Moscow was, under the sheer white snow. It was the more difficult to penetrate because I met people who were thriving in this absurd world. It had an obvious appeal for the creative community, for whom the very fact of living out a looking-glass existence had its own resonance. A rash of previously unperformed plays, by Beckett and Ionesco, were running in the capital. I went one day to a production of Ionesco's *The Chairs*, a play about an old couple living out a fantasy world in which the chairs became their guests at a lavish soirée. The woman who sat next to me confided afterwards that, although she had been unable to make head or tail of the play, she recognized the characters. They were, she said, 'real Moscow out-of-town types'.

There were many intellectuals who, as long as their material aspirations were modest, made the most of a surreal existence which had the advantages of childhood. Knowing nothing, they were responsible for nothing. They could take the bits they wanted and complain about the rest. My attempts to understand were not only pointless, but in some way subversive.

This conspiracy of silence left me demoralized. What was I doing trying to write a book about this country, when what understanding I had seemed to dissolve day by day? Once I was driving with Elena's son-in-law through the centre of Moscow. Grisha's ten-year-old car had sputtered to a halt in a backstreet of the old city. On any journey round Moscow, the battered Zaporezhets would stop once or twice. Grisha knew how to fix it. But each time was a reminder of the car's mortality. We had stopped, Grisha noticed, near the flat of a friend. 'He's a violin-maker. Let's go and visit him. I warn you, he's quite mad, but he's nice.' In Moscow there was always time to follow an impulse and always time for friendship.

A man with a fluff of grey encircling his mild face blinked at us from a doorway. The spacious room behind was on the *piano nobile* of an old house. On the wall hung a lute, and various baroque instruments. His wife, though much younger, was a female replica of him: plump and pale with an abstracted expression. They lived and worked in this noble room with its tall window looking on to the street. Vitaly made one instrument a year for a state workshop. The rest of the time he worked on private commissions. For the past five years, since the rage for playing baroque instruments had begun, he had been unable to keep up with the demand.

We found Vitaly very shaken up. He had just come back from a hospital: 'Well, they call it a hospital. In fact it's a central dump for attempted suicides. I had to go and get this friend out. Otherwise, I suspect, he'd have stayed there for good. Some time ago, he got married to his American girl-friend and moved to the States. They told him he was free to come and go to Moscow as he pleased. But he hadn't actually got round to taking out American citizenship before his marriage split up. Now he's involved with someone else in the States. But he came over here for a visit and now of course they won't let him out again. He's in love with this girl, so he got into a terrible funk. He drank himself senseless and ended up in that dump.' Vitaly sighed and watched his cat tear apart a fish head amid the wood shavings on the floor. 'It was hell. In this huge room, where the lights burn day and night behind wire netting, the corpses of the successful suicides lie beside those who didn't make it. The self-poisoned, the self-stabbed. One man who looked like a corpse kept groaning. Another was saying, "Where am I? Where am I?" It's a morgue. There's no way out of a place like that unless someone comes and hauls you out.' His wife rustled up some food, as Russians will whatever time of day or night you drop by. Vitaly sat at the table shaking his head. 'You don't understand,' he said to me. 'You can't understand. This country *is* a madhouse. It was the sane people who were lying there.'

Over a fresh mackerel, Vitaly cheered up enough to start explaining to me the meaning of human existence. He drew a diagram on a small blackboard behind him:

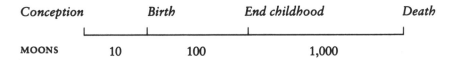

Conception	Birth	End childhood	Death
MOONS 10	100	1,000	

'The great question is what happens before that point,' he fixed me with his insistent gaze as he indicated the end of the line on the left: Conception. 'And what happens after that point.' He pointed to the end of the line on the right: Death. 'The process of development from the purely mineral through to the biological, the molecular and finally to the spiritual, is one that happens at first very slowly – nine months from mineral to biological.' He pointed to the bit of line with a 10 under it: Birth. 'Then the coming to consciousness takes about ten years.' He moved his pencil to the right. 'The next stage, the development of the spirit, may either happen or not. It's a process that is absolutely independent of the world around –

whether a person lives in California or Kuibyshev. It's simply a matter of whether a person bothers to bring their spiritual life into being, or whether food and reproduction remain the point of the whole cycle for them.'

With his wife curled up on the large bed behind him, feeding pieces of fish to herself and to her cat, he went on to expound his metaphysical beliefs. I found myself drawn towards his absolute certainty. A great weariness had come over me in the course of the last few days. I was tired of understanding so little. I longed to curl up, like his wife, on the bed.

Vitaly turned the conversation towards me. 'What are you doing here?' he asked. It was not the right moment for the question. I had known what I was doing here, but just now I was not sure. I said something evasive. Vitaly got up and fetched a half-made violin. 'What is the form of your search? I mean, when I set out to make a violin, it is clear that I won't end up making a guitar. I must start by cutting out the template and round that I build the sides of the violin and only then do I begin to carve the front. Once, I did manage to instruct a friend of mine who had never made a violin how to make one for himself. He succeeded. But of course there are many who will try to make their violin and who will fail.'

I opened my mouth, but the conviction had drained out of me. What was it that I should have known about Russia, about myself, before I embarked on this journey? I tried to explain what had been happening; how every day I seemed to understand less and less of what went on around me, how the ordinary transactions of everyday life worked . . . 'Understand!' this mild-mannered man broke in, incensed at the word. 'You are speaking like a Westerner! Logically! But life here is not logical! Understanding immobilizes! Once you understand the problem here you know that it is irremediable. It is better not to understand too much if you want to remain free to act.'

There was nothing more to say. The light was failing in the high-ceilinged room. Vitaly had put on a record of contemplative modern piano variations on a Bach theme. Shaken, I got myself out of his flat with difficulty. At that moment, I envied his wife her placid happiness. Within the force field of the violin-maker's certainty, I had been mesmerized by the logic of what he said. How, then, was I to proceed in this looking-glass land? I had been brought up to believe that, except towards the edges of the scientific and the spiritual, whatever exists is knowable. Now I was being warned that, in a looking-glass land, the closer I came, the further away I would be.

I must have looked miserable as I stood there in the snow, as Grisha said comfortingly: 'I warned you he was mad.'

Despite the violin-maker's advice, I persisted in trying to get some primitive understanding of how this hidden economy had come about. There was much to be learned from the way people talked about their experience of work. A worker's contribution was judged, it seemed, not in terms of productivity, but by virtue of physical presence. A worker was literally, in the eloquent phrase we use to describe life in prison, 'doing time'. The more talented a person was, the harder it became to live within the system. Ideology had won over economics. A bright woman who had worked as an architect for several years before she could bear it no longer, gave me a chilling account of her day: 'It was deadening. A routine not of work, but of pretence. We had to arrive at 8.30 on the dot, and if we didn't file into our places as the bell sounded, if we were two minutes late, we had to report to our boss after work. We stayed in our places until 5.30, with thirty-seven minutes off for lunch. If you went out for a bit, no one stopped you, but there was an informer who ran and told the boss. And what did we do all day? We were given any number of irrelevant, mechanical jobs. Mine involved copying corrections from one sheet to another identical one. And that was considered a "good" job. I had graduated well and was in the fast stream. Qualified architects ten years older than me thought themselves lucky to be given that job.

'I can't tell you what you feel like at the end of a day spent not working. Day in, day out, it's utterly demoralizing. If they'd given us proper work, I'd have done it with pleasure. I loved the maths and the detailed realization of an architectural idea. As it was, I worked out my own method of resistance. I found it so awful, so frustrating, to turn up for a day's work like that fresh and full of energy that I would go to sleep for two or three hours when I got home; get up, do a few hours sewing, knitting or whatever. Then I'd stay up all night and have a good time. By the morning, when it was time to go to work, I was exhausted. That is to say, I was ready for work. There were some people who managed to sleep during the day, but I couldn't. A few years working like that destroys a person's self-respect entirely. I had to get out.'

It was a system in which the worst sufferers were always those who enjoyed work. One young man who was later awarded distinctions for the quality of his work described how, after his first month in a factory, when he had worked twice as hard as anyone on the line, he was not only paid the minimum but told that he would have to sustain the same rate of work, that is to say double that of anyone else, in order to continue qualifying for the minimum wage. As a result of this active discouragement of productivity 'the law of the slowest worker' prevailed. People quickly learned to take their rate of work off the drunkest or most incompetent worker, who became, in this sense, the key worker, the post-Stakhanovite linchpin.

Under these circumstances, human ingenuity being what it is, the concept of productivity had not disappeared. It had acquired a bizarre new twist in the informal economy which had subverted whole factories. Where quality was not controlled by the market, where it was therefore of no importance to anyone in the production process whether or not the goods produced were usable, 'productivity' had been hijacked by the workers for their own ends. No matter that the scam cannibalized production, at least it saw some return for each worker. As it was explained to me it was quite simple: 'If you are in charge of a shoe factory that turns out, say, seventy pairs of shoes a day, it is going to be worth it for your employees to produce not seventy, but ninety-five pairs a day, using the same resources. What you do is to trade in the original materials for more of inferior quality; you use a little less glue, rotten thread, and at once you have a system out of which someone is getting something. You have twenty-five pairs of shoes which the workers can sell for themselves, on the side. It's not much, but it helps. None of the employees is going to wear the shoes, of course, because they all know that they will fall to pieces in no time. But the money will come in useful, and it will go towards buying a foreign pair for yourself.' No wonder no one could afford to take an overview of a system in which the continued well-being of the employees could only be ensured by the destruction of the factory's output. The concept of the absurd had become central to the experience of work.

During those first, miserably confusing weeks of my residence in Moscow, there was one person who did not find my desire to understand offensive. It was Grisha, the journalist who had taken me to visit the violin-maker. He now took pity on me and appointed himself as my tubby, bespectacled Virgil. 'First of all, you must stop minding about understanding nothing. The laws of socialism are still very mysterious. It's like being a doctor trying to cure a Martian of a terminal illness. You don't even know where the heart is. Is it in the front or the back?'

The popular scapegoat for the shortages that bedevilled the economy was of course the cooperatives. In fact the causes lay in the abuses to which any monopoly system was vulnerable. The problems had been building up for the last thirty years. Before then, as everyone old enough to remember knew, the basic necessities of life (and more) had all been available, in uniform quality, from end to end of the Soviet Union. For all its brutality, the Stalinist economy had worked.

84

Only now did it become completely clear to me what the function of fear had been. It had been the only motor of the economy. The camps had been essential to the system; not because slave labour was effective, but because fear was. Fear had kept people working, and kept in check the abuses to which the monopoly system later fell victim. When the fear relaxed, the problems began.

The partial process of de-Stalinization that had been started by Khrushchev had laid the seeds of the new deficit economy. It was Khrushchev who had first introduced the idea that some products were no longer to be available to everyone, but required the production of a residence card. It did Khrushchev great political damage, and it gave bureaucrats a control that was to become central to the deficit economy. In the Brezhnev years, the inclusion in a circle of distribution became a function of privilege, and subject to political control. The result, which had a stunning simplicity about it, was that the less that was made, the more status was accorded to those who had access to things. An economy had been conceived whose ideal was progressively to minimize its own output. 'Every year', as Grisha put it, 'we continue our struggle towards the ideal of the least amount of goods in the shops. Soon we will have reached our ideal. There will be nothing in the shops but bread and milk. Then we'll be content . . .'

As a visitor from an economy based on the creation of artificial needs, I had years ago discovered that the Soviet system had some charming by-products. Once it was in no one's interest to work better or faster, work had become of secondary importance in most people's lives. People had had unlimited time to cultivate private delights, like conversation. But as the economy moved inexorably into what seemed like its final desperate phase, people were no longer freed by this process. The pursuit of ever more scarce supplies was consuming more and more time, leaving people depressed and exhausted. There were only two ways out: to become rich, which meant becoming corrupt enough not to need to stand in line all day. Or to do without.

But this collapsed, surreal 'system' had one extraordinary by-product of which I was the direct beneficiary. In accepting Elena's invitation to come and live in her flat, I had unwittingly put myself in the slip-stream of the one motivating force left in the society, friendship. For people sickened by exhortations to sacrifice themselves for ends in which no one believed, friendship remained a currency that was true. It was the one balm that could be applied to all the hurts.

It was also extremely useful. In a system that did not work, things could still be made to happen through friendship. Scarce travel tickets could be obtained; doctors could be found when they were needed. The principle of friendship was one which seemed capable of almost infinite extension. As I had already found, people would put themselves out to help perfect strangers as well as friends, if a personal appeal was made to them. 'For a glimpse of the person behind the mask, people will get something done,' as Grisha put it. 'You can stop anyone in the street with an "Excuse me, brother, would you mind giving me a cigarette, three roubles for a bottle . . ." It works every time. It leaves us with this extraordinary cult of sincerity. The trouble is,' he added ruefully, 'that friendship is all very well, but in economic terms, it has no end product!'

The Reinvention of
the Ordinary

The first time I went to Grisha's flat I noticed the faded black-and-white photograph on the wall. Grisha's baby father was balanced on his mother's knee while the little boy's parents presented their country faces to the camera in a belligerent stare. 'Grandpa was about twenty at the time of the Civil War,' Grisha commented, as I looked at the picture of the slim young man and his round-faced wife. 'He joined the Reds. When they turned up at a town not far from his home, there was this ravishing girl, whom they were all after. That's her. You can't see from the photo, but she was extremely pretty. He shot a couple of his rivals and got the girl.' Grisha paused and sighed: 'What can I say? He was young and they'd all been living by the gun for some years.'

By dint of being a third-generation Muscovite, Grisha belonged to something of an élite. Even in the early years, it had not been easy to get to Moscow from the countryside. 'They brought in this strict system of passports after the Revolution. So my grandmother and another enterprising young woman dressed up one day and started chatting up the official in charge of passports. The two girls played this game with him, flirting and passing him from one to the other until he'd simply had enough, he was so frustrated. Then the girls said yes, they'd sleep with him if he'd give them passports. He got out all the kit and was just about to write them out when they knocked him over the head; once, twice and he was out cold. They took a whole notebook from him and stamped every page. Then they raced off, gave one to each of their relations and legged it to Moscow before he had even come round! She was that kind of woman, tough, enterprising. My grandfather was an altogether gentler character.' Yes, this was still the same grandfather he was talking about. This gentle character was the one who had killed two men for nothing, to impress a girl. The man was not extraordinary, but the times in which he lived were.

Over the months, Grisha told me little things about his peasant grandparents which brought them to life for me as characters: 'In the twenties, my grandfather got a job in Moscow guarding the warehouse where they used to bring things that had been confiscated from the intelligentsia and the rich. He used to describe that warehouse to me again and again when I was a boy. He used to tell me what it was like when he was left all alone at night with this vast collection of pictures. Think of the opportunities he had to enrich himself over the years. But there was nothing of value in his home at all. It was his first encounter with beauty, with art. He used to say to me, with tears in his eyes, "What do you want to be when you grow up? Couldn't you become a painter?" Out of the sum total of his experience, it was the beauty of those pictures that he wanted to leave his grandson with.'

The course of Grisha's life had been affected by those conversations with his grandfather about beauty, he said. He was a romantic too, but the legacy of his down-to-earth grandmother was just as strong in him. He saw things as they were: 'When my grandfather used to talk about the countryside where he was born, it was always a sunlit land, where the melons were as fat as piglets. And my grandmother used to interrupt him and say: "It's all complete nonsense. You forget that I was there. There used to be one pair of trousers in your house between the whole lot of you. Anyone who had to go out, man or boy, used to put them on. And the same with shoes . . ."'

*

Grisha and I had met in the autumn at Elena's flat. I had gone back to Elena's to collect the money I had forgotten to take the first time I visited her. Thanks to Grisha's appearance, I forgot about it again. Grisha had dropped by to collect his laundry from his mother-in-law. Elena's daughter Ira was away working and, like most Russian men, he was unable to cope on a domestic level without her. A short, spherical man with eyes that twinkled behind his glasses, he had sat balanced on a stool and announced that he had decided to put himself forward as a People's Deputy. 'Ah, how wonderful!' we chorused. 'It's not wonderful at all,' he responded. 'I won't get past first base. But as a journalist, I'm interested to know who will stop me and how.' In a country where people seemed to ask so few questions, I had found a questioning man.

That evening, Elena and Grisha appeared to decide spontaneously and without consulting each other to adopt me into their family. When I came to live with Elena, it was Grisha who took it upon himself not only to try to explain the inexplicable but to broaden my acquaintance beyond the limits that my random approach could yield.

As well as being a journalist and an occasional documentary film maker, Grisha was senior editor for a magazine with the unpromising title of *Country Youth*. In order to accept this promotion, he had been obliged to enter the Party at a moment when membership had become at best something to be lived down with humour, at worst an ordeal. Party membership was one of the few subjects about which Grisha was touchy. It represented a strategic decision which set him apart from most of the intellectuals I had met. He had staked everything on the possibility of change and he had done so knowing the risk he ran: 'If things do not change soon it will be too late for me,' he confessed at a low moment. 'What do you mean?' 'Because by that time, I will have become the thing I'm fighting against.' It was a fear that haunted him.

As a journalist, his concern was to see how far he could use the growing power of the Fourth Estate to champion be-leaguered individuals pressing for change. This crusading role had developed as a result of an initiative he had taken the summer before I arrived. At the special Party conference called by Gorbachev in June 1988 to try to mobilize the Party behind his reforms, his section of the Union of Journalists had found that their choice of a representative had been pre-empted. The man who was being sent on their behalf was an old Stalinist called Ivanov who was known for having informed on the enlightened editor and poet Tvardovsky. Grisha caught the attention of the magazine *Ogonyok* by submitting a striking article entitled 'The Two Ivanovs', in which he described two separate characters: the brilliant writer and prize-winner of the official profile and the disreputable hack who was the other Ivanov.

'After that all hell broke loose. It looked as if I might be thrown out of the Party . . .' 'That was the only time of our lives when we used to go to bed at night and not know what lay in store for us next day,' Ira, his wife, interjected. 'You couldn't exactly call it fear, but it was an alarming time.' 'Someone denounced me to the regional Party committee. It was not a personal denunciation, but a demand for "an explana-tion of the contents of Comrade Kakovkin's article . . ."'

'They called me in for "a chat". There were three of them and they had the article there, with words and phrases heavily underlined and the margins dotted with question marks. They said that my article "raised a lot of questions" and asked me to explain myself. I said that if they could formulate those ques-tions I would be able to answer, but that I could not respond to question marks in margins. If I wrote "Comrade X came into the room and shut the door" that was that. It was not something amenable to further explanation. "No, no, you've got the whole thing upside-down. Don't you see," they cried, slapping me on the back, "that this isn't some kind of interrogation, it's just a chat between friends." Well, the "chat" went on for four hours and ended with their asking me, there and then, to write them an explanation. I said I couldn't. I'd have to go home and make a considered response.'

The upshot was that instead of the cringing explanation which they had expected, Grisha wrote another article as outspoken as the first. He delivered it to them, keeping copies which would be sent off for publication in case of trouble. This pugnacity saved his career: 'They were dumbfounded. They didn't know how to respond. There was an attempt to mobilize the journalists who work for our group of magazines against me. But, unusually, they supported me. If they hadn't, things would have gone badly for me.'

'Most moving of all,' Ira took over again, 'a young girl whom Grisha had never even spoken to – she worked in the typing pool – stood up at the meeting and said to the man from the Party regional office: "You should be ashamed of yourself. I feel sorry for you. You can't possibly believe in what you're doing. I can say this to you," she went on, "because I'm a nobody, so I'm free. There's nothing you can take from me, as I have nothing." It was an astonishing outburst. All the journalists had been making these well-argued contributions and there was this young girl, with no education, with nothing, who went straight to the heart of the matter. The Party official was stumped. If it had been a man, a professional, he would have known what to do. But against her he had no defence.'

The outcome followed a pattern with which I was to become familiar. A minor victory concealed the larger defeat. Grisha was saved and went on to enjoy widespread support from the new radical political groupings that were beginning to emerge. From then on, people started to refer cases of injustice from all over the Union to him. But this did not stop Ivanov from representing the journalists at the Party conference.

It was not Grisha who told me about the institute in Moscow whose researchers were employed in reinventing basic agricultural implements like the spade. But it might have been. In his moments of gloom, Grisha despaired of his fellow countrymen,

91

who, taking their cue from Jean-Jacques Rousseau, had sought to reinvent the world: 'We had to think up everything ourselves: we strained our starved minds, we sweated, we searched for the right words, but what we came up with turned out to be worse than what existed already.'

At other times, he found in this same observation a reason for optimism: 'We have spent our entire history being special. Chaadaev was the one who said it first before this terrible century began. He said that we were doomed to act as a laboratory for the world's ideas. Because people here have always been ultimately more interested in ideas than in real life. And I don't just mean the intelligentsia. Which is why we condemned ourselves to live out the great idea of the twentieth century to the bitter end of the experiment. Now at last people are tired. What they want most of all is to be ordinary, to live like people in the West, with a house, a car and a nice dull life.' The question was, could this ordinary dream be realized now by ordinary means.

Two Faces of a Village

Early in the morning Grisha and I got on a train for Zagorsk and took a taxi from there deep into the country. The sun was shining and the snow was disappearing fast. This year the thaw was a month earlier than usual. The taxi took us through fine wooded countryside interspersed with villages that straggled along the road. In one after another, the burnt-out shape of an onion-domed church stood out against the skyline like the ribs of an animal picked clean.

We were going to visit Valery. Six months ago he had left the state farm for which he had always worked, to farm on his own. He was only putting Gorbachev's reforms into practice, but his action was remarkable enough for Grisha to have made a television documentary about him back in the autumn. A law had been passed which was designed to stimulate private enterprise. But none of the other laws had changed. For seventy years, the state had been the only employer in the Soviet Union and even now no legal framework yet existed to accommodate the idea of work independently executed. This had made Valery an easy target for harassment. As soon as he had surrendered his work book, which he had to do on leaving the state farm, he had become a 'parasite' from a legal point of view. The local authorities felt free to arrest him and imprison him for three weeks on this charge. When this did not deter him, they cut off the water supply without which his smallholding could not survive. Or so they thought. But Valery carried the water in buckets. He had calculated that by the end of the year he

93

would have spent a total of fifty-two days, in hours, carrying water. There was more than casual malice in this harassment. Valery represented a threat. If he were to succeed, others would follow. Already, after only six months, he had produced more than twice what he would have on the state farm. No one in the community was on his side, not even, it was rumoured, his wife.

I had briefly met Valery in the autumn, when he was in Moscow for the last day's filming of the programme about him. It had been an odd encounter. On our way to the television centre to join up with the crew, Grisha had hailed a young man in a fur hat at a bus-stop and we had all got into a taxi together. The young man had been in high spirits. He was fair, with large, grey-blue eyes and the straight-featured looks of a medieval prince on a Palekh box. I had taken him for a member of the crew. As we waited for the others, the 'prince' had chattered and bounded around with animal exuberance. He had prattled of Balzac and Dickens and boasted of his Beatles records. I paid little attention to him. Moscow's gilded youth had a way of getting on my nerves. When the bus arrived to take us to the location, I asked Grisha when he would meet Valery. 'But that's him,' he had replied. This milk-fed boy was the traduced independent farmer of whom Grisha had spoken! It was the first time that I was to be so taken in. But it was to happen again. In this extraordinary country, it was never safe to make assumptions about people's social standing on the basis of their literary tastes or the nobility of their bearing.

Grisha and I were on our way to the village of Konstantinovo that morning to visit my Palekh 'prince'. The taxi drew up at a small, one-storey wooden building on the outskirts of the village. Through a little courtyard stacked on three sides with firewood, a man in a vest was stretching in the open doorway. He appeared to have just woken up. I took him for Valery's father. But as Grisha greeted him, I realized that it was Valery himself. When I met him he had been wearing a fur hat.

Without it, his forehead could be seen to be deeply scored with lines. The top of his head was bald. But that was not all. The man I had met in the autumn had dipped and soared like a swallow. But this man seemed earthbound. His shoulders, though they looked immensely strong, were bowed. The pails of water with which he was still keeping his farm alive had taken their toll. Valery yawned. He looked exhausted. 'You've been working too hard,' I sympathized. 'On the contrary, I haven't done a stroke for days. That's probably why I'm so tired.'

Stepping over a cat who was giving birth to her first kitten on the doorstep, we went inside for a cup of coffee. The modest three-room house was loud with the sound of a Beatles song: 'All the lonely people . . .' The sound seemed to come from the shining metal proboscis of the home-made stove which ran from room to room. There was no one else at home. Valery's son and daughter were at school, and his wife was making post-boxes in the local factory. 'If only you'd given me a bit more warning, I'd have given you a proper welcome,' he grumbled. He did not have a telephone and he was clearly not pleased at having been taken by surprise.

Valery seemed proud of only one place in his house, his shoe-box of a study which doubled as a bedroom. An archive of yellowing newspaper cuttings was stashed on shelves along one wall. 'I scan the press for every reliable fact that can be gleaned about the countryside,' he explained. The wall behind his desk was dominated by the leonine head of Marx along with smaller ones of Lenin, Dostoevsky and the Beatles. He was the only man for miles around who worked on the land and had a higher education. The notebooks on his desk were the conversations of a lonely man with himself. But only a Westerner would have been tempted to see this fascination with ideas as being merely the response of an enterprising man to enforced inactivity. He was that most Russian of characters, a man in the grip of what his hero Dostoevsky had called 'the accursed questions'.

Over coffee, Valery read out to us from the pile of letters he had received in response to the television programme. 'They were mostly nasty, but that was to be expected. They called me a *chastnik*, a private trader, which is even worse than being a *kulak*. The term *kulak*, coined to designate the rich peasants, enemies of progress, was emotive enough in the Soviet Union. Six and a half million people had died in the name of Stalin's policy of 'smashing the *kulaks*' alone: '"It is people like you who are suffocating the system . . ."' he went on reading, and added in an aggrieved tone: 'I work far harder than anyone on the state farm. Just because I've got a car, they all think I'm so rich. But I've given up my pension rights and I could have my little field taken away at any time.' Valery seemed so wretched and so ill at ease at having me in the house, that I suggested we went outside.

We walked to the back of the house through an outhouse where Valery kept rabbits. The 'farm' consisted of two plots leading off from his bungalow in different directions. One was a neatly ploughed area smaller than a tennis court. Until he had started to work it, it had lain fallow. But Valery's continued use of it depended on the whim of the state farm, whose property it was: 'I know it doesn't look like much, but I can make quite a good living out of it. By the end of the winter everyone is suffering from such a serious vitamin deficiency that if I can get my potatoes in early enough, I can make a good price on them. If they're ready by early June, I can get 2.50 roubles a kilo for them, though by August they're worth only 30 kopecks.'

Valery's own plot was about the same size. Now that the snow had retreated into dirty patches of white, it had a dilapidated air. Tufts of dead grass jutted up like tousled hair between wooden frames, and a few puny apple-trees offered a distant promise of fruit. Valery had only been able to plant them recently, once the tax levied on every privately owned apple-tree had been removed. Broken by the weight of snow, polythene flapped on the wooden frames in which he would be planting cucumbers and tomatoes to sell in the market in Zagorsk. 'We're not really allowed more than twenty square metres of cold frames and I've got twice that. So I have to watch it. If I could farm this lot properly, I wouldn't even need the potato field. I'd be a rich man. I'd grow lots of flowers. I love flowers. I'd rear pigs over there,' he pointed to the end of the plot, 'and keep masses of rabbits, not just a few, as I do now. I'd build lots more frames, and fill them all with cucumbers and tomatoes . . . But I can't.' As he had been talking, he had looked boyish again. Now he seemed to wilt: 'I've got to sit here trying to remain poor. Otherwise they'll come down with the bulldozers and have the whole lot down. They've already threatened to.'

Valery's Great Dane, bought to deter the bulldozers, barked persistently at the end of its chain. It was a wearing sound. The day was cold and a rank smell wafted across from a shed in which the state farm reared calves. The life of an independent farmer here must have its moments, but they were not in evidence that day. As we walked back inside, Valery talked about the future: 'There aren't going to be many people leaving the state farms as I did while the local Party and state organizations are so dead set against us. All these reforms they keep passing, they're just new ways of avoiding giving the land back to people.' 'Come on,' I said, still the optimist; 'farming has been collectivized for more than half a century. Reform has only just begun. You can't expect too much. In ten years' time you'll begin to see some change . . .' 'But listen, I haven't got ten years. In ten years' time, it'll be too late for me. My daughter will have gone, brought up within all the old constraints, and with no more opportunities. As it is, I can't keep on like this. If I can't get anything going in the next few years, I'll give up and retire, beaten, to write my embittered notes.'

It was not just the regime that Valery was up against, but the weight of Russian history. The restraints on independent farmers had historical roots that pre-dated even serfdom. Serfdom had evolved into slavery out of seventeenth-century laws which had been less oppressive. They had tied the peasant to the soil, though not to the landowner. Even after the abolition of serfdom in 1861, the land had not gone to the peasants. The peasant became a free man, but even if he succeeded in paying off his landowner for the transfer of some land, he did not acquire full ownership of it. It was subsumed into communal ownership by the peasant commune, which would periodically redistribute the land to its members according to the size of their families.

Such was the attachment of the peasantry to these arrangements that in 1917 they had chosen to bring back the commune with all its inefficiencies, in a reversal of the reforms brought in by Stolypin. This remarkable statesman, who had been made prime minister in 1906 in a bid to save Russia from revolution, had attempted to repair the defects of the reforms of 1861 by bringing into being a new class of small landowners in Russia.

Valery offered to take us to our next destination in the village in his jeep. As a man obliged to aspire to something less than prosperity, until the thaw was completed he had time on his hands. Once we had left the house, he cheered up. I was glad to leave the house. I sensed that he had been looking at his life through my eyes and that the gap between his aspirations and the reality had been hard for him to bear.

That day in Moscow he had been free to be the person he aspired to be. However lonely he might be in this community, for us he had been special. There had also been the hope. If anything could have removed the obstacles that beset him, it should have been the power of television. Fearing his visibility, his enemies might back off. But the programme had changed nothing. It had merely made him more disliked in Konstantinovo.

The main road in Konstantinovo was the only metalled one.

As soon as the jeep turned off it, the mud was like uncooked cake. The red sun shone low through the bare trees as we approached the state farm to which Valery had once belonged. From a distance it was heralded by two tower blocks which jutted up from the other side of the wooded hillside, a reminder of the original Soviet ideal of industrializing the conditions of agricultural work.

We were going to visit a group of young men to whom Valery had introduced Grisha. They had given up their well-paid jobs in Moscow and moved out here, lured by the promise which had been held out to them by Gorbachev of being able to build their own houses and live as free men off the land. To leave Moscow? To build their own houses? These simple phrases expressed a notion that was extraordinary in Russia today. If you dig deep enough in an urban Englishman, they say, you find a dreamer for the pastoral life. But in Russia, the countryside had always been the place from which people dreamed of escaping. Those who worked the land had long been felt as a dark weight of ignorance, a class apart. In 1914, four-fifths of the country had still lived on the land. But the combination of ruthlessness and ineptitude that had character-ized Soviet agricultural policy had left the countryside drained of people and skill. Despite the system of internal passports which was meant to tie people to the land, the young managed to leave. The idea that anybody should give up coveted residence rights in Moscow to come out here was a startling one to the Russian mind.

We pulled up at a wooden hut. Outside it stood a car from under which a pair of muddy legs stuck out. We were greeted from the doorway by Bronislav, a swarthy Ukrainian bulldozer driver. Inside the hut, conditions were basic: a table, a few chairs and, in the next door room, six narrow iron beds, over which a fishing net was spread. Bronislav was making the net. The others were out on the building site. The muddy mechanic fetched the plans and we sat down to study them over a cup of herb tea.

I do not know quite what I had expected these young men to be building. Something, I suppose, that would betray the damage to the imagination wreaked by the impoverished example of decades of shoddy Soviet architecture. The drawings were a revelation. The boys each had a precise idea of what they wanted, which an architect had turned into a set of plans. Each house was spacious and imaginatively designed, with its own garden, outhouses and a communal barn. This was a country in which the wealthy aspired to make their lives look as miserable as anyone else's – from the outside. These drawings made no concession to that notion. The boys were going to build the houses of their dreams.

We were soon joined by the others. One of them, Slava, who carried the authority of the group, took it on himself to explain how they had all come to be there. He was an inspiring figure as he sat there in his filthy clothes, his face alive with excitement, wearing a straggling prophetic beard, intended, perhaps, to add weight to his young face: 'It all started about four years ago. I had a good job in Moscow, as a metal-worker. I had made friends with Victor,' he nodded towards the muddy mechanic who had shown us the drawings, 'who lived in the same block as me. We had met once or twice at meetings and liked the look of each other. It turned out that we were both from the countryside, and that we both had this dream of going back and making the life that our fathers never had. We'd had enough of living like slaves. But back then it wasn't at all like it is now. Nothing was happening and it seemed like a pipe-dream. All the same, we did go and take a look at one or two villages.

'Then came this declaration that they wanted to renew the countryside. They said that skilled workers were needed in the country, and that they should be allowed to build their own houses. "Well," we thought, "that's it. Let's do it." So we started going round the country within reach of Moscow, talking to the state farms. The man who runs this one, Komkov,

100

was enthusiastic. He promised us our own land, freedom to work for ourselves and for the farm, everything we could want, if only we'd come. He seemed a decent enough fellow, passionately pro-*perestroika* and all that. So we agreed.

'We needed some more workers, so we got this article into *Komsomolskaya Pravda*, asking for volunteers. We were inundated with replies – there was even one from the Arctic Circle. Then we all gave up our jobs, left our wives and children where they were and came. Only that makes it sound a lot simpler than it was. Because we all had good jobs. They thought we were off our heads. Take Bronislav – they wouldn't let him go at all to start with. He's a bulldozer driver, very highly skilled. He's been everywhere – the Yemen, Iraq. He had to take his boss to court in order to get free.'

The problems began once they arrived. Getting hold of building materials was one of them: 'We went along to the shops and everything was there in the window. But it didn't seem to be for sale. We kept going from shop to shop, until finally it dawned on us that it wasn't a question of availability. The stuff was there all right. It was just that no one was going to sell it to us unless we gave them huge bribes. We'd already borrowed huge sums of money from the bank, but we just had to go back and borrow a great deal more.

'Now it's all started to get messy. The local Executive Committee has accused us of wanting to build *dachas* for ourselves.' *Dacha* is the word used for the country house of a town dweller. 'They're trying to make out that we're sabotaging state production!' The local bureaucrats, realizing the threat to their edifice of power, had become indignant that the boys were primarily interested in working their own land, rather than producing much less working for the state. The agreement they had come to with Komkov, who ran the state farm, had involved their promising labour to the farm, but as free workers. Now Komkov was reneging on that agreement: 'He wants to bind us to the state farm, like the other workers. But it's absurd. We've already spent 30,000 roubles which is not our own. Now they're saying that we wouldn't be free to sell our houses if we wanted to, that in the end they'd belong to the state farm.' While Slava told their story, Valery sat with his head lowered, his elbows on his knees. None of this had come as a surprise to him. These were the same officials who had cut his water off and imprisoned him.

Grisha had heard the boys' story from Valery a week ago. Already, he had started making a documentary about their plight. He had interviewed the head of the state farm, Komkov. The effect had been electric. Despite the fact that it had not helped Valery, Komkov was still so jumpy about publicity that all obstacles in the boys' path had suddenly been lifted. The young men themselves, whose delighted welcome to Grisha I now understood, were bewildered by this new turn of events. They had a month now before the programme about them was due to go out, a month in which to conclude a contract with Komkov. But was there such a thing as a position of strength? They had begun to have their doubts: 'We were very naïve, of course, to believe everything Komkov said, without having anything on paper,' said Victor, the mechanic. 'But even if we had got a contract, even if we got one now, we realize that it wouldn't make a blind bit of difference. The state farm is the law around here.' The look on Valery's face confirmed this conclusion.

Bronislav took Grisha and me out to look at the site where they were due to begin building as soon as the ground had properly thawed. Past the modern tower blocks, past the bosses' prefabricated bungalows, the track led out to a site piled high with the precious bricks and breeze blocks. As I gazed at the muddy site where these boys were going to build their dreams, I committed myself to following the course of their project. This story at least promised to have a happy ending.

Before we left, I asked Bronislav how many houses the six of them thought they would be able to build in the course of a short Russian summer. 'We'll build them all, of course,' he replied. What? Six men would build themselves a house each in the course of five months? I was incredulous. 'They'll get it done,' said Grisha to me afterwards. 'I know this lot. They will work like Russians, day and night, without stopping.' Yes, he had said it, this man who had helped me to understand how his countrymen had been taught to live by 'the law of the slowest worker'. Grisha had said of Slava and the boys, 'They will work like Russians.' As we got into Valery's jeep and set off for our last appointment in Konstantinovo, I thought about his use of the phrase. It expressed what I most liked about Grisha. However pessimistic his analysis might be, his faith in people remained.

An Exigent Man of God

When we had arrived that morning in the taxi from Zagorsk, I had been surprised to see the dome of a large, freshly painted church glittering above the village. It was said that people from 117 villages around worshipped at the Church of Our Lady of Kazan'. As we approached it, I glimpsed that vision which, in the Middle Ages, the churches and cathedrals throughout Christendom must have seemed to embody. Everything that man had made in this beautiful, rolling countryside was shabby, impoverished and embedded in mud. Only the seventeenth-century church was immaculate. Time had left no trace on its white painted walls and huge gold dome which glowed in the last rays of the sun. It was the more extraordinary after the string of burnt-out churches we had passed that morning in village after village.

On our way to visit Slava and the boys, we had stopped at the church. The priest had invited us to pay him a visit later in the day. He was an impressive-looking man in his late thirties with a peaceful, broad face and long brown hair tucked under his robe at the back.

The freshly painted green, one-storey wooden house into which he invited us was built to one side of the church. Its window frames, white and hand-carved, looked like iced biscuits. Inside, it was cool and dark. In the large outer room, several women were sewing the vestments from which the church derived its income. Through this and other means, such as christenings and the sale of candles, the church made 40,000 roubles a year, which had to pay for the upkeep of the church and for its priest.

This most Russian of figures turned out to have been born in Kazakhstan, of German parents. His mother was Catholic and his father Lutheran. There had been Germans in Russia for a long time, ever since Catherine the Great had encouraged them to settle. They had acquired a not altogether favourable reputation among the xenophobic Russians, who resented their industry and their temperateness. After the Revolution, like other substantial minorities, they had been given a homeland on the Volga. But Stalin had uprooted them again during the war, and sent them into exile. Even there, it was said, their houses and gardens had been distinguished from those of other nationalities by their careful husbandry.

There was about the priest's manner as he ushered us through to his inner sanctum, eschewing his outer consulting room, something of the sense of ritual of the Orthodox service. As he held back the curtain in front of the door, I noticed the tattoos on his hand. I wondered what intervention in the life of a young German tearaway, exiled in a Muslim land, had called him to the beautiful, alien faith of Russian Orthodoxy? Had this been the way in which he had sought to throw in his lot with his adopted land? Ever since the Mongol invasion, the Orthodox faith had been essentially bound up with the notion of Russian identity. That had never been more true than today, as the Soviet Union reverted to its national entities.

The intransigent farmer Valery, Grisha and I were a strangely matched trio of visitors. But we all responded to the priest's sense of occasion. He settled behind a large desk that filled one end of the long room. The window behind him was doubly veiled from the outside world by a curtain of fine old lace lined with a thin material which suffused the room with pink light. One long wall of the room was covered with books. Against the other stood a harmonium, against which a life-sized wooden figure was leaning forward in a sorrowing attitude. It had once

105

been brightly coloured, but the paint had worn away, leaving only traces here and there. During our conversation, my eye kept on being caught by the figure in its attitude of grief. I kept thinking that one of the women from the outer room had crept in to listen to our conversation. But of course none of the priest's helpers would have disturbed his inner sanctum uninvited. It must have been a relic from one of the burned churches, many of which had been gathered here, at Our Lady of Kazan'.

The priest had deep brown eyes and a mesmerizing presence. His hands moved like tame white doves. When we had dropped by earlier to see the church, he had said dismissively that he was not interested in talking to people who were merely curious. For whatever reason, he had decided that we were worth his attention. The conversation was casual at first. He talked of the way in which his congregation had grown: 'Five years ago, I might have had one person at a regular service. A year ago, it was about eight. Now we get forty or so every time. They're nearly all women, of course.' He paused and added warmly, 'But when I get a man, he's worth ten women.' 'Why?' I asked defensively. 'Well, the babushkas are all very well. They keep up the rituals. But they're not strong.' My experience of Russian women was leading me to the opposite conclusion. For me, one Russian woman was stronger than ten men. But I kept my opinion to myself. 'When a man converts, he comes with his head and his heart. It's all right to belong emotionally, but what I want is the balance of head and heart.' He looked intently at Grisha and Valery. 'The one without the other is not good enough.'

So that was it. He was making a serious bid for the souls of my companions. He was a good judge of people. Grisha wore a cross concealed under his jersey and Valery looked susceptible. As he talked, the priest lovingly cleared to one side of his desk a fine collection of silver dogs; one was attached to an ink-well, one to a penholder and one to a pen-box. It was as though he

106

was intent on clearing all obstacles between us. One dog, the last to go, was prostrated in a position of abandon, its back legs stretched out behind as a dog will lie who has been running on a hot day. The priest placed it carefully to one side with his large white hand that bore the tattoo.

There was a pause. The priest was in control of this conversation and we waited for the cue from him. All three of us, I noticed, were sitting on the edges of our chairs like children who had been called to the headmaster's study. The priest turned his head slightly to the two men and asked them what their attitude was to the Church. Valery spoke in a rush: 'I've been interested for a long time. But I haven't quite got round to coming to see a priest.' He admitted that today was the first time he had ever entered the church. Considering how the building dominated the village, to live here without entering it did constitute a choice. There was another pause, again orchestrated by the priest, during which he gave Valery the time to consider this.

Valery took a deep breath and began again. He was twisting his hands together awkwardly in front of him: 'What I mean is,' he blurted out, 'is it too late for me?' The priest spoke as if he knew all about Valery: 'You must learn to take things calmly – not to fight everything and everybody.' Valery bent his head, in acknowledgement of the criticism. There was no knowing whether this remarkable man knew about Valery, who, having left the state farm, could hardly be an inconspicuous figure in the community, or whether he had just been watching him closely this afternoon. Valery started to expound his ideal of a commune, where all would work equally and share the fruits of their work. 'Could we do this under the aegis of the Church?' he asked. He was a man casting around for an outlet for his energies. The priest replied: 'I like the idea of your working for the Church. But you just want to be free to work your own plot, don't you? People who work for the Church can only work on Church land, for a wage.' Valery swiftly changed his ground. 'Well, I could work half my time on my own land and half for the Church, couldn't I? You must need things here, don't you?' 'Food is less important to me than flowers,' the priest responded. The conversation was taking on the character of a concrete negotiation. 'We'll always get food somehow or other. But I long to have fresh flowers in the church all year round,' said this exigent man of God, sitting in the island of order and beauty which he had summoned out of the muddy, demoralized Russian countryside. 'Could you do that for me?' Valery beamed.

We would have done anything for the priest that day. The quality of his spirituality drew us to him like moths to the light. For me, the last few weeks had been a bewildering experience of immersion in a world which did not make sense. The effect he had on me was to reconcile me to the insanity. At the time, this did not seem strange. It was only gradually, as I attended more Russian Orthodox services, that I began to suspect that this had always been the role of this Church's intoxicating ritual. For centuries, it had reconciled its congregation to the intolerable. As the acute Marquis de Custine observed a century and a half ago: 'They never preach in the Russian churches. The Gospels would reveal liberty to the Slavs.'

The Alternative is Slavery

I was on my way to see an exhibition at the Picture Gallery on the banks of the River Moskva. It was a Sunday. Krymsky Bridge was crowded with people, all walking my way. In Gor'kij Park, which runs along the river to the right, a dark crowd stood out against the green. The triumphal entrance to the park was closed. People were being admitted by ticket only. Three queues snaked away and buses full of policemen were waiting in rows. I asked my neighbour what was going on. Boris Yeltsin was holding a political meeting, he said. The first genuine election since 1917 was only a week away.

Over the road, on the bald expanse of ground in front of the looming block of the gallery, people unable to get into the meeting were standing in huddles. I wandered from group to group, listening. Everyone was talking about the news. The Central Committee had set up a commission to investigate whether remarks Yeltsin had made constituted a breach of Party doctrine. A woman was collecting signatures in support of him.

Without warning, a tight posse of men and women marched up the steps from the underpass, headed by an elderly man. 'For Yeltsin! For Yeltsin!' they chanted, holding flyers above their heads. A surprised hush fell on the crowd. After a moment's hesitation, people started to follow. 'Where are we going?' asked someone. 'I don't know, but I'm glad we're off at last,' said a middle-aged worker with warts on his face. I abandoned the idea of the exhibition. At the top of the steps leading on to Krymsky Bridge stood a well-dressed man wearing a Yeltsin badge: 'Don't go. It's a provocation. Can't you see? The buses are waiting!' He sounded desperate. Provoke, denounce, inform, trap, Them, Us. At this invocation of the familiar vocabulary of control people faltered, but the momentum was too strong.

'Yeltsin, Yeltsin!' The chants were rhythmic, caught up now by one part of the crowd, now by another, as the crowd swelled, moving faster and faster. We moved along Krymsky Val past the Union of Journalists. A couple of people looked sheepishly on from a crack in the front door. Did this constitute coverage, I wondered? 'Let's go to the Kremlin!' 'Down with the commission!' We marched along the pavement round the broad ring road, accompanied now by cars and buses full of policemen, and flowed into Kalinin Prospect which led directly to the Kremlin.

Up until now, the only mass demonstrations had been official ones. They had served two functions. They were displays of power intended to show the world that its future lay here in the Third Rome. They were also trials of popular obedience. It was along this street, Kalinin Prospect, the route of the great state parades, that I had walked on my first day, daunted by the shuttered faces of the pedestrians. Today, everyone was laughing and crying with joy, holding hands with strangers and embracing them. 'From here to Park Kultury it's solid with people,' said a boy who had just run up from the back of the crowd, dodging between the cars. 'There must be a million people.' Later, the Western papers said 10,000. Who is it, I wonder, who counts crowds? 'Down with Ligachev!' 'Yeltsin for President!' 'Down with the Jewish–Masonic conspiracy.' This last cry, by a man on my right, was taken up by no one. A woman weaved through the crowd shouting: 'Please, no "Down Withs", only "For Yeltsin" – it's vitally important, please.' The woman next to me seized my arm: 'Let's make a line. The alternative is slavery.'

110

Up until now, Muscovites had hung on to their electoral cynicism. Behind it, people were groping for a political language for the first time. The most common question being asked was whether a candidate was 'a good man'. 'I have to tell you,' a woman candidate had reminded a packed hall of radicals the day before, 'honesty and goodness are not going to be enough.' She had been greeted with disapproving silence. For the time being, honesty was enough. The announcement of the commission into Yeltsin's conduct had been felt like an electric shock. Timed, presumably, to discredit him, it had completed his apotheosis. People here might know nothing about politics, but they knew about victims. It was not the first time the establishment had turned on Yeltsin. After the emotional outburst which had led to his being stripped of his job at the head of the Moscow city Party in 1987, he had been sacked from the Politburo following a meeting at which friends and enemies had united in denouncing him. Now he was on his way back to power, standing as a candidate for the city, the country's largest constituency.

Where the understanding of democratic politics was so primitive, Yeltsin was not so much a political figure, he was an idol, he was a demon, he was the repository for grotesquely inflated hopes and fears. What did he stand for? He was against privilege. But beyond that, all was unclear. Was he, or was he not, for the multi-party system? One day he said one thing, another day he said something else.

There was not one Yeltsin, there were many Yeltsins abroad in those pre-electoral days. There was the dangerous and skilful demagogue about whom the educated talked a lot. I had not heard him. Indeed I was beginning to wonder whether he was anything but the product of their fears. There was the political opportunist, whose fortunes I had followed in the newspapers. There was the plodding voice of the official who I sensed had risen too high, which I kept hearing through crackling megaphones in overcrowded meetings. There was that miracle, the

111

honest functionary, about whom people from his home town Sverdlovsk had enthused to me. Who could put the pieces together? Each Yeltsin was on its own now. That was what happened to information here. Like the Nose that once adorned the face of Gogol's civil servant, it had declared its independence from its origins and established itself as a person too.

Even now, information was in short supply. At a Popular Front demonstration, I had watched what looked like a fight break out. The victors came away with crumpled pieces of paper. They were not reading them, but folding them up carefully and putting them away, as a hungry man will hoard a piece of bread. Of all the shortages, the shortage of information was still the one that most defined this society. But there had been a change since I was last here, a few months before. Those who had access to information seemed to have lost interest in any issue beyond their own lives. Those who had been used to living without it had difficulty knowing what to do with the information they had.

This came home to me when I paid calls on various people whom I had met in the autumn. With Anna, the blonde in the high-heeled boots, I went to see the writer Venedikt Yerofeev once more. This time he did not get out of bed. He did not look like a Teutonic knight any more. He just looked ill. We sat quietly while he talked with Anna, digging the battery-powered stick into his butchered throat to produce the high-pitched chant that was all he had left of a voice. When Anna wanted to smoke, we went into the living-room. The last time I was there, it had still looked like a writer's room. There were piles of fly-blown paper everywhere. Now it had become a cheap shrine. The paper had gone and the carved piano and other surfaces were covered in offerings: dolls, candlesticks, records, dead flowers, postcards, calendars.

I had by now read *From Moscow to Pyetushki*, which was, as a final irony, being serialized in a journal called *Sobriety and Culture*. This time I understood why Volodya stood in awe of

Yerofeev. Out of his vagrant life, Yerofeev had produced an epic poem, an odyssey into a Russia where the intelligentsia would never venture and which no foreigner would reach. In the form of an inspired, blaspheming monologue, it told the story of a train journey from Kursk Station in Moscow to Pyetushki, some seventy miles away: the comical–lyrical account of a journey into delirium tremens.

The last time we had been here, I had not been able to work out Anna's attitude to Yerofeev. Today she was in a reflective mood as we stood in the shrine having a smoke: 'I can't help seeing it as a punishment, the cancer. He used to be so proud, so indifferent, so beautiful. You could spend a whole evening with him and he would not address a single word to you. He would just look you up and down with those brazen eyes. It's only since he was so ill that he has needed people around.' The more I saw of Anna, the more I warmed to her. Her respect and pity for Yerofeev were boundless. But his belated fame did not make her uncritical. Her response to the claim he made on her was deeply feminine, however. Even now, before she entered the bedroom, she had fluffed up her shoulder-length blonde hair and put on fresh lipstick like a teenage girl.

From his prostrate position, Yerofeev was flirting happily with her when more visitors arrived. There were three of them: another writer, whose tweed jacket and nonconformist credentials were impeccable; a bald philosopher with a condescending smile; and a strapping fellow, an artist, who had left for Israel seven years before. The 'Israeli' sat with his legs apart radiating health in the dying light. He had brought a feast from the hard-currency shop. The tins were opened and the cognac was poured. The writer mentioned that the last time he had seen Yerofeev, he was standing on a platform, answering a question about his opinion of Lenin: 'He produced a swear word which went on for five minutes without a single break, I promise you! Everyone clapped and cheered and the Party organizer felt obliged to walk out.'

113

They talked about Yerofeev as if he was not there. The 'Israeli' asked what the etymology was of the word *mat*, which means swearing in Russian. 'I know it means doormat. But why has it come to mean swearing?' The writer suggested that it was derived from the Russian word for mother, *mat'*. The bald man turned to Yerofeev: 'You're the philologist, you tell us.' Burying the electric stick into his ravaged neck Yerofeev had begun to answer, in his parody of an Orthodox chant. But the writer and the 'Israeli' had gone on with their conversation. Yerofeev became upset. He hurled his stick against the wall, or rather at the end of the bed. His face was clotted with painful emotions, but his throw was more careful than it looked. He was not going to risk breaking his 'voice'. He buried his head in the pillow.

No one was quite sure what to do. The conversation continued in a constrained way. With the first round of cognac, cracks had begun to appear in the surface conviviality. Yerofeev, the loner who had been rendered completely dependent, despised us all and longed to be alone with Anna. Anna looked as if she wished the three men would go to hell. Galya, Yerofeev's wife, doubtless wished Anna would do the same. They all appeared to resent the 'Israeli' for having left Russia and for having done so well. I had not gone down well either, having lived up to their stereotype of the English. They had asked me what I was doing there and my explanation had proved that I was hopelessly naïve. I had withdrawn to the point where I was almost invisible. 'Foggy Albion,' the writer teased me, trying to draw me out, but I felt too uncomfortable.

He and the bald man with the condescending smile continued to talk about Yerofeev in his presence as though he were simple. They did not appear to like him much either. I had the feeling that they were here in order to be able to say, as they sat around in someone else's room in a day or two: 'When we were round at Venedikt's the other day ...' It was not fair, of course. We were all, perhaps, more hard-working, perhaps

114

kinder than Yerofeev, this profligate, blasphemous, dying drunk. But he had been given the gift.

Yerofeev still lay with his head buried in the pillow. Anna was tickling his ear and laughing at him gently, as a mother will when bathing her baby. After a while it appeared that he was laughing too. But the atmosphere did not improve. The writer's way out was to keep filling everyone's glasses, particularly Yerofeev's. Each time he did, Galya flinched. Only the Israeli seemed impervious to the mood of the room. He liked everyone. He was here to have a good time and to show how well he was doing. The visiting men had nothing to talk about and yet they talked. It was a conversation that had gone on for years. Today it was taking place at Yerofeev's. Tomorrow it would be somewhere else.

These men were creatures of the Brezhnev period. One of them had got out. The one with talent had destroyed himself with concoctions of brake fluid and glue. His old drinking companions had even had to 'pay' him a glass per page to get *Walpurgis Night* out of him. The two remaining men in the room had come here, it seemed, to gloat. They were, after all, the survivors.

Out there, the first free election was happening in a week's time. But no one in here had talked of anything but themselves. It was not done in these circles to show interest in politics. It would look too like an admission of hope. Galya, who had been looking miserable as they got Yerofeev drunk, left the room. The writer and the 'Israeli' went next door for a smoke. Yerofeev resumed his flirtation with Anna, expressing his affection through a torrent of swear-words. 'It's like a Chekhov play,' said the bald man to the two of them. 'You are on stage and we are the spectators.'

I also went to visit Bella, the beautiful girl who, back in the autumn, had helped me find the theatre where the Kiev group was playing. I had hoped to have a chance of seeing her on her own. I really did not want to see her husband Andrei again. I was not feeling strong enough to deal with his primitive stereotypes as I had last time. But she begged me to come over on Saturday afternoon to spend the rest of the day with the family. I arrived late.

For all his grave face and stilted manners, Andrei greeted me almost warmly. But no sooner had I taken off my coat than Bella declared that she had to put in a token appearance at the House of Culture, where she worked. Andrei offered to take me to what he called a *vernissage* in Izmaylovo Park. I had little choice but to put on my coat again.

It was nearly dark by the time we arrived in the park. Under deep snow, it looked spectacular, with the bare trees outlined against the failing light. The *vernissage* turned out to be no more than an open market. The people who had been selling pictures, carved wooden knick-knacks and kebabs were packing up their wares. I was amused at the fate of the word *vernissage*. Where in the West it denoted something exclusive, the invited opening to an exhibition, here a little had to go a long way. The use of the word 'première' of a play here, I had been intrigued to notice, meant the whole first season.

As we wandered between the rows of canvases, Andrei asked me whether I had heard of a society called the Open Heart: 'It's been going for some time, but it's only just been given official status here. People are now allowed to belong. The idea', he said, overcome by a fit of shyness, 'is to get people in different countries thinking of each other at the same time. What do you think?' In retrospect, it was clear that Andrei was making a move in my direction, to which there could only be one response. The man clearly felt badly about having been so suspicious of me when we first met. But I was not feeling well disposed towards him. I was in a churlish mood. All I could think of was that Andrei still seemed wedded to the notion that things did not properly exist until they had been given official endorsement. I cannot remember what answer I gave. It was at

116

best noncommittal, probably patronizing. Andrei continued encouragingly: 'It is such a short time ago that foreigners were enemies . . .' But I was not feeling generous towards him that day.

Andrei bought me a little green jointed wooden snake of the kind that a wooden Eve might have listened to, and we made our way home. In the Metro, he returned to the subject of the Open Heart. 'What I want to know is this: is the Open Heart the same as a religion? My mother is very religious and I watch the way she goes off to church weighed down by the cares of life. Then I see how she comes back transformed, happy and strong. Isn't that what the Open Heart is trying to do?' Andrei did have a way of asking a question which made it sound rhetorical, but that was no excuse for my failure to respond. There are conversations that we regret, and for me, this was one of them. I had noticed Andrei turning over little crucifixes in an experimental way at the 'vernissage'. He had made a cry for help. But I did not care enough about him to try to bridge the gap between my understanding of religion and his. 'I suppose it is,' I said without much thought. 'So why is the Open Heart not a religion?' Whatever answer I gave, it was not adequate. I was not taking Bella's husband seriously.

By the time we arrived home, Bella was back preparing a meal and the little boys, who had been with Andrei's mother, were racing round the flat. As Andrei played with them, I had to concede that his attitude was in marked contrast to the barbarous manners that distinguished so many, even sophisticated, Russian men towards their families. He was an affectionate and helpful family man. As we settled down to eat buckwheat porridge with lumps of melting butter, I noticed a samizdat edition of the Gulag Archipelago on the other side. I began to be ashamed of my offhand behaviour towards him. Perhaps I was the one who had been left behind.

'People are already beginning to get tired of all this talk of the past,' he said about Solzhenitsyn's book. 'That's very dangerous, because they really know nothing about what happened.' I could not believe my ears. He paused, and then went on, shyly: 'You know, I really did believe in Brezhnev. Honestly. When they made jokes at his expense at work, of course I would laugh. But I never repeated them. That would have been wrong. Until a year ago, Bella and I didn't know there were prostitutes in the Soviet Union. We'd been told there weren't, so why should we doubt what we had been told? It's all very well being told to think for ourselves now. But no one ever taught us how to do that. In our education system they told us what to like. There was only ever one answer.' My irritation with Andrei vanished. Remembering the first evening we spent together, I could only admire his courage in talking to me so openly.

I began to get some inkling of the difficulty of Andrei's life. Every one of the propositions, like the Open Heart, that was put to him, every book he read, represented not an offer of information, with its own bias, but an invitation to belief. No wonder he had been so strange with me when we first met. When I had read *1984*, I had not, of course, read it literally. But here I sat with a man for whom Orwell's concept of the Two Minute Hate had worked. As long as we, the enemy, had remained the visible obstacle to the realization of the dream of universal justice, local injustices had paled to insignificance. Privations had been nothing more than sacrifices in a noble cause. I smiled at Andrei, pleased no longer to be the object of hatred.

The meal was punctuated by repeated raids from the two small boys on our plates and persons. I was often taken by surprise at the licence Russians gave their children. There was more to it than ordinary indulgence. It was disproportionate, as though the parents wished to compensate in the few years the children were in their control for the lifetime of constraint which they knew lay ahead of them. Not until four-year-old Ryurik had finally collapsed on the sofa, naked except for his T-shirt, did we have a chance to sustain anything like a conversation. Then Andrei, who today had his agenda carefully worked out, turned to me: 'Susan, what is *svingerstvo?*' I looked blank. 'It is an American word, I think.' Except that it was clearly derived from the word 'swinger', I could make nothing of it. Andrei, ever the earnest bookworm, fetched a volume entitled *The Crisis in the American Family.* Like the last book which Andrei had showed me, it was heavily underlined. It was also full of newspaper cuttings about America. Reading the word in context, it became clear that *svingerstvo* meant wife-swapping. This was described as 'a type of marriage contract characteristic of capitalist America'. I read on: 'Bourgeois society has given birth to these moral deformities because it is, in itself, deformed to its roots.' I looked at the flyleaf and saw that the book had only been published in 1985, the year Gorbachev came to power.

I looked at the expectant face of this decent man striving to re-educate himself and I was filled with fury on his behalf. As Bella and Andrei looked on in astonishment, I found myself standing in the middle of their little room raging against O.G. Kuryanova, the author of the book, venting my accumulated anger for all the craziness I had been meeting day after day whose origin was ideological. The voice of O. G. Kuryanova was that of the bad old days. I was horrified to think of Andrei trying to orientate himself between the violently different points of view expressed by this woman and Solzhenitsyn.

Kuryanova's starting-point was a theoretical one. Wife-swapping was the inevitable by-product of the mutilation of personal relationships that was bound to occur in a society based on private ownership. Logically satisfactory as it was to the author's analysis, *svingerstvo* had been inflated to the point where, for a reader like Andrei, it seemed like a massive sociological phenomenon. Of course, there was an element of truth in her thesis. Property obviously did play an unattractive part in divorce in the West. It was easier to get divorced in a society where no one owned much. But the high divorce rate in the USSR – two out of five marriages in the late seventies – did not suggest that Soviet society had found solutions to the problem of the family.

Kuryanova's account, chained as it was to theoretical starting-points, had no place in it for the concept of human frailty. What is more, she had evidently been to America. But rather than come to grips with the intractable problems of family life in that country, she had preferred the theory. The other approach would have had the intolerable effect of showing how many of the problems were common to both countries.

I sat down, embarrassed to have lost my temper. Although Andrei had looked a little alarmed at my display of anger, he gave me a brave smile. It was a difficult business, living. But now that I knew that he knew that we were on the same side, we could at least begin to become friends.

III

BAKU

Too Salty

I would wake early and lie on my back on the sofa in the living-room, wondering how to get out. From where I lay, the reason for my desire to flee, amounting almost to panic, was not obvious. After my cramped little hutch in Moscow, where morning after morning I would wake to the grumblings of the old woman through the wall, all was peace and elegance in Baku. The room was light, high-ceilinged, with dark furniture and plants that carpeted the deep sills of the windows with green. Down the hill, a big ship boomed as it left port. The wind buffeted against the wall of the house, and the flame in the boiler roared. The name Baku, I had learned, means 'windy town'.

My invitation to Baku, from a friend of friends in Moscow, had been unexpected. I had leapt at the chance, even though it meant leaving Moscow the day before elections to the new parliament. Why, after only three days here, should I be desperate to get out? The feeling was grotesquely out of proportion, or so it seemed as I lay there, listening to the roar of the wind. It was only later, much later, that I began to get any perspective on the strength of my own reaction. The feeling had not been my own. I had absorbed it from the atmosphere. But it was the more powerful for never having been expressed by my generous and charming hosts.

Arriving from Moscow, I found Baku a delightful surprise. I felt as if I was back in familiar territory, in the extended Europe of the Levant. The city stands on a steep hillside leading down to the port. I walked with my hostess inside the old Muslim citadel, enclosed within finely ornamented thirteenth-century walls. The invasions of the Arabs in the eighth century and the Seljuk Turks in the ninth had laid the religious and linguistic basis for a flowering of culture which had been interrupted but not halted by the devastation of the Mongols. After visiting the magnificent fourteenth/fifteenth-century palace of the Khans of the Shirvan province, we wandered down the narrow, cobbled streets of the old town. The smells were ancient ones: damp stone, candles and charred meat. The life of the old town was hidden behind high walls on either side, but there were occasional flashes of movement and colour up long alleyways, through half-open doors: bare-legged children, scrawny cats and gaudy washing that flapped in the wind. Throughout my stay, my understanding of this town would be snatched from just such occasional glimpses. The sun was bright but the wind howled round the town, like a genie out of a bottle.

Of the army presence in the city I saw nothing that day. Despite the check-points on every entrance to the city and the curfew that was imposed at night, they were keeping themselves discreetly tucked away. In Baku, the Soviet army were behaving as though they had learned the first lesson of this town, the importance of appearances. Below the citadel, we followed the slope down to the Caspian, past handsome late-nineteenth-century buildings that were a reminder of the strong European presence that had characterized the heyday of the city's power. In 1898, roughly half the world's supply of oil had come from the Baku wells.

We had made our way home to the pleasant tree-lined street where my hostess lived. It looked down the steep hill on to the curve of the natural harbour. The pink paint of the low old houses had mellowed to terracotta. The corner shop sold delicious, flat unleavened bread. Just round the headland, the city ended abruptly and the shore was grazed by a flock of oil wells with nodding heads. Those were the oil wells from which had sprung the wealth of Alfred Bernhard Nobel, founder of the prizes and inventor of dynamite. It seemed a peaceful and prosperous scene.

I was the guest of an astonishingly beautiful woman called Tatyana, who lived with her mother in a three-room flat. She was tall and dark, with a strong face and large, watchful eyes. She carried herself with a sense of occasion. But if she caught sight of herself in a mirror or a sheet of glass, she would turn away as if from something monstrous. She was half Armenian, half Russian. Her height and pale skin distinguished her from the plump honey-coloured Azeri women. Yet, in those days before catastrophe had overwhelmed the city, even though thousands of Armenians had already fled their homes, Tatyana seemed on the surface to be totally assimilated. Her friends were all Azeris; she spoke the language; and she talked of the Armenians as the 'others', as if she were herself Azeri.

Tatyana was a talented set designer with Baku's Puppet Theatre. Although she was not well off, she had style of a kind that did not seem to come naturally to the Russians. Her bookshelves were full of translations of modern literature from all over the world. I had the immediate feeling of having arrived somewhere which was beyond the reach of Soviet culture, somewhere which, for all its exotic charm, seemed familiar. Her widowed Armenian mother was a retired architect and an inspired cook. I liked them both enormously.

But I had to get out. Something was going on in that flat, something unbearably painful. I was caught in the cross-fire of an endless, wearing battle between the two women. On the face of it it was just a family matter, a struggle between a protective mother and her daughter, a professional single woman in her thirties who wanted some life of her own. But, as I was to discover slowly, the lines of every larger battle that was being fought out in Azerbaijan ran through that flat.

As a household, it was distinctive in two ways. There were

no men in it, and it was an Armenian household. Of the two, it was the lack of men that seemed to me in those first few days to pose the more immediate problem. I had been taken by surprise to discover that women in this richest and most advanced of the Muslim Soviet republics were, at least notionally, still so much regarded as the property of men that they were not meant to go out of their houses unaccompanied. They were not meant to drive or smoke, or appear in public places such as cinemas or cafés. Women could still be 'stolen', as Tatyana's great-grandmother had been, by any man who wanted a wife. Her husband and three daughters never heard of her again after she was abducted from her hospital bed. Things had not changed so much, it seemed. As a result of these unexpected restrictions, I could not get out of the cross-fire between the two women by going out on my own, even for a breath of air.

This traditionally Islamic attitude to women did not seem to fit together with what I knew of Soviet Azerbaijan, the northern part of a country which had been ceded by the Persians to the Russian Empire in 1828. It was by far the richest and most progressive of the Muslim republics. By the 1860s, foreign capital had started the process of rapid industrialization that was bound to accompany the international exploitation of Baku's oil. By the end of the century the workers of all nationalities, who had been attracted to this scene of opportunities, numbered 60,000. The bad conditions of early industrialization, exacerbated by old feudal abuses and abetted by newer colonial ones, had provided the ideal breeding-ground for revolutionary agitation. By 1920 the new Soviet government was in control, supported by the population. In this context, unique among the otherwise backward Muslim republics of the Soviet Union, it had never occurred to me that the hold of Islamic custom would be so strong. Nor was there any evidence of an upsurge of religious feeling in the city at that stage. The mosques were conspicuously empty.

126

As the days wore on, my suspicion grew that this traditionalism reflected something complex. It seemed to have become a bulwark of resistance to a rule that was universally regarded as colonial. The words Soviet and Russian were treated as though they were synonymous. People saw their rich country as having been robbed of oil, poisoned with insecticides and given nothing in return. The Russians were spoken of with a contempt that reserved its greatest scorn for those who were working for reform. 'Poor man,' as someone said to me of my friend Grisha in Moscow, 'he's labouring under the delusion that he can be an honest Party member!' In the disillusionment here, there was no loss of faith, for faith had been lost long ago. The cynicism was arid, unrelieved.

In flying from Moscow to Baku I appeared to have leapt forward in time. Here I glimpsed the cynicism that would settle on Russia if reform continued to bring no substantial change: 'What can *perestroika* possibly mean down here? We long since ceased to believe in the system.' Tatyana was no longer even capable of becoming angry: 'You can't expect us to believe it capable of reform either. What Russia is going through now, we went through thirty years ago – the disillusionment and the development of a widespread counter-system. My father, who would have been in his late fifties now, was in the Party. His was the last generation that could possibly have pinned its hopes on socialism. After the war there was a genuine upsurge of idealism. But down here, anyone in my generation who says they are a socialist is a fool or a liar.'

This contempt extended to all aspects of Russo-Soviet culture. Russians were numskulls who did not know how to behave, how to cook, how to dress, or indeed how to protect a woman. In defending their own attitude to women, the comparison was always with the Russians. 'What have Russian women got out of their so-called liberation?' as Tatyana put it to me. 'Nothing but drudgery.' I ended up agreeing. The abuses to which Soviet life exposed Russian women offered nothing which could be preferred to the protected status of Azeri women.

After I had recovered from the shock of adjustment, I began to appreciate another twist. As befitted a social development whose origin lay not in religion but in the resistance which Azeri culture had put up to Sovietization, the customs which dominated the lives of women in this worldly culture were far more sophisticated than they looked at first. They involved an elaborate and deeply oriental play between appearance and reality, rules and exceptions.

A woman was not allowed to walk unaccompanied in the streets – but she could go shopping or to work. She could not appear in a public place like a cinema, theatre, restaurant or café. But, as the days unfolded, I gathered that there were one or two theatres that were considered respectable if a woman was properly accompanied by a man. Although restaurants and cafés were off limits, particularly for women on their own, Tatyana took me to one or two which for one reason or another proved to be exceptions to this rule. The ban on smoking remained absolute, of course. But it only applied to company, and above all to mixed company. Every lavatory and woman's bedroom was thick with smoke. As for the concept of virginity before marriage, it was still of enormous importance, and a bridegroom's relations could indeed demand the conventional proof before a wedding. But this custom served only to infuse with vigour the extra-marital whirl of Baku's social life. Its clandestine character added zest to the game. As for the tradition of stealing women, it had become a device whereby the young whose parents opposed their marriage could overcome those objections by dint of the young man arranging to 'steal' his bride. Traditional customs, in other words, mostly seemed to have been turned from being restrictions into being refinements, capable of keeping the play between the sexes in perpetual motion.

In the coming months, I was to meet many single women in

128

Russia who lived desperately lonely lives. The Azeri extended family offered an alternative that had much to be said for it. I caught a tantalizing glimpse of this one day when Tatyana took me to call on friends of hers in the old citadel. During the first month of the Muslim New Year, it was the custom to pay such visits, and to eat of the ritual dish of dried fruits, symbolically adorned with a tuft of growing wheat. Soviet Muslims had never stopped observing the tradition, but that year they had been granted official permission to celebrate it for the first time.

Raul's family lived in the heart of the old citadel. The façade of the house with its arched windows and crisply dressed masonry made a statement that was wasted on the narrow, cobbled alley outside. Before the Revolution, the house, which now contained seven families, had belonged to them. Luckily, Raul's extended family was big enough to occupy the whole of the first floor. The life of the household faced inwards, on to an open courtyard. Instead of the grand old stone staircase, which had been demolished, flimsy wooden steps led up to a wooden gallery which ran round the courtyard, connecting the rooms.

We had called at an exciting moment. The first-floor women were scurrying to and fro along the gallery, engaged in preparations for a family wedding next day. We were met by Raul and his handsome father, who got up to greet us with the exquisite manners so common here, manners which in Europe had disappeared with my grandfather's generation. The appearance of the two generations of men was in striking contrast one to the other, a contrast which expressed the rise and fall of the Soviet empire. The tubby Raul had let himself go. His uncombed hair and dishevelled appearance declared his bachelor state. But his handsome father, a well-known actor, was smart in a shirt and waistcoat and striped-cotton pyjama bottoms. These were like the ones my brother used to wear as a boy. Pyjama? But of course, the word had its origin in the Persian word for leg garment. With that scavenging instinct of our pragmatic tradition, we had brought the idea back in the early nineteenth century, added jackets and adopted them for nocturnal wear.

The large living-room was sparsely furnished with sofas around two sides. But the long wall was set on fire by a red-and-blue modern carpet that hung on it. A case containing a few pieces of fine cut glass dated back to a more prosperous time. Before the Revolution, the family business had been accountancy. On the walls hung several calendars and a plastic picture of basset-hounds in relief.

Raul's father produced the family photograph album. It too was an eloquent window on the rise and fall of a period of history. The early pages were full of pictures of beautiful, laughing young actors and actresses from the twenties. Their faces had the confidence of people who believed in the new world they were building. But as I turned the pages of the second, more formal phase of group photographs, dating from the thirties, the expressions changed. The faces gazed out solemnly. Here and there one had been scratched out, leaving a white hole above a body. It had been an arrestable offence to be caught with the picture of a forbidden person in the house.

The worst effects of the Terror appear to have been mitigated by the strength of the traditional family structure. Sons did not denounce fathers or neighbours betray each other with quite the compulsion that they did in Russia. But none the less, the old man's brother-in-law had been given ten years for an instance of Crimespeak, as Orwell called it: 'He was the best runner in Azerbaijan,' Raul explained. 'One day, at a grand parade, he said to the man standing next to him that it looked as if Stalin had not shaved that day. He didn't even have time to get home before they took him away. For days, his wife had no idea where he was.'

In the next-door room, a conspiracy of women and children was busy with preparations for the wedding. Raul's sister, a mountainous woman dressed in black, flitted with abundant good humour between the two rooms, plying us with tea and sticky cakes. Following in the family tradition, she was a successful actress. She was single, but the extended family had even managed to provide her with a baby, a robust boy bequeathed by one of her married sisters.

The next day, at the wedding, I watched her dancing with her twelve-year-old nephew, to music which reminded me of the pastoral origins of the Azeris. The long tune lines wound their way like sheep tracks up a hill. As she slowly turned to the music, her arms as supple as tendrils, her great body clad in dark green silk was as ripe as a watermelon. I watched her move confidently between the twittering women, putting shy ones at ease and making them laugh. It seemed to me that she had found a way of being single as well as free in this society. She belonged to no one but, contained within the extended family, she posed a threat to no one.

The contrast to the household in which I was living was inescapable. Essentially, the freedom of a woman here depended upon her belonging to a man, or within a structure presided over by a man. Tatyana did not. Her independence outside the extended family was a violation of the social order that left her dangerously exposed. Her mother's anxious shadowing of Tatyana's movements was based not on neurosis but on genuine fear. Tatyana had been stolen once, but her abductors had forgotten to lock the door of the car and she had thrown herself out of it when it slowed down for a traffic light. The combination of her daughter's beauty and her single unprotected state contravened all the unwritten rules.

The play of appearance and reality that operated so generously in favour of Azeri women who were supported by a family worked in the other direction in Tatyana's life. She was less, not more free than she looked. She depended for her entertainment and her mobility upon her beauty, which drew around her many cavaliers. No wonder this proud woman felt so ambivalent about her looks that she would turn away from her reflection in the glass. She lived in a society whose cult of beauty was tyrannical. 'A woman does not need a mirror to tell her she is beautiful here,' as Tatyana put it. 'From childhood on, she is told it every day.' In this country, a woman's beauty had little to do with her looks. It depended on her attitude of mind. Tatyana, whose mind was as trained as any man's, knew about that trap. But painful as it was to be beautiful, she could not afford not to be.

In those first few days, I met none of her cavaliers. By some unhappy chance, they were otherwise occupied and did not happen to ring up. It later transpired that one of them had spent the time in prison on my, or rather Tatyana's, behalf. Tatyana had asked him to procure a sturgeon in honour of my visit. He had driven out of town and bought one directly off a fisherman. But the soldiers at the check-point had found it in the boot. Just as swans in England belong to the Queen, so sturgeon belong to the socialist state and no private trade is allowed. 'Apparently it was a gorgeous fish. If it had been the police, they would have been fine,' lamented Tatyana, going on to say with true Azeri disdain: 'But these poor Russian soldiers, from the depths of the Russian countryside, they haven't a clue how the system works.'

Without her cavaliers, Tatyana was helpless. The rules of her dependent independence, as far as I could observe, involved her having to wait until they rang her. The reasons she gave were clues to an opaque culture. She would say, for instance: 'I never know where people will be in the daytime.' In time I realized that in this republic that was thirty years ahead of Moscow, the ideal of economic stasis seemed almost to have been achieved. No wonder Tatyana did not know where her friends were in the daytime. Attendance at work seemed by no means obligatory. Her friends were architects who put up no buildings, directors who directed no films, writers whose books were always about to be finished. She had other reasons as well to explain her reluctance to pick up the telephone. She would say, for instance: 'I don't like leaving my name, because it's not Azeri.' A chance remark like this would unexpectedly illuminate a sensitivity about her nationality to which she would not normally admit. Her surname, like her first name, was not Armenian, but Russian.

The true fears of these two women were not expressed by what they said directly. They were silent about those. About everything else, they argued incessantly. Yesterday's skirmish, for example, occurred when we had come home from the museum to find that we had just missed one of the cavaliers, Rasim, who had been waiting for two hours. His tea was still warm. I had heard about Rasim. He occupied a post in the Pleasure Park with the intriguing title of Director of Free Time. It would have been nice to meet him. I had talked to no one but Tatyana and her mother for the last three days. Normally, according to Tatyana and her mother, her flat was full of admirers night after night. But Rasim's warm cup of tea was the closest I had got to meeting one of them.

We had arrived back just in time for supper. Although I had done nothing but eat since I arrived, the smell in the flat, a delicate combination of spices, made me hungry. Mother brought in a dish of chicken with bitter cherries. Her cooking made the cuisines of India, Europe and the Arab lands look primitive. In this rich agricultural land spices were not required to drown the taste of the ingredients, but to embellish it

Tatyana (tasting the sauce): 'No, this is not right. You've used the wrong recipe.'

Mother: 'I got it off Marina.'

Tatyana: 'Then it's your fault, not the recipe.'

Mother: 'Was that Mahmoud on the phone?'

Tatyana: 'Don't you think you're rather overstepping the mark in your role of social secretary?'

(Tatyana tried the pilau rice, the ultimate test of a Middle East cook. It was so succulent that it belonged to a different order from any rice dish I had ever eaten.) 'Too salty.' (She unwrapped a boiled sweet from a bowl on the table and left her plate untouched.)

Mother (after a pause): 'Raul's such a charming man. Emil also called.'

Tatyana: 'Which one?'

Mother: 'How would I know?'

Tatyana: 'Did he say Tanya or Tatyana?'

Mother: 'I don't remember. Then there was another one who wouldn't say a word. The telephone never stopped ringing and I've been feeling bad all day.' (To me) 'I get these pains up my side . . .'

Tatyana: 'Mother, you're like a bottle that's been uncorked.' (This caused a lull in the conversation. Mother and I got on with our food.)

Mother: 'You must be frozen, walking out there all afternoon.'

(Tatyana remained obstinately silent.)

Me (after a pause): 'Well, no, we were actually indoors most of the time. We've been to . . .'

Tatyana (interrupting): 'Would you like to hear some jazz after supper?'

Me: 'I'd love to.'

Mother: 'You can't have been on your own all that time —'

Me: 'Well, actually . . .'

Tatyana (interrupting again, to mother): 'Why do you have to keep butting into our conversation?' (To me) 'For a long time I couldn't make head or tail of jazz. Then suddenly it clicked into place . . .'

Mother: 'All day I've been on my own. Not a soul to . . .'

Tatyana: 'But you said that Seryozha came round with the telephone. And Raul was here . . .' (Seryozha, Tatyana's twelve-year-old nephew, had come round with another telephone, in response to Tatyana's fear that the bell of theirs was not working.)

Mother: 'Seryozha only came at five and Raul at six . . .'

134

Tatyana (accusingly): 'You've been talking non-stop for three hours.' (To me, in a different voice) 'What would you like to hear? I used to have this whole cupboard full, but people kept borrowing them . . .'

Mother: 'I ironed five sheets, four towels, nine washing-up cloths . . .'

Tatyana: 'Then it's your own fault you're feeling bad . . .'

Mother: 'Tomorrow's going to be a real holiday, without the ironing.'

Tatyana: 'Tomorrow we'll lay it all out: five sheets, four towels, the lot, all over the living-room floor. And we'll trample on it. So that you've got something to do.' (She laughed to show that this was a joke. It did not sound like one.) 'I could put Count Basie on, but you're probably fed up with that sort of . . .'

Mother (as if to herself): 'Tomorrow I'll do some cooking. I'll do dolmades.'

Tatyana: 'No, don't do that. You'll do it all wrong. Do beef.'

Mother: 'We've just had beef.'

After the meal, Tatyana and I were clearing the table. Mother was in the kitchen. 'I've got good qualities too, you know,' said Tatyana, reading the look on my face. 'I can be good and sweet too. But when I give in to them, it is my undoing. The only way I've won myself the little bit of freedom I have is by telling her nothing at all. If she gets the slightest morsel of information, she falls on it and pushes and pushes.' I went into the kitchen with some plates. It was mother's turn: 'I know nothing about her life at all. She tells me nothing. I just take the messages from all these Rauls and Mahmouds. She tells me to tell Raul that she'll be at home at six. The phone rings. It's Raul. "Tatyana says she'll be at home at six." "Oh, that's nice," Raul sounds a bit surprised. Have I said the wrong thing? An hour later, the telephone rings again. "It's Raul." A different voice. What am I to say? Should I repeat the same message? It turns out that I did give the message to the wrong Raul. She is furious. How was I to know?'

Tatyana and I retired to her bedroom for a cigarette. Her mother 'does not know' about her smoking. 'She is a complete despot, I tell you. I ring up when I am going to leave work and she is in a panic if I am five minutes late arriving back. A while back I met a girl-friend on the street when I was on my way home. She was in a terrible state. Her marriage had just broken up. She just stood there and talked and talked. I tried to get her to come home, but she refused. What could I do? I couldn't just leave her and say, "I'm sorry, but my mother will be worried." In fact I knew what my mother would be doing. She would be ringing round all my friends to see if I was there. And when she found I wasn't, she'd have rung the police. I was right. In the end, a whole lot of my friends converged on the corner where we were standing. They were all out looking for me!'

Words like these filled their time between the first great exodus of Armenians from Azerbaijan, in December 1988, and the second, in January 1990. That second time, Tatyana and her mother had no choice but to go. No wonder Tatyana hated Chekhov's plays. When the two women were together, they spoke like Chekhov's characters. Theirs was the kind of unhappiness which was too deep to be put into words. Every day it lapped away at me, like water at the side of a lake. I felt it, but the real cause of it was obscured, because they spoke of everything but that. Baku was their beloved town. They had no other home. They did not define themselves in any way separately, as immigrants will. Of the figure of 200,000 displaced Armenians, they would be just two.

Easygoing People

The Apsheron Hotel has the only discothèque where a decent Azeri woman would be seen, suitably accompanied. The night before, an Azeri friend of Tatyana's called Rauf took us there. Tall and darkly handsome, dressed with Edwardian style, he was a dashing escort. The hotel stands on the main square in the centre of Baku. Newspaper photographs have made it familiar to people all round the world. Here, where the statue of Lenin stands with upraised arm in front of an imposing government building, thousands of Azeri men have massed again and again to bay for Armenian blood. Last night, the great space was empty. The lamplight gleamed on the gun barrels of the tanks that stood in rows in the corner of the square, waiting for the next wave of hatred to reduce men to the level of animals.

It was not easy to get into the Apsheron. The Soviet Army had its headquarters in the hotel. But Rauf, a regular visitor, was greeted warmly by the Russian major in charge. A stout, blond man who looked like a giant teddy bear, he was depressed. 'It's spring,' he said with a sigh. 'I should be at home, planting out my garden.' The hotel was not the place to cheer him up. With its bleak, monumental furnishings and high ceilings, it had the air of a luxurious prison.

The discothèque had succeeded in its aim of looking like discothèques all over the world. That is to say, we could make out little in the gloom. As we sat drinking champagne, bombarded by noise and strafed by lights, the Russian disc jockey Sergei, who confessed to having gone deaf in one ear in the line of duty, turned up the volume still further on a new record. The people at neighbouring tables rose to dance, chanting happily: 'An Englishman in New York . . .' It was the theme tune of *Stars and Bars*, the film I had made the year before. It had only come out a few months earlier in England. I was seized by a jangle of discordant emotions as the bitter-sweet experience came back to me. I must have changed colour. 'What's the matter? Are you feeling all right? Is the music too loud? It's all the rage, this song.' Rauf, the attentive cavalier, was solicitous. My companions looked astonished at my explanation. Suddenly I saw myself through their eyes: a visiting Englishwoman, dressed almost as badly as a Russian, could I really be a Western film producer? If I was telling the truth, what on earth was I doing here, in a remote provincial city in the Soviet Union, when I might be producing films in the West?

How could I start to explain? The very fact that I had a choice summed up the difference between our positions. As for my simple clothes, they were not intended as a disguise, but they were a camouflage. In Russia it served its purpose. But I had not reckoned on this proud republic being so different. Here, even on our outings to the country, I had seen no one who would have been caught wearing Soviet-made clothes. How people could afford to dress with such style, I had no idea. But I had come to understand that sartorial elegance was the most obvious expression of the Azeri preoccupation with appearances. Here my dull camouflage had the effect of making me look conspicuous.

Later in the evening, this lesson on the fragility of role-playing was reinforced by another reminder. Rauf, who had been dancing with each of us in turn, had taken the floor with Tatyana. An Azeri who had been keeping an eye on our table approached, bowed low and invited me to dance. Before I had even had time to decline the man's invitation, Rauf was by my side. He marched the man off and gave him a furious wigging. Poor fellow. He had obviously thought I was Russian. Russian

138

women, as I knew, were fair game. He could hardly have known that although I was dressed like a Russian I was in fact an Englishwoman. But Rauf was right to be furious with him. The man knew that whether or not I was a foreigner, as long as I was in Rauf's company I was an honorary Azeri.

Early next morning I sat on my sofa bed, enjoying the peace of the house. This was the only time of day that I could be alone. The days started late in Baku. Two pale brown doves were cooing in the open vent of the storm window. The wind that had been raging every day had dropped and the air was clear. From the window I could see out over the Caspian, which gleamed like a gun barrel. Like my view of Baku, it was restricted. But if you looked carefully, I was beginning to find you could see a long way. Ever since I had given in to the restrictions on my movements, life in Baku had miraculously improved. I was enjoying being a pampered Islamic woman.

Tatyana's cavaliers had reappeared in the last few days. They had been taking our pleasure seriously. Like Rauf, they were witty, well-educated and seemed to have unlimited time at their disposal in which to exercise the art of conversation and escort us on delightful outings. Their outlook and cultural references were international, in a way that was not true of the educated Russians whom I knew. They had old-fashioned manners, slim figures and the looks of matinée idols. They were also astonishingly well dressed, in pale, freshly pressed linen jackets and trousers, clearly of Western origin.

These days had been like stepping into a Jamesian novel. I was living outside time, in a world whose connection to any economic reality was obscure. Tatyana's cavaliers were no more privileged than my Russian friends. But they apparently enjoyed wealth and leisure of a different order than did anyone I knew in Russia. Partly, of course, this was a question of style, that is to say, of appearances. Tatyana's friends were gentlemen and they would never have allowed a guest, or a woman for that matter, to pay, or even to guess that it was difficult for them to pay. But even to enter such a game required more money than any of my Russian friends had.

This comparative ease did nothing to soften the edge of their cynicism about Soviet power. Their detachment from political developments in the Soviet Union was unnerving. Election day had passed unmentioned by anyone except me. Tatyana and her friends had not voted. They had not bothered to find out the results. From their point of view, that of the colonized, there was no difference between this election and every other conflict-free election they had known.

As for Tatyana, she specialized in getting through her days without making any contact with a wider world. She did not read a newspaper, watch the television news or listen to the radio: 'If anything interesting happens, someone will tell me,' she told me, grandly. If the radio were on in the kitchen when we returned from one of our outings, she would rush to turn it off. 'I used to listen, once,' she explained. 'Then I realized that they were playing the same songs, in ancient recordings, day in day out. They play not only the same songs from the same operas, but even the same excerpts from the same songs from the same operas . . . They break off at the very same place, in the middle of the song, each time. It drives you mad! This repertoire is only interrupted by the news; always the same voice, funereal yet joyful, announcing' (her voice became that of a mature robot) ' "And now the news from the fields: a harvest of X million tons of millet and Y million tons of cotton has been brought in . . ." All these crops and still nothing in the shops! You're right, I do react as if I've got an allergy . . .'

As I sat there listening to the doves, my thoughts returned to the dissociations that I was beginning to sense around me, between appearances and realities. Underneath the polished veneer of my new friends there were tensions. At the mention of the word 'Armenian' their indifference cracked, giving way to an overwhelming sense of grievance. Their injured tone was

140

a complex response to the facts behind the present conflict between the two nationalities.

The issue was not new. It concerned political control over the 4,400 square kilometres of rocky land that constitutes the province of Nagorny-Karabakh. Standing as it does at the ancient juncture between the Christian West and the Islamic East, the territory had been fought over throughout recorded history. Although a majority of the population had always been Armenian, the territory lies well within the confines of present-day Azerbaijan. But the Armenians had been using the opportunity afforded by *glasnost'* to change the map.

It is said that the Communist leadership of Azerbaijan had actually offered the territory back to Armenia in 1920, after the 11th Red Army had claimed both republics for the new Union of Soviet Republics. According to this version Stalin, then Commissar for Nationalities, dithered for three years before leaving it under Azerbaijan's control. A glance at the underlying political realities of the time makes this seem plausible.

Not long before, the Ottoman Armenians who had lived in what is now Eastern Turkey had lost something like a million people in three massacres by the Turks between 1895 and 1915. The survivors had been obliged to be grateful for the shelter afforded them by the barren fragment of their territory which had belonged to the Russian Empire and which was conquered by the 11th Red Army in December 1920. Azerbaijan's position had been quite different. The oil wells of Baku were crucial for the survival of the new Soviet regime. Indeed, until after the Second World War, when the output of the Volga–Ural fields rose, Baku continued to supply three-quarters of Soviet oil. Was Stalin likely to have weighed up the claims of the two republics dispassionately?

Fortune had also played cruelly with the Armenian republic more recently. There had been a moment, in February 1988, when the Politburo had appeared about to cede Nagorny-Karabakh to Armenia. Then the death of two Azeris in the

141

course of a mass protest in Nagorny-Karabakh that month had sparked off a pogrom resulting in the death of twenty-six Armenians and six Azeris in the industrial town of Sumgait, north of Baku. Terrified, the Armenian population in Azerbaijan, which numbered nearly half a million, began to leave their homes, as did the Azeris in Armenia. When the Armenian earthquake of December that year killed 50,000 and left 400,000 homeless, the disaster spiralled further out of control.

In the middle of these events, knowing nothing of the context behind them, I was shocked at the way my civilized Azeri friends talked as if they, not the Armenians, were the victims of history. How had they ended up in this emotionally embattled position? Or was my own perception coloured by an instinctive sympathy for the Armenians because of their Job-like afflictions? I had no confidence in the explanations my civilized friends offered. In those charged days, each explanation, however scholarly, had its own top-spin. Searching for clues that would explain their baffled rage, I listened to the refrains through which they expressed their national grievance.

The first refrain went like this: 'They're great stirrers, the Armenians.' This had a number of variations: 'Moscow's full of Armenians . . . It's they who've stirred the whole thing up'; 'They're clannish, always boasting, always stirring the pot . . .'; or even, 'They're playing a dirty political game. If they got hold of Nagorny-Karabakh, it wouldn't stop there. Next it would be Sochi, or Krasnodar . . .' Although I listened to these refrains with scepticism, I later discovered that there was a sense in which this complaint was justified. Ever since 1985, when Gorbachev had come to power, the Armenian campaign had been a concerted one. Collectively and individually, Armenians had bombarded the government and Party in Moscow with petitions by the thousand. Orchestrating the sympathy due to them on other issues, they had won the propaganda battle in Russian and Western eyes.

I was ashamed to find that British foreign policy in the late nineteenth century had played its part in creating the Armenian reputation for being a nation of 'stirrers'. As the Ottoman Empire had moved into the final stage of its long disintegration, the Russian army had moved south in 1877 to occupy part of the Armenian territory under Ottoman control. Britain, seeing it as against her Indian interests to allow the Ottoman Empire to collapse, had intervened to force Russia to retreat. In the resulting treaty, Britain had assumed the role of protector of Christians in Asia Minor. For his part, the Sultan had agreed to allow the Armenians a greater degree of self-government. Through this bit of manoeuvring, Britain managed to remove from the scene the one power that would have been capable of ensuring the security of the Armenian population. In its place it offered only postures.

Even that posturing had its own aggravating effect on the situation. It encouraged Armenian revolutionary groups to build European intervention into their plans and to believe that making a noise would further their cause. But where the Europeans had no intention of doing anything but increase their exhortations to the Turks, the Armenian 'stirring' aggravated Turkish hostility. It helped precipitate not the reforms, but the massacres.

The second refrain which I kept hearing was revealing about the Azeri self-image. The cavaliers kept describing the Azeri violence, which had made thousands of people flee their homes three months earlier, as an 'aberration'. 'No one really understands it. It goes against everything the Azeris are.' 'We are such an easygoing people, we have always lived with other nationalities.' 'We would never have started the violence . . .' The image the Azeris had of themselves as lazy, peaceful people, to which they disdainfully compared the industry of the implicitly plebeian Armenians, related to the traditional division of labour between the two peoples. The Azeris had grazed the flocks, while the Armenians had tilled the soil and built the houses. To some extent, this is still true today.

This self-image was rooted in another historical difference between the two peoples. In their time, they had both fought the Romans, Persians, Arabs, Mongols and Turks. But the pattern of the one history had been as exclusive as the other had been inclusive. The Armenians' traditional territory had lain well to the south of Soviet Armenia in eastern Turkey. It had always been distinguished by being a buffer between the empires of East and West. Their adoption of Christianity and an alphabet of their own as early as AD 301, even before the Roman Empire, had both defined their separateness and underlined their vulnerability.

The people situated to the east in present-day Azerbaijan had survived by adopting the opposite principle: they had assimilated the new blood of conquerors or refugees, wave after wave. In the veins of the modern Azeri, there was little left now of the blood of the tall, well-made sun-worshippers whom Strabo had admiringly described, let alone of the huntsmen whose vivid sixth-century rock drawings adorn the mountain of Kobustan. When the wars between Persia and Byzantium began in the sixth century, the first wave of Turkic peoples had arrived in Azerbaijan. Between the invasions of the Arabs, who left their religion behind, and the Mongols, the Seljuk Turks had arrived in the eleventh century, bringing their language with them. When the Persian Safavids took control four centuries later, they had confirmed the domination of the Turkic people over the rest of the population by promoting them as soldiers.

Through this history of inclusion and adoption, the Turkic population had steadily gained control. The ascendancy of the Turkic Azeris had been confirmed in their republic by Soviet power. As long as this was not threatened, the Azeris had little reason to be anything but easygoing. But there were terms. The appearance of Azeri ascendancy had to be maintained. As Tatyana put it in a telling remark: 'I've got a Jewish friend here who is a musician and composer. He has always been free to

144

play and to compose. But they wouldn't let him publish his music under his own name. They wanted him to use an Azeri one. Did I ever hear him complain? He just got on with it. Now if he'd been an Armenian we'd never have heard the end of it . . .'

Tatyana's own attitude illustrated the delicate balance between Azeri tolerance and ascendancy. Her pale-skinned beauty marked her as Armenian, but she had put herself under the protection of the Azeris. 'The other day', she remarked to me, 'my boss, who was introducing me to someone, said: "This is Tatyana. She's Azeri." It's quite obvious that I'm not, of course. But it was his way of saying "She's one of us". It's all a matter of attitude. Armenians who don't get on here have only themselves to blame.' That was all very well unless, as her mother feared, she happened to come across an Azeri who did not happen to know that, despite her Armenian blood, she was 'one of them'.

When Tatyana's mother took me to the market in the city centre, we passed a wall which looked as if it was white. In fact it was made up of thousands of scraps of fluttering paper. Each announced the availability of a home from which an Armenian family had fled. Yesterday, Tatyana had shown me one such house. It was so singular that no Azeri had dared to appropriate it.

We had been on our way back from visiting the Zoroastrian shrine at Šurakhany when, acting on a vague memory, Tatyana had asked the driver to turn off the road. We were in an unprepossessing residential area where houses were surrounded by high garden walls made from sheets of rusting metal. 'Ah, stop! There it is,' said Tatyana, pointing towards a scrubby patch of land at something that might have been a gibbet. Figures were hanging suspended in the air. As the car approached, this melancholy impression gave way to an enchanting sight: a constellation of airborne beasts and characters that looked like the spontaneous realization of a dream hovered in the air within the narrow confines of a high-walled property. Primitive life-sized figures in painted clay stood rigidly to attention on the surrounding wall: gowned ladies, a bewigged judge and mustachioed men. A happy couple balanced upon each gatepost thrust forward rigid arms upon which lay an astonished baby. Behind them more men and women, with proud faces and bemedalled fronts, rose in a pyramid. It was a pantheon of Soviet heroes. Round it, to the frozen music of a turbaned piper, gambolled antlered Scythian deer and a pair of spotted panthers. On a nearby post a man with a gun uselessly strapped to his back stood locked in combat with a maned lion.

This creation was the work of an illiterate Armenian, driven to put form on the creatures crowding inside his head after the death of a beloved daughter. Despite the resentment of his sons, who minded doing his work for him; despite the resistance of the authorities, who at one stage forbade him to pick up the bits from building sites which were his material, he had persevered in the realization of his dream. It was dedicated to the ideal of Soviet power. But now the Soviet dream had failed and he and his family had had to flee for their lives.

As I was gazing at this flying circus, I realized what had been bothering me for days. I had been infuriated by the cavaliers' insistence that the Azeri violence was 'an aberration'. But they were right. There was something incomprehensible about the brutality which had torn all these families from their roots. For all the clues which history yielded, the upsurge of violence between the Azeris and the Armenians was out of all proportion to the cause. What then was the real cause? 'No one in this country is genuinely happy,' the words of one of the cavaliers, an erudite and thoughtful man, came back to me: 'Whatever people show on the outside, they feel an inner disquiet. Where all power is distributed from the centre on a political basis, no one, even the most fortunate, is secure. The political spectrum has only to shift a little and a whole lifetime's work crashes to the ground.'

146

The cause was not the illiterate genius and his family, who had been forced to flee for their lives. They were only the scapegoats. The cause was rage, rage against the beautiful dream, the Soviet dream, which had betrayed them all. Tatyana's cavalier had been right. The political spectrum had shifted a little, and an entire regime was crashing to the ground.

IV

MOSCOW

A Potential Traitor

'If words are not concerned with deeds and do not lead to change, then what good are they? They are no more use than the barking of village dogs in the night.'

Alexander Solzhenitsyn

Moscow was full of badly dressed, ugly people. But I felt as if I had come home. Little more than a month before, when I had arrived in Moscow, I had been dismayed to find that I understood nothing. But after Baku, Moscow seemed as easy to read as a child's book. I had stayed long enough in Baku to have felt the desperation underneath the elegance. Baku was an elephant trap, its surface strewn with luxuriant grass. Marvelling at the grass, I had fallen into the pit underneath. My escape seemed miraculous.

The contrast between the colony and the capital leapt out at me. Here at the centre of the disintegrating empire, positive change still seemed worth striving for. When I had left Moscow just before the elections to the new parliament even the cynical had been struggling to resist the contagious atmosphere of hope. More than a week had passed since that first test of the popular will for change. But when in Baku I had, perforce, lived like the Bakunites. Their indifference to all things Soviet was not casual, it was a mark of self-respect. I returned to the capital with no idea at all of the election results.

A Moscow election official had dropped dead of a heart attack as he opened his mouth to read out the results. So too, for opposite reasons, had a crooked official in Kazakhstan on learning that he had succeeded in bending the system yet again. The list of Communist grandees who had failed to secure their seats for the new Congress of People's Deputies was long. It included Moscow's mayor and his deputy; Leningrad's regional Party first secretary, city Party chief, and mayor; the mayor and local Party chief of Kiev; the Prime Ministers of Latvia and Lithuania; the general in command of the army in the Far East, the admiral in command of the Pacific Fleet ... Thanks to the commission convoked in order to discredit Yeltsin, he was in by 89 per cent, the highest vote in the country.

I had arrived back to find that spring had been routed by winter again. But it did not last. Now the snow was thawing fast once more. As I walked through the centre of Moscow, chutes of impacted snow would dislodge themselves from the roof-tops and land with force on the pavement. I stood in the brittle sunshine and slush at the foot of Pushkin's statue, waiting for Vika. I had come to the Soviet Union to find the answer to the question: when Gorbachev came to power, had there been people who still believed in the Soviet dream? Nowhere in Azerbaijan, my friends had told me, would I have found such a creature. But the empire was Russian, and so was the capacity for belief. Vika was only in her twenties and she was a bright girl. But she had believed. I had met her through her husband, who was a dancer with the Bolshoi. She too had been trained as a dancer, but when her husband got into the prestigious school in the capital, she had been obliged to give up her career in order to keep the family together. Not that it was exactly together now. Wives and children were not allowed to live in the students' residence. She lived there illegally, in a partitioned corner of the room which her husband shared with two other students. She divided her time between her husband

and her daughter, who lived with Vika's parents, both miners, deep in the countryside.

Vika had warned me that she might be late, as she was coming straight off the train. She had been spending the last few days with her daughter. The wooden seating round Pushkin's monument had been ripped out for winter so I stood in the slush, shifting from foot to foot. Now I saw her, walking fast, weaving through the pedestrians on Gor'kij Street, her long dancer's neck bandaged in a home-knitted brown scarf. She looked far more relaxed today than when we first met. With her neat-featured good looks and hair tied back, she could only have been a dancer, but she could have been of any nationality. What was Russian about her was the expression of vulnerability, which had drawn me to her when we first met.

Then, she and her husband had taken me to see the staircase off which the writer Bulgakov used to have a flat. For years, it had served as a shrine. But by the time I saw it, its time had passed. While earnest foreigners scrutinized the graffiti, half sacred, half profane, scrawled over the walls, there had been young Georgians sitting on the ill-lit stairs, drinking from a bottle of port and boasting about their conquests. Vika and I had been standing at the foot of the staircase when she suddenly started to try and put words to the pain I had seen in her face: 'It's very hard for me to live now. You see, I used to believe in it all.' She whispered. The half-light had fallen on her girlish face. Her voice was full of tears: 'I was one of the masses, marching cheerfully in step! Yes, I was one of them. And then we discover that everything, everything we believed in was a lie. It hurts so much, because I believed in my heart.' She paused. 'It's easier for my husband, a little, because he uses his head. He can think it through. But with me' – she put both her hands on her heart, as though the wound were physical – 'as for me, I feel it all. It has become so hard to go on.'

Today, Vika took me to an ice-cream parlour on Gor'kij Street. Miraculously, there was no queue and we found a table in a room in which it was no punishment to sit. The ceiling was not too high, nor the music too loud. The waiter was surprisingly friendly as Vika ordered Russian champagne, pomegranate juice and ice cream. Moscow was smiling on us. I asked Vika what she felt about the election. With a characteristically Russian seriousness, she answered not the question I had asked, but the one which I had wanted to ask, the one I could never have brought myself to put into words: how did a girl as intelligent and sensitive ever come to be, as she had put it, 'one of the masses, marching cheerfully in step'?

'At school, we were not allowed to think up our own answer to a question. There was always a right answer and a wrong one, black and white. But I was never sure. Take Lermontov's Pechorin.' Pechorin is the Byronic figure at the centre of his novel *A Hero of Our Time*. 'We were given this essay to write about him. You were meant to say that he was riddled with evil from head to foot. But he didn't strike me like that at all. I was sorry for him and I said so. I got a two.' Two out of five is a bad mark. 'Or take Raskolnikov in *Crime and Punishment*. He, believe it or not, was a revolutionary!' Raskolnikov had murdered an old lady for no other reason than to prove that he could. 'And it wasn't just literature. It was everything.

'It hasn't changed much, either. A friend of mine told me how her twelve-year-old daughter burst into tears the other day when faced with the task of having to write her opinion of some Soviet painting of a train travelling through the countryside: "But Mama, it's so ugly!" she said. All the same, what she did write was just what they wanted. You know the sort of stuff: "In this masterly painting, the artist has depicted the train, symbol of progress, racing through the countryside without disturbing the beauty of nature . . ." and so on. She was only twelve, but she had already learned how to think one thing and say another.

'I was always unsure at school. But we were never allowed to doubt. That was considered unprincipled. "Doubt is the first step to treachery," they used to tell us. They accused me of being an intellectual – and that was a term of abuse. How could I have been an intellectual? My parents had only four years of schooling before they went down the mines. It was wartime and they were short of labour.

'I came to think of myself as a potential traitor. It was very painful. I kept watching myself, never trusting my own re-actions. Now that it's all changed and I am grown-up, with a child of my own, I find that all those years of education had their effect. Now that I have to live in a world without answers I don't trust myself. It's painful to get through every day. You asked about the election. Well, to tell you the truth, I didn't vote in the end. I'm afraid of myself. I would have voted for Yeltsin. But I've avoided getting to know too much about him, because I'm afraid I'll take him to my heart and make an idol of him.'

I had never imagined that I would meet so many people, including bright young people like Vika, whose instincts had been effectively cauterized by the experience of totalitarianism. But I had also never imagined that such people would be able to talk of the experience with such lucid candour. Honesty like that is not met often in the West. It was as if people like Vika, deprived of the overview with which we grow up in the West, focused on self-knowledge with a different intensity. Whatever political catastrophes might overwhelm Russia, this at least would last for a few generations, this liberation of people's heads and hearts. For a long time to come, there would only be one way of visiting oppression on these people and that was from the outside. They would know what was being done to them.

A Tiny Movement of the Head

Last night on television, I saw Grisha's programme about the boys in Konstantinovo who were building their own houses. It was to have been shown a few days ago, while I was still away. But at the last moment, it had been pulled. From a distance, *glasnost'* might seem to have made steady progress in establishing itself. But living here I watched how every week brought triumphs and reversals. While I had been here, the first criticism of the Party had appeared in print, followed by the first criticism of Gorbachev. But after the election, there had been a moment when the fragile new freedom of television seemed under threat. The response of right-wing politicians like Ligachev to the results had been to demand access to television on their own terms. For the first time in their political lives, they were feeling the need to reach out to the electorate.

Grisha had not been surprised when his documentary about the boys had been withdrawn from the schedule at the last moment. His editor's nervousness was a reaction to a law that was coming into effect redefining anti-Soviet activities. Public appeals to change the Soviet regime, 'in a manner contradicting the USSR constitution', were to be punishable by ten years' imprisonment. In Moscow, there had been a ripple of panic. No one was clear what constituted a public appeal to change the system. All over the country, people were making these daily, hourly. Did the new law signal a return to the old days, or would it be as unenforceable as Canute's command to the waves? It is only afterwards that the answer seems obvious.

Ten minutes of the most outspoken material of Grisha's film had been cut before last night's transmission.

What had surprised Grisha was the pressure from the boys themselves to suppress the programme. Komkov, the head of the state farm where they were building their houses, had promised them anything if only they would get the programme stopped. 'When will they learn?' Grisha lamented. 'Komkov has only to be nice to them and they believe him.'

Even with ten minutes cut, the film was stronger than anything I had seen on Moscow television. Interrupting one another, unabashed by the presence of the cameras, the boys had described how they had given up their well-paid jobs in response to Gorbachev's appeal. 'Mikhail Sergeevich said that all help should be given to people who wanted to leave the city to bring fresh blood to the countryside and build their own houses . . . Now we're accused of wanting to build "country houses" for ourselves . . . Not a single promise that was made to us has been kept . . . They're saying we are making an "assault on state production", just because we want to work our own land and not produce much less working for the state . . . Effectively, we've been told we're criminals . . .' Most of this was not new to me. But Komkov's interview with Grisha contained the immortal line: 'Our society has not yet developed to the point where people can work their own land with their own hands.' Behind his words I sensed 'the backward half look over the shoulder, towards the primitive terror' as T. S. Eliot called it.

A couple of days later, I met up with Slava, the young man who had talked with such authority in Konstantinovo that day. He had come into Moscow to see his wife and son. At first I had not recognized the young man with the trim beard and high cheek-bones who stood over me smiling in the sunshine as I waited by Pushkin's monument. The last time, he had been wearing a long straggling beard which, together with his burning eyes and filthy working-clothes, had given him a prophetic air. We sat on a bench in the sunshine and talked. Slava was in holiday mood. Following the programme, someone who was out to get Komkov had unearthed a file of complaints about him. It looked as if he was on the point of losing his job. I could hardly believe Slava's magnanimity: 'I feel sorry for him,' he said. 'I wish there was something I could do to help.'

For all his buoyancy, life out at Konstantinovo was anything but easy. The central difficulty was no nearer a solution. Before they could start building, they still had to get an agreement from the state farm which would secure their position as free men with the right to build their own houses. Meanwhile, the boys led isolated lives: 'People don't want to be seen to be connected with us. For the teenagers, the only thing of any importance in the world is getting away to the city. They think we're mad. There aren't any people of our age at all on the farm. The rest of them are too scared to want to make friends with us. There are one or two exceptions, but not many. What is it about my countrymen that makes us so slave-like? Maybe it's genetic. Maybe it'll never change . . .' Slava was good company. His instincts about power seemed to have left him unsurprised by the revelations of the last few years. 'It's not that I knew anything more than anyone else. I just knew what They were like.' His combination of scepticism and energy had left him apparently unmarked by the experience of totalitarianism. His background was not privileged. He had grown up on a collective farm. His father had been an alcoholic. But he had done well enough at school to get into a Moscow institute. There, he had met his Armenian wife, a bright girl who had arrived at the institute from an equally humble background. 'Once I'd met her, the whole business of getting a diploma seemed beside the point.' When he mentioned his wife, his voice changed. 'We decided to start a family, and both dropped out of our institutes. What good would a diploma have done me? I didn't want to be a boss, or a bureaucrat. All I wanted was to be free.' It was rare in this culture to find a man who would admit to the importance of the woman in his life. But Slava was exceptional. Like my Russian mother Elena, he had known enough about power to avoid the seduction of being made a boss.

Once they had dropped out of college, what had Slava and his wife done next, I asked him. 'The next problem was how to get Moscow residence. It takes years. What they need most is construction workers, so that's what we became.' There could not be many couples confident enough in their own direction to give up the chance of higher education in order to become *limitchiki*, Moscow's slave labourers. Slava had not remained one for long. With difficulty I prised the explanation out of him. It turned out that he had been so highly valued as a worker that he had soon been offered permanent residence in Moscow. This distinction only made it more remarkable that he had kept to his resolve of leaving Moscow for the countryside, in pursuit of his ideal of freedom. 'I wanted my children to have the experience of the countryside which I never had.'

Slava knew enough about power not to become a boss. But, in moving to the countryside, it looked as if he had taken one step too many in the direction of making himself a free man. To me his dream of building his own house and supporting his family by the work of his hands might have seemed realizable. Only now did I begin to understand what a threat the boys posed. Over the last couple of days, Komkov had mobilized the forces of the fearful state-farm workers and launched his counter-attack. The little wooden house in which the boys lived had been under siege by workers. The television station had received a telegram, signed by 200 people, 'demanding' that the pro-gramme's second transmission be cancelled. Astonishingly, it looked as though the station was going to accede to this demand.

Now that things had turned nasty, the real problem was going to be the agreement which Komkov had forced the boys to sign when they arrived. This committed them to working as ordinary members of the state farm. Komkov had assured them

159

that, although it had no meaning, it was the only way that they could be given land that belonged to the state farm. They would remain free, he had insisted, to sell their houses, and their labour, wherever they chose. Over the last couple of days, this 'meaningless' paper had suddenly acquired meaning. Things looked bad for the boys. The only hope lay in the fact that the newspaper *Izvestia*, alerted by Grisha's programme, looked as if it would be publishing an article about the story.

I was sitting in the packed minibus that was ferrying people from the end of the Metro line on the outskirts of Moscow. The little road zigzagged with mathematical precision through a jungle of tower blocks. I was going to meet Slava's wife. I recognized her immediately. Her pale beauty was distinctively Armenian. She stood caught in the wind that was channelled between the tower blocks. Her long dark hair blew around her face. Her cheeks were dimpled and her eyes turned up at the corners when she smiled. Standing in this windswept landscape of minimal shelters for massed human beings, she seemed like an exotic fantasy, a creature made for pleasure. Yet she was merely a *limitchik*, one of the army of poorly paid labourers of whom one catches sight from the street when, high above on some scaffolding, a figure in heavy work-clothes looks down to reveal a delicate face.

Natasha seemed unperturbed by her husband's difficulties in Konstantinovo. For the last few months her sister Valya and three sons had been living with her. They were refugees from Sumgait, the industrial town just north of Baku, where the first massacre of Armenians had happened in February a year before. What was the threat of losing something that had never been more than a dream, in comparison with losing all that you had?

We were accompanied back to the flat, through the melting snow, by three little boys, Natasha's son and his cousins. Although the cousins were about the same age as Natasha's boy, they were shorter and painfully thin. The skin seemed too tightly stretched over their skulls and their eyes loomed in their pointed faces. We made our way up to the seventeenth floor of one of the tower blocks, to the two rooms in which the sisters and their children lived. Valya carried a third son in her arms. She was plump and equable, with reddish hair caught back in a bun. We settled in a small and sparsely furnished room. Apart from a table, the only furniture was a sofa and a narrow iron bedstead. The room next door in the communal flat was occupied by someone else. 'If you think we're crowded now, imagine what it's going to be like when my mother and father arrive.' Natasha knew what I was thinking. 'They wanted to stay in Azerbaijan. But it's no good, it's just getting worse every day. Their luggage should be arriving any day now.' From her phlegmatic tone, it sounded as if they were coming because the weather was too hot.

Natasha went to the kitchen and Valya, dandling her lively baby on her knee, began to talk: 'The anti-Armenian feeling had been on the increase, but you did not run your life by it. It didn't used to be like that. No one was aware of things like that. When other boys in the street beat up my eldest for being a "filthy Armenian", he said, "But I'm Russian!" His father's Russian and no one had ever talked about nationality at home. But the other boys knew the score: "Your mother's Armenian," they said. "We know . . ."

'I'm the same age as the town of Sumgait. It was founded in 1949. My father was one of the flood of workers who came from all over Azerbaijan to work in the new town. The population was mostly Russian and Armenian then, as well as Jewish. Only about five per cent were Azeri. It was a kind of model town then; wonderful beaches, plenty of work and well-stocked shops. Even fifteen years ago you could buy sturgeon and caviare any day. It was a good place to live.

'Then the population started to change. The criminal element arrived. People with prison sentences were sent to Sumgait to work out their time on building projects. The educational

161

standards dropped. And over the last fifteen years it has become the most polluted town in the Soviet Union.' That explained the emaciated look of Valya's older sons. 'Where we used to have lovely golden beaches, they are now covered in dead fish and oil slick. You have to go a long way from Sumgait to bathe now. The town is full of chemical factories. My father has to visit one where they work with mercury, making things like thermometers. After a day working there, he comes away feeling terrible and spitting blood. Nothing grows round the factory.

'All that pollution had a lot to do with the February events, of course. So did the state of provisions in the town. How can you be expected to feed a family of two adults and three growing boys on two kilos of meat a month? Even then, each ration usually turns out to have half a kilo of bones buried in the pack. You can't tell till you open it up. There's meat around all right, just not in the shops. You can get it by the crateful if you have the contacts or the money.'

Natasha came bringing *golubtsi*, meatballs wrapped in cabbage leaves. I had tried to choose a time of day to visit when there would be no excuse to feed me, but as usual I was outwitted by a tradition of hospitality which did not allow a visitor to leave without being fed. 'The riots weren't spontaneous, I'm sure you know that. They', Valya jerked her chin up, indicating somewhere up there, 'knew exactly what they were doing. You know who was out there on the streets, leading the riots that first night? The First Secretary of the Communist Party for Sumgait town. Everyone in Sumgait knows that. But there was nothing in the papers about it.' I mentioned the official death toll, which stood at thirty-two dead, twenty-six of them Armenian. Valya smiled. Between her and her friends alone, they personally knew of more than eighty dead.

'My parents live just outside Sumgait. One morning I had to collect the children from my mother. For some reason the idea of my going on this occasion made my husband uneasy. He

162

didn't want me to. But anyway, off I went. And as I went down the street I found myself thinking: "I didn't have any idea the place had become as run-down as this." There was broken glass everywhere. And there didn't seem to be anyone around. I waited and waited for a bus. After about twenty minutes I asked a woman. She looked at me oddly and sort of winced and backed away: "There was trouble in the night. You'd better go home," she said. It was only then that I realized what had been happening. Anyone who had been caught outside had been beaten or killed and the women raped with bottles and sticks.

'We spent a week locked in the flat, the boys and I. My husband and I don't live together any more. We don't get on. But he made this sort of spear for us, by strapping together a whole lot of kitchen knives. As he said: "If they come, this won't save you, but may I be allowed the sinful thought that at least one of them will share your fate?" We kept the spear, together with a pile of hammers and knives and stuff by the front door, which we reinforced and nailed up to make it a bit harder for them to get through. What they would do was just rush the front doors, raping and killing everyone they found inside. The looters would follow afterwards. A woman we know was lying on the sofa dying after being raped and they just stripped the place round her. The neighbours would tip them off as to which were the Armenian flats.' She hesitated 'Well, they didn't all do that. There were plenty of exceptions. They threatened one of our neighbours, who was hiding Armenians in her flat. They tried to frighten her into telling them where they lived and she just folded her arms and said, "Never." But there were others who just tipped them the wink. It takes no more than a tiny movement of the head.'

Valya talked almost without emotion, as if she were talking about a natural disaster somewhere a long way off, not about the violence that had uprooted her and her children from their home town. At the moment she was more upset by being unable to get a job, although she was a computer operator: 'They're crying out for them here. But the trouble is that if they give me a job, they're obliged to house me, so I'm stuck.' At that moment the three boys rushed in: 'Mama, Mama, look what we found!' Natasha's son put something shiny into her hand. It was a silvery brooch with paste diamonds. 'We found it just outside, by the rubbish tip.' Natasha looked at it, enchanted. Neither she nor Valya was wearing any jewellery. 'What luck you've brought us. It's beautiful. It's the first time they've ever found anything worth while . . .' There was a pause, then she went on. 'Here, you take it. I was worried that we didn't have anything to give you. And now, you see, we have! I know it's not much, but please, take it.'

A Country of Miracles

Elena returned from work the other evening in distress. An important film director had a première the day after tomorrow in some distant Soviet city. Elena was responsible for issuing his wife with a plane ticket so that she could join him. She gave the money to a man in the office who ran such errands and asked him to bring her the ticket in the afternoon. When he returned, he stood by her desk, dead drunk, with no ticket.

'"Where's the money?" I asked him. He gave me a charming smile and said: "I do hate you so much. I always have." He had drunk every penny of it. I couldn't believe it. Normally he's a quiet, reliable little man. Now I didn't know what to do. There was no way I could get hold of more money. I just told him to have the ticket by the following morning, no questions asked, or else. Though what good my saying that would do, I didn't know. He'd got no money of his own.'

The next day, the man turned up with a ticket. The problem had been resolved in the most Soviet way, through friendship. A friend of his in the airline office had taken pity on him and given it to him, free. Elena sighed: 'It's a country of miracles.' It was a phrase she often used.

On top of Elena's fridge sat an indented gold tray of paper from a smart box of chocolates I had given her when I arrived. It had been there for weeks. 'It seems a pity to throw it away,' Elena explained. 'It looks so nice.' The role of packaging was an ideologically revealing one. In the West I had always resented the expensive, wasteful veneer it provided for goods which did not live up to their promise. After some time here, however, my resistance was beginning to soften and I caught myself returning to the chocolate tray with pleasure. The eye tired of mangled chicken corpses whose splayed limbs lay in the shops in genocidal heaps; piles of frost-bitten cabbage and paper bags full of eggs which had to be carried home whole, giving such everyday transactions the quality of an egg-and-spoon race.

The absence of packaging here also carried its own false promise. It seemed to offer itself as evidence of the unexploitative nature of the transaction between shop and citizen in a socialist state. At a time when the shops were visibly emptying month after month as a result of the corrupt sale of goods through the back door, this stylistic humbug had a particular edge.

Packaging had some interesting functions here however:

(1) When used by the élite, its purpose was not display but concealment. For instance, luxurious provisions for the entire extended family of the chosen one were brought by car to the flat every week in unmarked packages whose function is to conceal the contents from the envious gaze of ordinary people.

(2) Ordinary people also used packaging in this way, though to different ends. It was customary, for instance, to circumvent the petty regulations of the Metro by carrying your dog in a bag. Often the only sign of this was a pink tongue protruding from a hole below the zipper.

(3) Packaging did have protective functions, though not for objects belonging to the state, as these were without value until they fell into private hands. Until then they could be spoiled at will. People carried their personal effects, for instance, in suitcases which were often improbably wrapped in paper and tied with string. This surreal notion of the packaged package was only equalled by the sight of lovingly bandaged brooms, skis, shovels and fishing-rods. According to the regulations of the Metro, all sharp objects had to be wrapped.

*

Rereading Orwell's *Road to Wigan Pier* recently, I could not help being struck by Orwell's perspective on socialism from the late thirties, the heyday of Soviet socialism. His assumption, comical today, was that this system was bound to lead by the shortest possible route to the mechanization of every aspect of life. He examined the paradox that, despite the ostensibly desirable nature of this goal, it was one that every thinking man must dread. For the qualities we admire, the qualities of the gods, were quite different. They were to be brave, generous and physically strong: 'In tying yourself to the ideal of mechanical efficiency, you tie yourself to the ideal of softness. But softness is repulsive; thus all progress is seen to be a frantic struggle towards an objective which you hope and pray will never be reached.'

It turned out not to be socialism but capitalism which had taken us, or at least the lucky ones among us, along this equivocal path towards 'the ideal of softness'. But precisely because the socialist path to industrialization had failed so catastrophically, daily life here continued to bring out in people the qualities of an older age, those of endurance, generosity and ingenuity.

Every day provided its own examples. When Elena was preparing a special feast recently, she got time off from work and queued for three hours at the only shop in Moscow where Chinese meat dumplings were sold. During the third hour, she wept. But when she came home bearing the dumplings, she was as exultant as a hunter who has brought home the bear. Her clothes offered another example. If she dressed better than most Soviet women, this was not because she had money. She earned little more than the minimum wage. But she was tireless and ingenious and made all her wardrobe, including the winter coat. She had just finished knitting a smart jersey whose wool came from three old jumpers which she had unravelled and redyed. Now the hunt for the buttons was beginning.

Today the window-cleaner was due to come at some stage,

so I stayed in all day. Elena, who was away, had left me with a challenge. I had to suppress all trace of her new Japanese television set. Its existence in her flat could cause problems. If word got round that such a prize was to be found at Flat Three, Staircase Four, it would be gone within days. Had I known when I bought it for her what a burden it would be, I might have thought twice. It had been hard enough to pick a moment to rush it from the car into the flat without it being seen by all the neighbours in the first place.

Now there was the problem of hiding it and its stand, which did not look like an occasional table. It was a large television. There were few options in the modest two-room flat. I ended up putting it in Elena's cupboard, balanced on top of the sheets, swaddled in jerseys, with the stand on top. I could not get the door to lock.

At any other time, I would have enjoyed talking to the fat, garrulous woman – who incidentally earned a good deal more than Elena. But throughout her visit I was on edge. The cupboard was so full that I was holding my breath, fearing lest the door should burst open, spilling clothes, sheets and a television at her feet. As I fidgeted around, I was aware of being watched by Pasternak's noble sorrowing face from the wall.

The rise in crime was a frequent topic of conversation. Today's *Moscow Evening News* reported a 42·9 per cent increase in the first three months of this year over the same time last year. But was this a real rise, or simply the revelation of what had been hidden before? What constituted a crime anyway? State socialism had confused the issue. Stealing from the state was really hardly a crime, was it, when the means of production belonged to the people?

What shocked people was the idea that Soviet citizens could steal off each other. The other evening, Grisha had been describing how, when he was married to his first wife, some provincial relations of hers had come to stay out of the blue. 'We were entertaining friends when they arrived. The man behaved very oddly. He went round the room fastening watches on people's wrists. He wore them all up his arm in a row. I couldn't think what was going on. He didn't look particularly rich and the watches weren't new either. The straps were worn and the faces scratched. Then I discovered that he was a policeman. He was the first policeman I had ever met socially and he was my guest! Suddenly it dawned on me: they were watches he had taken off drunkards "in the course of duty"!'

Much of the crime in Moscow was being committed by organized gangs of provincials, particularly from the Caucasus. The tradition of brigandage was older than that of socialism there. The Caucasian speciality seemed to be lifting fur hats off people's heads and coats off their backs in the street. This was the subject of much horrified gossip at bus-stops. I wondered that such a book-loving population should be surprised. This particular crime had a distinguished literary tradition. Had they forgotten the vengeful ghost at the end of Gogol's story 'The Overcoat'?

Yesterday, the second round of voting was held for the seats in which there had been no outright winner In the first round of the elections. I accompanied Elena when she went to vote. The weather was warm. But Moscow was at its ugliest. Where the earth had been laid bare by the retreating snow, exhausted debris lay revealed. The school near our flat which was serving as a polling station was decked out with little flags and red banners. Breezy music tinkled out over the street.

Elena went in to cross out our two Tweedledum and Tweedledee candidates, who should never have been offered to the voters a second time. There has been much complaint that no fresh candidates were allowed to be put forward this time. I waited for her in the reception area, marvelling at the freshly made cakes and soft drinks which had been laid to lure in the voter. Elena came out with a look of disbelief on her face: 'They were so polite, so grateful to me for coming! It was embarrassing.' Later Grisha, despairing of his mother-in-law's innocence, explained why they had been so polite. The tactic of protest in this second round of the voting had been a mass boycott of the election, wherever no worthy candidates were being offered. 'Every voter who turns up and registers only lends the election credibility,' he said sternly.

But as we walked away from the polling station to the sound of the jolly music, Elena was still wide-eyed. It was the first time in her life that she had not been forced to vote. 'There used to be this rush for the booth at 6.30 in the morning, for fear that you would be suspected of lack of enthusiasm. No one used to get much sleep the night before.' Today, in the spring sunshine, the level at which totalitarian control had been imposed seemed puerile. But this collective fear had worked effectively against the autonomy of even the most resilient characters, as an election story I heard the other day illustrated: 'Right after the war,' a writer told me, 'I used to live near an old man, an officer in his sixties, who had lost his wife and two sons in the war. He had no one left. On election day, he did not turn up at the polling booth until 11 o'clock at night, an hour before it closed. He had always intended to vote. He had just wanted to register his protest. There was a terrible rumpus. The neighbours had been petrified that they would be put inside because he did not turn up to vote! Do you know what happened to him at the next election? They locked him up in prison for the duration, for fear that the scandal would repeat itself.'

It is this that gives the particular flavour to everyday life under totalitarianism. There were the occasional petty sabo- teurs, like the old officer, or Elena's drunken messenger, who would set the place on fire because they could not take it any more. And there were those who spent their lives searching out other people's boxes of matches, for fear that if the matches were ever used, they might be accused of arson themselves.

Vast Resources of Healing Power

The Rusakov House of Culture was teeming with life on a Saturday afternoon. I was sitting in the cafeteria with Bella. It was some time since I had seen her and Andrei. I was anxious to find out how he was managing. I already knew that Andrei had changed a lot. But I shared the concern Vera had expressed when we first met: as a man who had believed all his life, how would he cope in a world of doubt? Would he again reach for belief of some kind?

It was hard to hear what Bella was saying. The boys in the adjoining hall were warming up on their electric guitars. A few teenage girls stood around at the other end of the hall, mesmerized by the possibility that something might be about to begin. Now and then a girl with artfully untidy hair broke into an angular dance.

Every district and factory supported its own House of Culture. They were the Soviet version of community centres, but they were taken more seriously. Bella worked here, in the famous hexagonal building that was erected in 1929 by the constructivist Melnikov. It was about to be restored, she said. 'We want to make it into a centre for the study of constructivism. We're trying to get rid of people like that.' She indicated the boys with guitars. 'But where will they go?' I asked. 'Oh, I don't know.' It was becoming clearer every day that, whatever the future held for Russia in general, life was going to get steadily worse for the people to whom it already offered least, the very young and the very old.

From the room next door a haunting melody could be heard between the blocks of electric sound. We opened the door a crack. Dancers in red and blue costumes shuttled back and forth across the room. This was where urban Ossetians came together to teach the traditional Caucasian dances to a younger generation who had no other contact with their culture. In the room on the other side of the foyer, past the long Honours Board, where pictures of this month's most productive lathe turners at the local factory gazed out at us, the old people were having their regular Saturday afternoon dance. Numbers were down, Bella said, because the price of admission had been raised as part of the new policy of economic self-sufficiency.

I was swept into a waltz by a trim old man who guided me through solid pairs of dancing women. The atmosphere was cheerful but my partner was discontented. 'Why can't the old ladies keep their figures? Look at them, they're like sacks.' Bella led me away. She had brought me here to hear the Great Shatalova. Although the name meant nothing to me, I knew she was great because of the way Bella said Shatalova, with an exaggerated emphasis on the middle 'a', as we would say McCartney in the West when we meant not any old McCartney, but Paul.

Shatalova stood on the stage, a handsome woman with a grey cap of hair. Bella whispered to me that she was seventy-three. She bounded with energy. Just the woman my cavalier was looking for. Shatalova was lecturing her audience on breathing, exercise, deportment and feeding habits. Her tone was political. 'Above all you must take responsibility for your-selves,' she insisted. 'We are only ill if we want to be ill. At this critical time we have a responsibility to be healthy. How else can we hope to renew ourselves? Once, we were famed for our health. May we be once more! My central principle is that we derive the greatest energy from the least food. You, on the other hand, live by the opposite principle, that of deriving the least energy from the greatest amount of food.' Bella whispered

172

in my ear that Shatalova, a surgeon by training, had become a non-surgical healer. Her message, though familiar in the West, was new here.

The dietary aspect of the deficit economy had not occurred to me. But from what I had gleaned of this mysterious economy, it made sense that people should aspire to eat more and more, the less there was in the shops. This could only hasten the steady movement of the economy towards immobility. No wonder Shatalova's ideas had received no official recognition.

The woman was a born performer. She declaimed, she charmed, but she was stern. She was now gaily telling her pale, dumpy, aching audience that they must give up tea, coffee, alcohol, milk products, eggs, salt, sugar, white bread and meat. 'We have but to slough off the habits we picked up off the Germans, the meat-eating Germans, and return to our old ways!' A bemused silence settled as Shatalova finished her speech. This list comprehensively covered not the everyday diet of her audience, but the diet to which these people would aspire if only there were the tea, coffee, alcohol, sugar and above all meat, in the shops. Here in Moscow some of these foods could still be found, but elsewhere people had not seen them for months. Eventually one man brought himself to ask the question for everyone: 'What is there left to eat then?' Nuts? Fresh vegetables? From the look on their faces at her answer, she might have been talking of seaweed and wild rice.

With her audience on the verge of rebellion, Shatalova changed key. She summoned two men on to the platform to testify to how she had saved them both from the jaws of death. 'Now I would like three volunteers from the audience, people with something seriously wrong with them.' She stood the first woman on one side of the stage and walked to the far side. Shatalova was going to examine the woman's biorhythms. She pointed a bent knitting needle at her as if it were a divining-rod and walked slowly towards her, searching, as she put it, for the edge of her aura. The belligerence of her audience had

173

evaporated. They were sitting forward in their chairs, each intent on their own ailments. The needle quivered and spun to the left. Shatalova shook her well-coiffured head. The news was clearly bad. The needle made a small lurch to the right. Did this mean there was hope? 'The problem is in your stomach.' The woman nodded her head and the audience relaxed. In diagnosing one, she had satisfied them all. Every nation has a favourite ailment. Just as the liver is to the French, the heart to the Germans, and the bowel to the Briton, here everyone had a stomach problem. After a more long-distance probing, Shatalova pronounced the woman as curable, as long as she submitted herself to a total personal revolution. 'Will you?' asked the healer. 'I will!' testified the saved woman.

Shatalova was impressive. She knew her audience. As the age of rationality came to a close in the Soviet Union, there was no point in talking to them about science. Rationality had failed them. It had led to the reign of the absurd. Although her dietary advice was sound, it had to be wrapped up in shamanism. I too knew enough about Soviet medicine by now to understand a little of what it meant to Shatalova's audience. It was not just that, despite being nationalized, medicine was not free. It was not just that every person who did anything for you, from the doctor who referred you for treatment, to the surgeon, the nurses, the anaesthetist, the physiotherapist, the whole cast of characters needed to be paid individually at an exorbitant rate in order to attend to you at all. In that respect, the system merely mirrored its American counterpart, although unofficially.

The reason this audience had no confidence in Soviet medicine was not even that it was starved of drugs and that doctors rarely used pain-killers. The Russians were a resilient people. It was the fact that, as one friend put it, 'You have to be very healthy to be able to be ill in the Soviet Union.' Because of the rich pickings to be had, this officially badly paid profession had for a number of years been attracting a different kind of 'doctor'. 'Like this friend of mine,' she went on to say. 'She is married and went through the motions of being a medical student. Then she bought her qualification. She's a nice enough girl, but I'd hate to be in her hands if there were anything really wrong with me. You have to be a psychologist when you consult the doctor here. Do they know what they're talking about or not? It does not say outside the door. If you don't like the look of a doctor, you get out quick.' The system whereby people bought their qualifications to practise medicine had been going on for long enough that there were now 'doctors' in teaching hospitals as well. Ironically the system of closed clinics and hospitals, whose purpose was to give the élite a superior service, also gave them a far higher proportion of 'doctors' as well. The richer pickings naturally attracted them.

At this stage in the evening, Shatalova had me in the palm of her hand. But from then onwards, my image of her began to get confused. Bella had invited us both to supper. She and Andrei had thrown their energies into the dietary revolution. I was the more surprised therefore to find Andrei looking haggard. He had also not shaved for several days, which seemed uncharacteristic. But my sympathy went down badly. It turned out that he had been trying to cultivate the hirsute look that used to go under the name 'designer stubble' in the West

Embarrassed, I followed Bella to the kitchen while Andrei entertained Shatalova. The healer had taken an immediate liking to him. Now, I hoped, I would have a chance to hear about the developments in Andrei's life since we last met. Things had not stood still for him. 'I know he'll want you to know,' Bella said with her usual delicacy, 'but I don't think he will manage to tell you himself. Andrei has lost his ambition.' She referred to it as if it had been a thing, like a wallet, or a diary. 'All these years we've been together, he's been off on one course after another. He was always wanting to learn and get ahead. He was in the Party even before he was called up by the Army. And he's done awfully well. He's one of the four

175

administrative bosses in his factory, as you know. It was only a matter of time before he was offered a good Party job. That was his ambition. Well, now they've offered it to him. It's the job he always wanted, in regional Party headquarters. And he's turned it down. He says he's not interested in anything now except us, his family. The revelations of the last year have done it. They have shattered his world and all his hopes.' I could not keep up with the speed at which he seemed to be building a new one.

When we rejoined the other two for supper, Andrei was sitting with his palm outstretched. Shatalova had suspended a ball and thread over it. She gave him a coquettish smile: 'Young man, you have vast resources of healing power.' Shatalova's contraption delivered a less favourable verdict on Bella, who had been nursing her husband through his ideological detoxification. Shatalova warned her that she was, in a negative sense, 'capable of becoming a witch'. I kept my hand to myself.

Having spent the evening lecturing us on the principle that the less you eat the better, Shatalova proceeded to endear herself to me again by eating vastly more than anyone else at the table. Once replenished, she treated us to a demonstration of her diagnostic power with the knitting needle. It seemed that she really believed in it. She asked Andrei to fetch two books wrapped in newspaper, one of which he thought 'good' and the other 'bad'. Her knitting needle would tell us which was which. After some time, he came back with two parcels. His choice of books would be revealing. Unerringly the knitting needle pronounced that the first parcel, which contained Bulgakov's *Master and Margarita*, was an evil book, and that the second was 'good'. It was called *A Handbook of Leadership for Officers* and I was pleased to see that Andrei too looked shocked at the needle's verdict. A few months ago he would have agreed with it. But Shatalova moved fast. She paused only momentarily before pronouncing: 'The needle cannot abide the Devil, you see.'

After Shatalova had left, Bella reiterated an invitation she

176

had made to me to join her on the trip she was about to make to her home town of Stavropol' in south Russia just north of the Caucasus. She was going down there so that her oldest son could spend a few days with his grandmother. Stavropol' sounded interesting. Set in the black-earth region, which contained the richest agricultural land in Russia, it was where Gorbachev and his wife had built their careers. We agreed that if I were to travel there at short notice, I would be better off going there by train, as I could go without a visa. Bella and Kostya would fly and I would meet them there.

At the end of the evening, Andrei offered to accompany me to the Metro. As we walked along the path under the bare trees, I finally had the chance to ask him what he thought of the elections. 'What is there to be so interested in?' he answered bitterly. 'It's not going to change anything, as it might in the West. Meanwhile, every day presents us with immediate problems, too many of them!' he sighed and seemed hesitant as to whether to go on. 'The real trouble is that when there are a limited number of things to go round in a society, the moral questions that arise out of everyday life become unbearable. Whose interests do you put first? Those of the general good, or those of your family? How can you not want the best for your family? But where would it lead me if I were to follow that principle? Black marketeering? Even racketeering?'

Andrei had only had one way of asking a question before, and that was rhetorically. But these were real questions. Andrei was in despair, and for the first time he did not mind my knowing it. 'We've got to the point where we see racketeers on television, saying just that – that they're doing it for the sake of their mothers!'

We found the Metro closed. As we waited for a taxi, he added in an anguished voice: 'I find life so hard. It was easier before. But there's no going back, of course. There never is.'

As I travelled in the taxi through the night streets of Moscow, I could not shake off Andrei's pain. When had I met him, he had

177

still been what Dostoevsky would have called 'a piano key', someone to be played on. Every day I lived here bore out what Andrei had said about the moral quality of life here. Morality was not a subject for a late-night conversation, or a question that arose after the first heart attack. Here, it was not possible to get through a single day without moral questions invading every shopping expedition and encounter at work. As technical director of a construction factory in a country desperate for building supplies, Andrei must daily be having to exercise that choice. But to hear the idea expressed by him of all people was extraordinary.

V

STAVROPOL'

The Vampire Style

'It's an apocalyptic time,' Elena's daughter Ira had said to me before I left. 'Feeling that, people draw opposite conclusions. Some think of nothing but themselves and others become saintly. There is little in between.' My sole travelling companion in the compartment on the Stavropol' train was not one of the saints.

With the prospect of a day and a half on the train, my immediate reaction had been one of relief on finding the four-bunk compartment empty except for a respectable woman of about sixty. She had wasted no time in making herself at home. As soon as the train pulled out of Pavelsky Station, she had changed into her *khalat*, the cotton shift that many women wear indoors. Then she had arranged for Larissa Andreevna, the attendant in charge of our compartment, to bring us two large glasses of tea and laid out a meal of bread, sausage and cucumber on the little table between us. 'Just fancy that! I've got her all to myself!' I overheard her saying to Larissa Andreevna. I should have been warned by that. Solemnly, she introduced herself as Marya, presented me with a small hard cake into which the word 'Peace' had been baked and invited me to eat. Since then she had not stopped talking.

How exactly can I describe Marya? I remember the difficulty I had as a teenager recalling the faces of the transitory objects of my affection in their absence. It was as if my feelings were so strong that they burned a hole in my memory. Marya's face eluded description for opposite reasons. She was neither fat nor

181

thin, short nor tall. Time had written little on it except the number of her years and her habit of being in control.

But it was not Marya's ordinariness that riled me. It was the gleam in her eye. Since the moment she had discovered that I was a foreigner, she had been after something. It was not understanding. She had started by watching me intently. Now that she was satisfied that capitalist women functioned in roughly the same way as others, her curiosity had dried up. Her conversation centred on her own life and that of her family. She was a retired economist and a Party member: 'But I'm afraid the Party is not what it was. Religion is the only power that can help us now. Not that I am a believer myself, of course, but the People have to fear something. Without fear, it all falls apart.' I longed to contradict her. For centuries, the rulers of this country had spoken with this voice. As far as I was concerned, that was the problem. For her, it was the answer.

Every now and then she would interrupt her own flow to return to the subject of her three daughters, and of Polya in particular: 'It's an odd thing,' she would say, putting her head on one side like a robin and gazing at me with a bright blank look, 'but you are so like my Polya – she's the one in Leningrad. The same hair! The same eyes! Such a talented girl! If only she could spend a few weeks in England . . .' She sighed and added, as if thinking out loud, 'But, of course, she would need an invitation . . .'

At least she was not going all the way to Stavropol'. I reckoned it would be about fifteen hours before she got off at Voronezh. Each time the train stopped, I hoped that our intimacy would be disturbed. But no one even looked into our compartment. Perhaps she had asked Larissa Andreevna to make sure that we were left in peace, I thought with horror. But that would not have been necessary. The train was not full. The children were still at school and the holiday season was some way off.

As she went on talking about her late husband, her late salary and Polya's accomplishments, I gazed out of the window. The train slowed down as it approached a river so broad that it seemed like a lake. Two boys were riding through the shallows on their bicycles, raising the water in a fan of spray. The evening sunlight caught the water in an amber light like that of memory. Travelling through this landscape, where mile upon mile of flat land was unbroken by the incident of hill or stream, the rhythm of the train brought back a poem of Pushkin's. He describes a journey by troika down a winter road. 'Monotonous, wearying, the little bell rings out. In the long-drawn-out songs of the coachmen, I hear something deeply familiar: abandoned revelry, the longing of the soul . . .' *Toska*, the Russians call that longing. The word, which has no real English translation, took on more meaning for me in this landscape that stretched away to an iron horizon. Here man could never forget the vastness of the land in which he lived. It was a force pressing on him, inviting him to seek comfort in oblivion. The monotony of the countryside was broken only by the beautiful names of the little villages through which we passed: Silver Ponds, Necklace, Dream. The Russian desire to find sanctuary in the beauty of words goes a long way back.

Eventually I staunched Marya's flow by offering her a copy of the radical journal *Ogonyok* to read. The train had stopped and I found myself gazing at a low, prefabricated concrete building, down whose wall an overflow pipe must have been pouring for days. The slovenliness might be Russian, but the relentless ugliness that covered this country like mould, that was Soviet. I was beginning to find it tiring.

The Revolution had inspired artists to reinvent the made world, reconceiving everything down to workers' clothing and cups. But as the regime had got into its stride, the vision of the constructivists had been superseded by its antithesis, the triumphalist style, which had glorified the People as Marya did, on condition that they did not step out of line. The attitude behind

183

this style was summed up in a phrase that had been coined to describe buildings like the handsome Stalinist skyscrapers that decorate the Moscow skyline: the vampire style. Fascist though it was, this style contained more care for people than what came afterwards.

At least in Stalin's day they had built well. Now buildings, furniture, clothes, all seemed to have been designed to cheat the eye of delight. But any attempt to credit Soviet design of the last few decades with intention was, I knew, fanciful. Although the result might be puritanical, it involved nothing as conceptually intriguing as a puritan search for forms which would not corrupt. Aesthetics had simply withered away. The only vision that could be tolerated by the looking-glass economy, in which the political had won over the economic, was a vision that involved the search for the lowest level of quality and choice sustainable in any artefact. In retrospect, what was so threatening about constructivism was that, like all original design, it had a vision of its own, rooted in the past, ambitious to shape the future. A painter had been telling me that even in Moscow there were only two colours of paint that were regularly in stock: one shade of green and red, the familiar shade of red. I could not help remembering the characteristic finality with which Tatyana in Baku had expressed her verdict on Soviet aesthetics: 'Taste? There's no such thing as taste in Soviet society. Taste, after all, involves discrimination and that is in itself an anti-Soviet concept.'

But no, I was forgetting the one style of decoration, if not design, that had been sanctioned and which could be seen from end to end of the Soviet Union, in every market and park. It was an ersatz peasant style, which limited itself to primary colours and aspired to make humans produce work which looked as if it could only have been conceived and executed by a machine. Even the ideological credentials of this style struck me as shaky, considering the epic campaign that had been fought to extirpate the peasantry and their culture in the thirties.

This cantankerous reflection had not been prompted just by Marya's company. The night before, a flash of beauty had crossed my path, upsetting my tolerance of ugliness. Over a bottle of Georgian wine in a Moscow flat, I had been listening to a woman musicologist singing songs which she had collected from remote parts of Russia. Their strange cadences and untamed scales were full of the sadness of the steppes, the *toska* of which Pushkin's coachman sang. The musicologist was lucky, she said. Before the fifties, it would have been impossible to collect such songs. Under Stalin, new pseudo folk traditions had been invented. The real thing had been considered far too dangerous. It still was. The wild beauty of the sound had made me freshly intolerant of the aesthetic cheat that had everywhere been perpetrated in this beautiful country.

The landscape this morning was as flat as ever, but now the fields were sprouting and the vegetable plots were planted. During the night, Marya had rolled up her mattress and left. It was not the last I was to hear of her. She took to ringing up Elena in Moscow and asking her advice as to how to get me to invite Polya to London.

Larissa Andreevna, our attendant, brought tea and stayed to chat, balanced on the opposite bunk. She was in her fifties, short and fat, with hennaed hair. No, Larissa Andreevna was not fat, she was sumptuous. Since I arrived I had been learning to look at fatness with a different eye. Bella, who was waiting for me in Stavropol', had told me that in her home village she had always been thought plain. The ancient equation between fatness and beauty still prevailed.

Even in Moscow there was a style among women which was strange to the Western eye. I thought of it as the Grushenka style, after the plump sexy minx at the centre of the rivalry between Karamazov father and son in Dostoevsky's novel. There were Grushenkas everywhere. They tended to have peroxide hair, thick make-up and generous figures. These were

185

poured into tight skirts, low-necked frilly shirts and high-heeled white boots. Grushenkas did not need to be young or even pretty. Their appeal was provocative yet ultimately maternal. Their model was the singer Alla Pugachova, a woman who looked like a tea-cosy and who had been Russia's most popular singer for a decade. Although Larissa Andreevna was a grandmother, she was also, I could see, a provincial Grushenka. After a day spent travelling through this featureless countryside I was beginning to understand the taste of Russian men for Grushenkas. I could see how a man might want to grow like ivy up the rock-like stability of a Grushenka's frame and seek oblivion in the effusion of her breasts.

As we sat and talked, little children were pulling their way slowly up and down the carriage, holding on to the rail. One stopped in the half-open doorway and looked at us impassively. Apart from children, only gods and animals gaze like that. The conversation turned to Elista, Larissa Andreevna's home town, where the train would stop. Recently it had become famous as the town where babies had contracted Aids after having been injected with dirty needles in the hospital. As she talked about the children, Larissa Andreevna's buoyancy gave way to an apocalyptic mood. 'Mark my words,' she said, 'the death of those babies is only the beginning. In a few years the disease will get us all.' There was a pause. The beat of the train measured the passing of time. Then she leapt up: 'Let's have a cup of tea!' and ran from the room. Tea! In a room where the conversation has become bleak someone can be relied upon to fetch strong Georgian tea. Tea is the antidote to gloom. Out there the country may hover on the edge of civil chaos, but the tea-drinkers have made a sanctuary. Thus comforted, Larissa Andreevna and I sat in silence and sipped our tea as the flat countryside slipped past.

In Search of the Soviet Experience

On my first day in Stavropol', Bella, who used to be a tour guide and had friends who still were, had made plans for me to get to know the town by joining a coach tour. She was so pleased at the arrangement that I could hardly refuse to go. From the moment she slipped me on to the bus at the last minute, the other tourists had turned their backs on me. They all knew each other, and I was not one of them. Besides, it was clear that I had not arrived by my holiday in the regular way, by putting my name down on the union's list and waiting all year to find out whether I had been allocated what I wanted, or something quite different. There was a deficit of desirable holidays as there was of everything else. I was clearly getting mine 'on the side'.

The group had arrived by plane from Moscow together. It consisted of twenty-eight women and three men. There were a number of young girls, with convalescent faces and permed, dyed hair. Off their drooping shoulders hung shapeless imitations of fashionable clothes. The middle-aged women were made of sterner stuff. They were no longer grieving for what might have been. Their perms had been stiffened for self-defence and their legs, thickened by years of standing in queues, would get them through anything.

At great speed, the bus drove us down empty streets lined with double rows of well-tended trees. It deposited us at a landscaped park, where we were photographed against a small monument to General Suvorov. 'It's beautiful,' murmured one

187

of the middle-aged women to another. After having fought Poland to reconquer the south-west Russian lands on behalf of Catherine the Great, Suvorov had come south. His mission was to destroy the Crimean Khanate, whose warlike incursions into Russian territory were a reminder of the Mongol invasion five centuries earlier. As late as 1750, Tatars were raiding the Ukraine. Their continued presence was hindering the economic development of south Russia. Suvorov had seized the Crimea in 1783, finally winning the Russian Empire a port to the south.

Stavropol' was founded then, as one of a line of forts stretching from the Black Sea to the Caspian. It was to become the military headquarters for the Russian offensive on the Caucasus which continued through the nineteenth century. For people like Tolstoy and Lermontov the town had been the last outpost of civilization before the journey into the Caucasian foothills, where mountain warriors were everywhere concealed. Stavropol' was the lively centre where the officers used to take their leave.

Of all this our tour guide said not a word as we toiled up the steps to another war memorial. It seemed possible that she did not know much of it. The Soviet school curriculum paid scant attention to pre-Revolutionary history. At the top of the steps stood a thirty-foot bronze soldier striding off the edge of a steep escarpment. It was a striking image to commemorate the final defeat of General Denikin's anti-Bolshevik forces in the south in the Civil War. After advancing north almost as far as Moscow, via Kharkov and Kiev, the White general had been forced back when his lines of communication had been severed. Though this memorial commemorated the victory of the Red Army over him, the bands of marauding peasants in his rear had been just as responsible for his defeat.

The afternoon had proceeded in a haze of war memorials. The remainder were all to the Second World War. Stavropol', lying as it does to the south and west of Stalingrad (or Volgograd, as it is now called) was caught in the German 6th Army's

188

push to remedy their desperate shortage of oil by gaining control of the Baku oilfields. They had entered Stavropol' on 3 August 1942 and left it when General von Paulus, starved of fuel and other supplies by the Red Army's encirclement, surrendered at Stalingrad in January 1943, turning the fortune of the war.

Bella's girl-friend, with whom we were staying, was Greek. I had expressed to her my surprise at the tenacity of this cult of war memorials, half a century after the last great war. 'Look at their history,' she had said. 'What else is there for them to be proud of?' She was right, of course, as to the official reason for the cult. But I had seen little evidence of pride from my fellow holiday-makers. They seemed obedient more than proud. They were not interested in the past. The chunks of stone seemed as remote from their original meaning as the bluestones of Stonehenge to the modern English tourist. But they clearly did derive some arcane pleasure from these pilgrimages to sites of carnage. When given the option, they had chosen to take in a couple of extra ones on the way home. Was it just for the fresh air? The full significance of these rituals had become impossible for the outsider to divine.

Beauty of a high order holds its own conviction. With Bella, unlike her awkward husband, it was all too easy to forget the gulf of experience that divided us. When she invited me down to Stavropol', she described all the Caucasian delights she longed for me to see. Kislovodsk, Piatigorsk – above all Dombai, 'the Switzerland of the Soviet Union', as she called it. She stood there among the bright birch-trees of Moscow's Izmaylova Park, looking like an antelope, her tawny hair looped around her face. She rolled her grey eyes and luxuriated in the word 'Dombaaaaai', and I was sold on all her Caucasian plans for me.

But on my second day in Stavropol', I had cause to remember that we came from different worlds. Anyone who could have believed all her life that prostitution was an ideological impossibility in her country had had practice at swallowing improbable propositions. I had not been able to find Dombai on the map and I was already on the way there before I learned that the day trip Bella had put me on involved ten hours' driving in a charabanc.

Dombai turned out to be about 200 miles south of Stavropol'. The scenery was quite like that of Switzerland. For two and a half hours I stood in the pouring rain appreciating it. The hotels refused entrance to people like us who were day trippers. The view from under the eaves of the hotel where I cowered would have been even more beautiful had it not been for the two prefabricated concrete tower blocks, and the messy building sites. Wet flocks of tourists were searching for places in which to hide from the rain as they scuttled along the concrete paths that led in small circles away from the bus park and back again. The one covered *shashlik* bar was full. Those, like me, who had exercised all the available options by walking as far as we were allowed to, were harassed by gypsy women trying to sell us acrylic jumpers which they told us were made of mountain wool. At the edges of the narrow valley, where the concrete paths doubled back again, the wooded mountain rose steeply on all sides. 'Walking forbidden', the notices said. The few tatty booths selling souvenirs were deserted because of the driving rain. My hostess had thoughtfully provided me with a packed lunch, which I ate under the dripping eaves, counting the minutes before I could get back into the bus again.

When our tour guide had told us how long the journey was on our way out of Stavropol' that morning, I had asked her if I could stay overnight. She had given me a strange look and her answer was curt: 'We don't have the manpower up there to look after all these tourists.' Her tone conveyed her meaning perfectly. It did not suit the employees of the tourist industry to spend their time in Dombai. Now I understood why. An hour of this was enough.

A few exclusive Soviet tourists in foreign ski outfits wandered past on their way back from the single ski lift and looked at me as if I was waiting for the opportunity to steal their skis. With nowhere to go and nothing to do I walked back to the bus early, or so I thought. I opened the door. A woman's face swelled up in front of me, purple and bulging with rage. Her frizzy hair stood on end like Medusa's snakes. Her teeth flashed gold. She was shouting, at me. Close to tears, I made my way down a gangway draped in wet macs, followed by hostile eyes. I appeared to have kept them waiting for half an hour, having misunderstood the instructions for our rendezvous. The linguistic misunderstanding had been compounded by a cultural one. I could not believe that anyone would have come so far in order to spend only two hours at their destination.

The bus started back for Stavropol' smelling of wet dog. Medusa's outburst was the first acknowledgement the group had made of my existence in the past two days. As soon as we had left the gloomy pines and low cloud of the Soviet Switzerland behind, the rain stopped. We crossed a mountain river rushing down a steep ravine. The bus was passing through the land of the Circassians, heading for the original home of the Karachai. A little further off were the lands of the Tatars, Cossacks, Chechens, Ingush, Avars, Ossetians, Abkhazians and Georgians. Through the hole I had made in the steamed-up window I watched as the close-cropped Caucasian foothills were taken away from me like a delicious, uneaten meal. I felt utterly miserable. Then it occurred to me. In my search for an understanding of the Soviet experience, maybe I had arrived.

A Father's Dowry

While I was in Dombai, my friend Bella and her son had taken a bus in the other direction to visit Bella's mother. I invited Bella's Greek friend Olga, with whom I was staying, out to dinner: 'Let's go to the grandest place in town.' Olga sighed and shook her hennaed head: 'You really don't understand, do you? There's nowhere you'd go out to for pleasure in Stavropol'.'

Olga's name was the only thing about her that was Russian. She was buxom, and with her full lips and eyes like Kalamáta olives, she had the beauty of a Coptic grave-painting. When she smiled, which she did a lot, her gold front tooth flashed. It was made, she told me proudly, from the last of the British gold coins which her grandfather had brought with him when the family had fled to the Crimea in the thirties. They had been expelled from Turkey together with more than a million compatriots following the abortive Greek invasion which had sought to exploit the collapse of the Ottoman Empire. 'It had a woman's head on it,' Olga explained of the coin. I could think of no better end to the foreign adventures of a Victorian gold sovereign. The other day, a Russian doctor had been recounting to me with amusement how an Armenian colleague had commiserated with him on still having all his own teeth. In the south, you replaced your teeth with gold ones as soon as you could afford to.

Olga, who worked for an airline office, was not rich. She had only two sets of outdoor clothes, which she wore on

192

alternate days and looked after meticulously, changing out of them as soon as she got home from work. But what money she had, she spent on clothes that no ordinary Russian would have chosen. They were sober and well-tailored, not Soviet of course. In them she looked like a prosperous Athenian matron.

I had particularly wanted to take Olga out to dinner because it was evident that she had only just moved house. She had only one room in a two-room communal flat, where the kitchen and bathroom were shared. From the doorway, her room looked like a vast relief model of the Caucasian mountain range through which I had been driving. The range upon range of craggy peaks and impassable valleys were her possessions, packed up in boxes and stacked round the edge of the room under brown blankets. Now I learned that Olga had lived like this for more than three months. She had an eight-year-old daughter who had been living with her grandmother down the road for all this time.

People in the Soviet Union seemed to be constantly on the move, trying to better their accommodation. In itself, this was enough to explain the makeshift air that characterized so many lodgings. But there were other reasons. Furniture was hard to find and even in an otherwise carefully furnished room some crucial item, like a table to eat off, would often be missing. Dedication was required, and anyone who was not obsessive tended to abandon the effort sooner or later. These genuine difficulties were compounded by the Russian phenomenon of *oblomovshchina*. This word describes an essential element in the Russian temperament; the easygoing, heedless, generous, lovable, slovenly characteristics of Goncharov's hero Oblomov in the novel of the same name.

If I made the initial mistake of assuming an element of *oblomovshchina* about the state of Olga's room, I soon realized how wrong I was. Olga, who had not a drop of Russian blood in her veins, suffered from the opposite disease. Her housing problem had arisen because she had striven too zealously to

193

better her accommodation. As a result, she had become enmeshed in a court case of Dickensian complexity. She had moved here from a larger room which she had taken great pains to decorate. This one was smaller than the space to which she was entitled. But when she had moved, the other room in the flat had been empty. She had swapped her fine room for this on the expectation that she would be able to take over the other one as well. To have a self-contained two-room flat on the ground floor of an old house would have been unbelievably luxurious in Soviet terms.

When she had already agreed to the move, everything had started to go wrong. An official in the Fraud Department had heard about the flat and decided to try to get hold of it for himself. He pulled strings to make sure that somebody was moved into the second room, and ensured that Olga was taken to court as a preliminary to getting her moved. As no one could get anything done in this country without breaking the rules, he knew that it would only require a little digging to discover some 'irregularities'.

Of course there had been irregularities. Olga had got 'married' to the son of a family friend, for instance, in order to win herself an entitlement to extra space. But the man from the Fraud Department had committed his fair share as well. In order to prevent Olga from moving into the second room, he had caused its status to be changed, so that it became a room tied to a factory rather than being in the gift of the housing department. The case was to have another hearing tomorrow.

'So you see why I haven't unpacked. I can't unpack until I've redecorated the rooms. But I can't bear the thought of doing all the work and then being forced to move.' There were no chairs in Olga's room. After supper, we sat on our beds on either side of the room while Olga outlined her plans: 'I shall block off this window with display shelving. And I shall put a dado round the walls and panelling above the dado.' As she unfolded her vision, I wondered if it was possible for *perestroika* to be totally successful in one flat or whether, like the principle of socialism in one country, it was to prove an impossibility. As Olga strode around, surveying the terrain like a general before battle, I felt a growing confidence. 'I'll put up proper curtains, with new curtain rails. And look what I found in Minsk, they're Indian . . .' She rummaged around under the blankets and pulled out some fancy brass door handles. There were advantages to working in an airline office. She could range widely in her search for furnishings. 'I don't know how to explain the look I'm after . . . Ah, wait a minute.' She took out of her handbag the packet she had saved off a cheap pair of French tights. On it was a photograph of a louche blonde sitting on a gilded Louis-Quinze divan. 'Yes, that's it. That's the style.'

In the course of looking for the door handles, Olga came across something else. Triumphantly, she pulled out a black tube out of which sprouted a bunch of soft plastic filaments. 'Look what I found in Leningrad last year. I was very lucky to get it. There can't be more than one or two of these in the whole of Russia. Just hang on, you'll never believe this . . .' As she placed the object upright on the table, the filaments arranged themselves like flowers in a vase. She plugged in a flex and switched off the overhead light. Specks of light, green, pink and white, travelled up and down each glittering strand and the vase began to turn, transforming the desolate room into a night-club. I had caught a glimpse of Olga's vision. She wanted to build herself a bunker against *oblomovshchina*.

In the course of explaining her housing saga to me, Olga mentioned that she had her father to thank for the room. 'When he was rehabilitated under Khrushchev, they started paying my mother a monthly pension and they gave her this housing entitlement. But she had married again by that time, so the housing passed to me.' It turned out that both her father and her grandfather had been arrested in 1938, in the Crimea. She seemed vaguely surprised that I should be interested 'in all that', as she put it.

In response to my interest, she went on: 'I can't remember what the charge was. What does it matter when they were all trumped up? But I do remember my grandfather saying that they'd accused him of setting fire to some factory or other. After a year in prison, my father spent the next seven in camp. Then he was exiled to Uzbekistan. After the war, Stalin exiled everyone from the Crimea who wasn't Russian on the grounds that if the Germans ever came again, it would be the non-Russians who would collaborate. While he was inside, his wife and children had left for Greece. They'd kept their Greek passports. He had changed his for a Soviet one. He must have got tired of checking in with the police every week, as you had to if you had a foreign passport.

'So he married my mother and started a second family. She was much younger than him and irresistible to men. She had this hour-glass figure and beautiful face with a long nose and thin cold lips.' A few days later I met Olga's mother. It was hard to fit the description to the squat mustachioed woman whose woollen hat was pulled down to her angry eyes. A lifetime of taking in laundry had worn her beauty away.

'I was only a year old when they arrested him again, so I remember nothing about him,' Olga went on. 'That second time, he was afraid of prison and tried to hang himself. But they found him in time. Soon afterwards he became ill and died in hospital. I think he just lost hope.' A clear, untamed voice sounded through the flat. 'Grandpa', the lorry driver who had been installed in the other room, was singing in the bath as he got himself ready to go out folk-dancing. He had come into the kitchen for a chat while we were having our supper. He was small and as bright-eyed as a bird and he looked as if he spent his days in the forest rather than in the cab of a lorry. He had buried his wife and sent his daughters out into the world. He seemed lightly attached to the earth himself. His room, unlike Olga's, was almost empty apart from the standard bed.

Despite the circumstances, Olga and he were fond of each

other. 'God sent him to me,' she said of him. 'If I had to share a flat with anyone, it's a blessing that it should be him. He doesn't drink either and that's practically unheard of among simple men . . .' He was singing a song full of yearning. Olga's cheerfulness had seemed unaffected by talking about her father. But as she joined in, her eyes clouded as she gave in to the emotion of the song.

We went to bed early. I was exhausted after my marathon journey to Dombai and back. It had been a curious evening. Olga had talked obsessively about the saga of her room. Yet when it came to the tragedy that had enveloped her family, she talked without emotion. She was clearly humouring me by telling the story at all. We lay in the dark, with the street light shining through the window on to the mountain range of Olga's belongings. I asked her what had happened after her father died. 'My mother married again. He was a good man, also Greek. I was fond of him. But he was a terrible drinker and after about five years he suddenly died. It was a tragedy for us. That was the only piece of happiness my mother had ever known.' Olga paused. The breeze blew through the open window and the thin curtain billowed into the room.

'Anyway, she was still very beautiful and before long another Greek, from Stavropol', wanted to marry her. That's how we ended up here. It was wonderful to get out of Uzbekistan. They're an ignorant lot, the Uzbeks, and life there is primitive. Not that my mother is an educated woman. She can't even read and write. But she's tremendously hard-working and she made a good home. All the same, it was a bad marriage. He was miserly.'

Olga went on, still sounding detached: 'He'd been married once before, when he was very young. Though he was from a simple background, he'd been a bright boy. He got into an institute in the Crimea and had a fling with a student from Leningrad, an intellectual down for the summer. Anyway, she ended up pregnant. Everyone was furious. Her family insisted that he do the right thing and marry her. His family was very anti the whole thing because she was Jewish. None the less, they got married though it didn't last long. The Germans killed her in the war for being a Jew, while he was sent to prison by us for being a Greek. After the war his mother thought he was dead, so – they still had their Greek passports – she left for Greece with the child, a little girl.

'It was only much later that his mother found out that he was still alive. By then times had changed. He'd had to get a Soviet passport and they wouldn't let him out. The girl is now grown up and works for radio in Athens. They did meet once, when she came here. It was a disaster. They hit it off very badly. She knew all about how he'd been to her mother and she wasn't at all keen on him. As for him, he wanted her to buy him diamonds and things. But she's an intellectual, she wasn't brought up in those peasant ways.'

We lay in silence for a while with the curtain billowing. The room seemed alive with the past. 'How is it that you talk so lightly of such a past?' I asked before we drifted off to sleep. 'Ah well,' she explained, 'if I felt these things all the time, I'd go to pieces. Besides, that's all history. It's the everyday problems like the flat that get me really upset.'

The next morning while Olga set off to attend her court hearing, I looked round the town. Olga had been thrown by my obstinate refusal to rejoin the tour group for further day trips to Kislovodsk, Pyatigorsk and other Caucasian beauty spots. The situation was awkward on both sides. What was she to do with me? She and Bella had evidently planned that I should spend the next few days sightseeing in the charabanc while Bella visited her mother, whose village lay a long way from Stavropol'. I could hardly tell Olga, whom I had only just met, that the treat she and Bella had organized for me had been a miserable experience and that nothing would induce me to mount the charabanc again. In the absence of any real explanation, my obstinacy must have seemed wilful. I made it clear that I would prefer to find some way of getting around on my own. This proposition only made things worse. It visibly alarmed Olga. To have an unknown foreigner staying with her was one thing. To have the foreigner, who had no visa and whom she thought of as her responsibility, wandering off all over the Caucasus on her own, that was too much. I surrendered quietly.

We settled for my exploring Stavropol' on my own. It did not take long. The town was in the heart of the richest farm land in Russia, and visibly prosperous. Its broad streets, lined with double rows of trees, were Germanically clean. The earth around the roots of even the full-grown trees had been dug, and the new buildings were more carefully constructed, out of better materials than they would have been in Moscow. But as I walked the regular grid of streets, down Lenin Street, across Marx Street, I felt no trace of the liveliness which Lermontov had enjoyed when he came here on leave from his regiment in the Caucasus. Then it had been a busy trading centre. Now the main railway line bypassed Stavropol'.

Except for the old men in overcoats who sat chatting all day on the benches underneath the trees, there were few people in the streets. Perhaps Olga had not been exaggerating when she had said that, in this town of 160,000 people, there was nowhere to go for the evening. Despite its theatre and its museums, despite its cleanliness and its prosperity, it had a feeling of no European town I knew, a feeling of being a long way from anywhere. As I walked, a misery descended on me like a cloud of flies, a misery that felt like the genius of the place. A pale echo of the feeling that pervades Chekhov's plays, it was rooted in a sense of ontological anxiety, a sense that history was going on unstoppably, somewhere else, without me. How do I get out? It was not a question but an irresistible need that was beginning to form itself. It was only in retrospect that I realized that I knew this feeling, from Baku. Misery makes itself felt each time as something particular.

199

Olga's day had been more successful than mine. She had managed to get her court hearing postponed. She had hopes of being able to take her case to a higher court where, because it was not local, the man from the Fraud Department would have no special purchase on the officials.

During the course of this second evening, I discovered what I should have been able to guess. Apart from her father, there was another man behind the saga of the flat. He was the 'irregularity' which she had not mentioned last night. 'He'd been thrown out by his wife, who bossed him around most terribly. He was a simple man from out of town. She thought she was better than him because she was educated.' This was a common problem in the Soviet Union where many more women than men went on to higher education and three-fifths of all places in intellectual employment were taken by women.

'Anyway, we started going out together and he moved in with me. Then he got this job in the organization that distributes flats. It was he who found the flat and told me to give up my old room for this place, which I could have all to myself. With his help, it was all set up and I was just about to move, when one evening he didn't come home. Nor the next night. For a week I heard not a word from him. Then one day when he thought I would be out at work, he came round to get his things. I ironed his shirt for him, gave him a clean pair of pants and socks and a good hot meal. All he said was: "Don't think badly of me for what I'm going to do. I'm in real difficulties." I didn't press him. It never occurred to me that there could be another woman. His divorce had gone through and he was so attentive, always bringing me flowers and paying me compliments. The men round here aren't like that.' Olga's account was not dispassionate this time. Whatever this man had done to her, she evidently still loved him.

'Then I heard from a friend that he'd gone straight off from my place to the register office and got married to his boss from Moscow. She'd come down here and found irregularities in his work. And she needed to get married to someone quickly so that she could get a flat in Moscow. So off he goes and I'm left here with all my things stacked around the wall, waiting for my case to come to court. It turned out that the man from the Fraud Department had heard that my boy-friend worked for the Housing Department and slipped a word to the court. As for my fella, he was soon back from Moscow. He sort of apologized. The trouble is that I understand so well why it all happened.' She gave a gusty sigh.

'That is my trouble. I always understand.' After a moment, she went on: 'He had been chucked out by his first wife. He had nowhere to live and I was a soft touch. Then he got into trouble with his boss, and this flat was one of the reasons. So he really had no choice. The silly thing is, he was fond of me. He says so himself. But he's a young man. He was ashamed of my being an older woman, with a daughter. It wasn't at all the image he wanted to project to his friends. He's a boss now. He wanted all the things that go with that. Parties, young girls and so on.'

Olga's love life consisted of variations on the theme of this story. At twenty, according to Bella, she had been the Brigitte Bardot of Stavropol'. At forty, her ample beauty was still ripe. She was a soft-hearted woman and a good home maker. Her only desire was to submit herself to the will of a good man, or at least a man. Most important of all in this land where the shortage of housing was the most painful of all the shortages, she had a flat of her own. In this way, her father had provided for her.

Why then was she on her own? The reason went back to the curse of being Greek: 'I was brought up to believe that I'd only get a husband if I remained a virgin. And I wanted to marry a Greek, for whom that is very important. So I waited for the right man to turn up until I was twenty-nine. But there aren't many Greeks around. Everyone thought I was off my rocker, waiting and waiting for nothing. In the end I realized that I'd

201

better at least have some fun before it was too late.' Once she had given up waiting for her Greek, Olga had gone out with a succession of men far younger than herself. All of them, including the father of her child, had shared her home as long as it suited them, then left to marry younger women.

Olga hid behind a firework display of cheerfulness. Only once did she give in to her unhappiness. Bella had returned, leaving Kostya with her mother. She was asleep in Olga's double bed, lying kipper-fashion with her head by Olga's feet. It was dark, unlike the night before. The street light had gone out. As we lay listening to the sound of her even breathing, Olga seemed almost to be talking to herself.

'There are days', she said in a distant voice, 'when I think of hanging myself. I can see no sense in going on living. Then I think of the shame my mother would have to live with. And my daughter too.' She paused. As she talked, her pain seemed to rise in the darkened room. I could find no position in the narrow bed that was comfortable. Surely her daughter gave her a positive reason for living, I suggested? 'I can't say she does. Because I know I am bringing up a girl to enter a world which will be even worse for her than it has been for me. Somehow, I know it will be her lot to play out once more the role of her mother and grandmother, the role of the woman abandoned by men. I can't say I live for her sake when I know perfectly well that in a few years I shall be a useless and terrible burden to her, as my mother is to me. I dread that. I would rather have brought up an unhappy child who was not my own, who would at least have been grateful to me. Who would be able to say, "Thanks to you, my life was transformed. I, who had no home, was taken in." Gratitude. It's not something I'm familiar with. It would be nice.'

As the days in Stavropol' drew on, I became more and more affected by Olga's mood. She was a brave girl, but now I could feel the unhappiness all the time, behind her defiant display of cheerfulness. The evening before we left for Moscow, when

202

Bella was out of the room for a minute, Olga looked over from her bed to mine. She said: 'What a sad face you have. Here I have been going on about myself all this time. But I can see that you have a secret sorrow too.' Her remark took me by surprise. I was not quick on the uptake. I started to explain that I had no secret sorrow. But my words dried up as I realized what I was saying. I should have told her sorrows worthy of her confidence. But it was already too late. She did not believe me and she was hurt. She thought that after all this time that we had spent together, I was refusing to share my pain. That any woman of her own age should be travelling far from home was in itself a symptom of distress. What was I in flight from? It was too much to expect that this woman for whom travel had always meant expulsion should understand my position. I felt free to travel for that most privileged of reasons, because I was not driven. I could not tell her that the pain she saw on my face was the imprint of her own pain.

Second Sight

It was our last full day in Stavropol'. Bella and I were shopping for the party Olga was giving for us when we met an old friend of Bella's in the street. Svetlana was dressed in the height of Soviet fashion, a long shiny leather coat, patterned stockings and high patent-leather shoes. As the three of us proceeded down the street, people turned to stare. She was a most unexpected sight in the sleepy town. Girls as well provided as her rarely walked anywhere.

The two girls had not seen each other in years. 'Well, what happened to you, then?' Bella asked straightforwardly. Svetlana had harsh peroxide blonde hair and pink eye make-up which put two wounds where her eyes should have been. Beneath the disguise, she was good-looking with an intelligent face. She explained that she was going out with a foreigner, a middle-aged Swiss computer consultant who was living in Stavropol' for nine months. 'He wants to marry me and take me home with him at the end of the year.' Svetlana shrugged. She was not overwhelmed by her good fortune: 'We'll see. I don't love him, but he's a good man and what is there for me here? I'd rather have married a Russian. But there are no men here. And I'd do anything to get out of Stavropol'.' Promising to try and look in on the party, she went on her way.

This chance encounter made more of an impression on me in retrospect, after I had met Ivetta. Ivetta was Olga's best friend. She lived on the seventeenth floor of a new block on the edge of town. Because of the state of Olga's room, the party was being held at Ivetta's. She was an attractive woman in her thirties, of Cossack and Ukrainian origin. Her hair was almost black, and her swarthy face was covered in faint blotches that looked like the scars of ancient kisses. She had a ten-year-old son called Ivan and a Bulgarian boy-friend, of whom she seemed slightly ashamed. 'He's a good man, my Zhenya, a real family man. He gives me all his wages every week. But I don't know. He and Ivan used to get on like a house on fire. They're both into body-building. But Ivan can't stand him in the house any more ... If only he weren't so dark ...' I suspected that Ivetta had arranged the time of our party so that Zhenya would be at work. But just as we were leaving, he arrived back.

He was a simple man with perfect manners and the physique of an athlete. As he shook hands, the muscles on his upper arm rippled under the skin. Shy-eyed, he kept looking at Ivetta for approval. But Ivetta was not to be charmed. For years it seemed that her boy-friends had been guest workers. The last had also been a Bulgarian, 'Not dark like this one, but fair, very handsome,' she had been saying earlier. 'Oh! that was something else. I've never been in love like that before. It was an illness. The day he left it all went dark. For a month I couldn't eat ...' The father of her son Ivan had been a Yugo-slav. 'He's always asking me, "Why can't you find yourself a Russian, Mama?" The truth is, I don't know why. These dark foreigners just seem to buzz around me like bees round a honey-pot.'

Again and again over the last days the conversation had gone back to the shortage of men in Stavropol' and in Russia at large. This shortage dated back to the war, my friends kept telling me. It took me a while to understand that they meant the Second World War, which happened long before they were born. Their explanation, though fanciful, showed how deep the historical scars went. The mothers and grandmothers of these women had been bereaved again and again. But the official death toll of seven million in the Second World War was nothing next to the thirty million people who, like Olga's father and grandfather, had lost their lives in prison, exile and in camp.

Everywhere that I went in the Soviet Union I was to meet beautiful, able women on their own. The haemorrhage of the male population had been stopped and there was no statistical shortage. But there did seem to be a shortage of marriageable men. Though the educational imbalance was one factor accounting for a mismatch between the sexes, there seemed to be a deeper cause, one that had roots in a history in which there had not been enough men to go round. Even now, men were being spoilt by women as though they were a rarity. They also found themselves marginalized by a sex that had developed the habit of managing on its own and had handed the habit down to the next generation of women. Treated like children, men seemed liable to crises of identity which increased their vulnerability to the traditional Slav weakness for alcohol.

Now there were drugs too. Olga's favourite boy-friend had been a good example. He had become a drug addict as an Army conscript before they ever met. She knew nothing about it, although they lived together. They had been happy until her mother had accidentally found out: 'Then he became pathetic and said he wasn't worthy of me. I said I'd help him come off it. But he'd found a new pusher by that time and he said that nothing in the world would make him stop. He just took off one day. I never heard from him again.'

Once we had eaten, Ivetta turned our coffee cups upside-down and read our fortunes in the pattern left by the finely ground sediment. For these women, the figure of fate hung over everything. Clues were left in the palms of hands, in stars, in cards and coffee cups. As a companion, I was something of a disappointment for, apart from my scepticism, I brought with me no foreign knowledge on how to read the seeds of time. It would have been hard for me to take the divinations of my friends entirely seriously, because the futures they outlined for

206

me all focused on miraculous solutions to the problems of men and housing.

Lovable though my new friends were, they had traits that were starting to get on my nerves. They spent a great deal of time chattering about things they knew nothing about. Sometimes their ignorance was endearing, as when Olga the proud Greek, living in the heart of Russia's most fertile black-earth region, remarked that 'Greece is such a rich country. You can grow anything on that dark soil.' I always became uncomfortable when the subject of national characteristics came up, which it did every day. 'I used to like the French, but I have gone right off them now,' Olga was saying, as though 'the French' were an unreliable family living down the road: 'They'll be smiling at you one moment, but they'll betray you the next for sure.' 'It's curious that the English have such large families, when they don't like children at all,' Ivetta commented at some point, oblivious of the strangeness of uttering this remark in the presence of the only English person she had ever met.

To start with, my friends had been interested to hear what I had to say about the people in countries in which I had lived and travelled. But the information that came from me was unsatisfactory. I cavilled at their generalizations. It was churlish on my part as it spoiled their pleasure without illuminating the causes of my irritation. They soon reverted to their original guide, Olga's book on national characteristics.

The heightened racial sensibility of these three women, one Greek, one Russian, one Cossack–Ukrainian, should not have taken me so by surprise. After all, they had been brought up in the frontier territory between the Christian empire of the Russians and the Islamic mountain tribes to the south. Each had her own experience of the sharp end of racial coexistence. When Olga offended my Western sensibilities by calling the Muslims 'dirty, ignorant people', she was talking about the people among whom she had been forced to live as an exile, in the lands where her father and her stepfather had died, victims

207

themselves of an arbitrary diktat exercised on racist grounds. Day by day, these women had to face the contrast between their poverty and the wealth of the republics to the south. Here, bright Russians trying to enter the medical college, or the prestigious agricultural college which Gorbachev had attended, had to face competition from Georgians whose fathers could back their candidature with bribes of up to 10,000 roubles. Distasteful as it was, I had to admit that my own Olympian attitudes to race, rooted as they were in an experience of security, might have been different if I had felt cheated of my right to education by a neighbour of another race. But no such understanding thoughts occurred to me at the time. I reacted to these conversations with an irritation that was childish. No wonder they came to treat me with the special, propitiatory indulgence which they extended to those unreliable creatures, men. Nor did this feeling of being patronized help, though it gave me a curious insight into the self-perpetuating dynamics of the sexual politics around me. The more irritated I became, the more they indulged me. My awareness of this process undermined me still further.

When, for instance, Ivetta discovered that my husband was American, she asked a question that was perfectly natural for a Soviet citizen to ask: 'What nationality is he?' 'He's American,' I answered. 'Yes, but what nationality?' 'American,' I repeated obstinately, although I understood her meaning perfectly well. Had my husband been born in this country, his passport would have said that he was a Jew. Race, which, significantly, they call nationality, has since the Revolution been the first point of definition for its citizens here. But in this company nothing would have induced me to give my husband's 'nationality'.

I had been put on my guard by a strange exchange between Olga and me on the subject of history when I first arrived. 'Of course, the Revolution was organized by the Jews,' she had said to me, as though she were talking of the influence of the moon on the tides. 'Ordinary Russians would never have organized something like that, would they? What would they have stood to gain? It's only the rich who are interested in revolution.' 'Why on earth should the rich be interested?' I asked. 'Oh, I suppose they could sell guns to people, things like that. Don't ask me. I'm an intuitive person. I don't know why they did it. I just know that they did. It was a dreadful thing to do, to break off people's traditions like that . . .'

Lenin's solution to the problem of how to turn a colonial empire into a socialist society had seemed in many respects progressive. The creation of a union of socialist republics had given power to ethnic minorities who had before been subject peoples. But their power was confined by a swingeing new colonial measure, which had enshrined the dominance of the Russians in the Soviet Communist Party. The ethnic power bases had been intended to be of transitory political importance. At the point where the political programme became a religious one lay the assumption that they would wither away. In fact the reverse occurred. The notion of a set of political structures defined on ethnic grounds not only gave a continuing focus to nationalist aspirations generally: for each ethnic group, and there are one hundred in the Soviet Union, the only hope of bringing pressure to bear on the state lay in its ethnicity.

One long-standing symptom of the continuing significance of ethnic identity is the comparative rarity of intermarriage, despite official encouragement. To take but one example, between 1926 and 1970 only two per cent of the non-Russian population assumed Russian identity. Of these, the vast majority came from groups like the Ukrainians and Byelorussians whose culture and language are close to that of Russia, or from groups whose position is particular, such as the Jews and Germans. Among most of the other groups, assimilation has been almost unknown.

Why was I so riled by Olga and Ivetta's chattering? At a politically uncertain time for Britain, Orwell had written an essay on the English language which came back to me now: 'It

209

becomes ugly and inaccurate because our thoughts are foolish, but the slovenliness of our language makes it easier for us to have foolish thoughts.' I was living with the evidence of how gossip and a highly tuned racial awareness, while remaining harmless for most of the time, had the potential, as Olga's remark about the Jews illustrated, to degenerate into something nastier at a time of change. Behind such remarks were stacked syllogistically muddled connections of thought, ones which were comforting if you happened either to be Russian, or to live in a country where it was a help not to have to blame the Russians for everything.

At 5 a.m. on the day Bella and I were due to return to Moscow, Bella's mother rang up in a state of alarm. Kostya, Bella's six-year-old, had been due to spend a few weeks in the country with his grandmother. Now she was ringing to say that he was fretting for his mother in the evenings. This news caused an immediate change of plan. Bella was a Russian mother, that is to say one who considers that a child, and particularly a male child, should never have his will crossed. It was hastily arranged that Bella's brother should bring the boy back to Stavropol' by car.

When Ivetta and I came back from the market, she and Bella settled down to help Olga prepare our farewell lunch in the kitchen. As usual, I was not allowed to help. Feeling in the way, I went next door to pack my bag. Kostya and his uncle Arkady were fighting playfully on the double bed. All of a sudden, Arkady stopped, turned his head towards me and started to whisper rapidly, running his words together so that it was hard to hear what he said. His appearance was arresting. He was a tall and abnormally thin young man, still hollow with the effort of so much upward growth. His curly hair cast tendrils in all directions and his dark eyes, set in an ascetic face, were at once childish and scalding in their intensity. 'If you think it's bad here' (I had not said a word to him, beyond a

210

greeting) 'you should see what it's like in the countryside. Not one of the old Brezhnevite bosses has gone. In some ways it's got much worse. For instance, over the last month there have been these night raids. People in police uniforms, with black bags over their heads and slits for eyes, carrying guns . . .' His sister came in to see how her son was and he started to play with Kostya again. I started to say something and he made violent throat-slitting gestures behind Bella's back. After she had gone and closed the door, he explained, hurling his energy into his words, eyes burning: 'You can trust no one, no one . . . They break into people's houses at night and force them to hand over money, jewellery, everything. It's a new development. No, they're not police, no one knows who they are.' Arkady leapt from topic to topic with such urgency that it was as if he expected a knock on the door any minute, as if he needed to leave something with me. His passion was electrifying. He wanted, in this brief moment, to impress upon me his whole life. His gabble was so deliberately encoded for the sake of the child that I kept losing the thread of his words, and having to ask him to repeat things, like an old woman: 'It's all going to end very badly, you know. In terrible bloodshed. But after that, there'll be a cataclysm. Something like an earthquake, I don't know quite what, that will shake the world. And those who survive will be a new people, cleansed of corruption . . .'

I remembered now how, when I had first arrived in Stavropol', Bella had told me about her brother Arkady's second sight. Without ever having been to this flat, she said, he had described to his mother the flat in which his sister was staying, giving meticulous details of the layout of the rooms. 'The only ambition I have left in life', Arkady was saying, his eyes shining with excitement, 'is to live honestly. Nothing else has any meaning in these days. I stay alive in that hole thanks to my friends. There are half a dozen of us. Never a day passes but two or three of us get together. Without each other we would

211

have nothing. We have our ways of getting hold of the books that we need. A network. The currency isn't money. We don't have money, and anyway books are priceless to us. The currency is exchange. It took a long time to get hold of Nietzsche, but we got him in the end. Schopenhauer was hard.' It turned out that although this boy spoke not a word of English or German, he could get through dense tracts in both languages. 'I'm exploring in a different direction now. Man's inner capacities. We've hardly begun to discover those . . .'

This remarkable young man, a chess instructor on a remote collective farm, talked on about yoga, Buddhism and tantra as though they could save him from drowning. As he spoke, I recalled something that Bella had told me. Although Arkady was good at chess, the real player of the family was her older brother Petya. As a child, Petya used to take on Bella, Arkady and their schoolteacher father together as they sat over their boards in one room while he sat next door with no board, visualizing all three games and beating them every time. 'He used to write beautiful poetry,' Bella had said of Petya. 'Now? Well, how can I explain. He's . . . living right out in the countryside, miles from anywhere, making . . .' She had paused. It was evidently painful for her to tell this story. '. . . wire gratings. He's been there for some years now. He cut himself off from all of us. He's a brilliant boy, absolutely brilliant. But when he left school and came face to face with Soviet reality he . . . couldn't take it. We grew up way out in the countryside, you know. My parents were both teachers. They loved their work and they were very honest. Petya had no idea what the real world was like. None of us did.'

This was a story that I was to hear again and again, the story of the traumatic induction of Soviet children into the real world on leaving school. There was a price to be paid for the overprotectiveness of parents. 'Petya went up to Moscow for his interview at the Law Faculty. Something happened there. I'll never know exactly what. He won't talk about it. But it was the year of the Moscow Olympics. For some reason they weren't taking anyone but Muscovites that year, no one at all from out of town. He was far brighter than most of the students. I only know that he spent a little time up there, ran out of money and ended up sleeping rough at the station. He was befriended by some rich Georgians. You know the Georgians and Armenians – they're so rich that they can buy up anyone and anything. He was so shocked by the corruption that he . . . well, he dropped out. He was just too sensitive . . .'

After our meal, we ordered a couple of taxis to take us to the airport. In order to have a little more time in the company of Bella's other remarkable brother, I let her, Olga and Ivetta go on in the first taxi and travelled in the second with Arkady. It was a luxury to talk about something other than astrology and the characteristics of the Germans. As we left Stavropol''s leafy prosperity behind, Arkady was inveighing against the materialism that was corroding his countrymen. 'It is the same everywhere,' I warned him. 'My country is more materialistic than ever . . .' 'You know why that is?' Arkady interrupted me. He leaned over and whispered in my ear so that the taxi-driver would not hear: 'It's your Mrs Thatcher. She's fallen into the hands of the Jews, those Rothschilds . . .'

213

VI

MOSCOW

The Shrivelled Self

Spring had finally won in Moscow. The cramped life of the apartments had spilled out on to the common ground between the blocks. The grey faces, the grey coats had all gone. A little old lady with rouged cheeks walked along the street wearing red shoes, a pink mac and a matching pink hat. Several people hurried past carrying bushes in their shopping-baskets. A young man sloped off with his friend to consume a bottle of white wine wrapped up in a copy of that day's newspaper. A row of old women sat on the benches, hands clasped in front of them, hypnotized by the sun. Even the vengeful tone of the old lady through the wall in Elena's flat had softened.

It was wonderful to see Elena again. After a week of never being on my own, I was suffering from claustrophobia. I had been longing to get back to the little flat. Elena's company was never obtrusive. She knew the art of living in proximity. To live with her was like playing a duet, in which both players are always listening for a change of mood. Until a few years ago, Elena and her daughter Ira had lived in a flat as small as this with the intractable mother of her ex-husband, a woman so difficult that her son would have nothing to do with her. Now what Elena dreaded was solitude.

Elena was welcoming, but she looked worn out. Typically, the only complaint she would make was that a favourite dream was eluding her. 'All my life I have had this flying dream,' she told me. 'But recently, night after night, I can't get up off the ground. The people around are laughing at me. When I do manage, they catch hold of me, try and hold me down. I try and try to get up high, but something is stopping me.'

We idled over breakfast this morning, catching up on each other's news over coffee with hot cabbage pancakes and sour cream. Good food had never tasted better than it did here, where it was scarce. The air was warm through the open window. We could hear the children playing on the swings. In the course of telling Elena about my trip, I mentioned the anti-Semitic remarks which had bothered me. This prompted Elena to recall how the Germans had rounded up the Jews in Brest, her home town on the Russian–Polish frontier.

'They put them in this ghetto in the middle of town. They were there for a long time. They were in a terrible state, with nothing to eat. I had this friend called Rai, who used to creep out of the ghetto at night and come and eat with us. I used to take food to her and hand it through the fence. Rai didn't look Jewish at all, and my grandmother and I tried to persuade her to come and live with us. They'd never have known. But she wouldn't. "Whatever fate lies ahead for my family I must share," she would say. After they were taken away the ghetto was guarded for a long time, because people used to go in and steal. I went in one night to find something to remember her by. It was very brave . . . No, that's not true. I had no idea what I was doing. But in fact, they used to hang anyone whom they caught. I took a photograph of Rai and her little sister, and a doll. But there was one man, I remember, I saw him as he came out. He had watches all up his arm. I saw them cut off his sleeve and string him up on a tree.

'Lots of people did escape from the ghetto, though. They dug holes in the ground and lived in them. One day I shall never forget. My grandmother and I used to go to the sawmill at night to collect bark for winter fuel. One morning I woke at dawn and thought, "She'll think I'm so clever if I go on my own and get back before it's properly light." So I set off. I could see the smoke coming from holes in the ground where Jews were

218

cooking for themselves. That's how they found them, of course. Further on, there were two men who had been killed, lying in the road. One man was very old. I could hear these terrible wailings, heart-rending cries. Then this soldier shouted at me to get out of the way. I ran towards him. It's a miracle he didn't shoot. They had no way of knowing that I wasn't Jewish. Then I saw them. A crowd of men and women. Some were so thin and so old that they could hardly stand. They'd rounded them up from their hiding-places. The soldiers all around had these great guard dogs. One soldier was Jewish, I recognized him. He wasn't a soldier. He'd been a sort of ghetto commandant, helping the Germans. He chased me with his dog. I don't know how I got away, but I did. I remember thinking as I ran, "What is this all about? What is this Jew doing, in German clothes, chasing me, a Russian?" It was then that I started to want to understand why they hated the Jews so much. I started to read the Bible and books on Jewish history.' She paused to pour us another cup of coffee. 'But of course, it wasn't just the Germans. I remember a very red-haired man going down this beautiful tree-lined boulevard in Brest. And round his neck was this card saying "Juden". And all along the road people, Russians, were throwing stones at him.' The long silence was broken by Elena's plastic cuckoo clock, which announced the half-hour. Elena was late for work.

I dressed slowly, unable to believe in the luxury of being alone. The real reason for my short temper over the last few days in Stavropol' had been claustrophobia. I was ashamed to have been irritable with those great-hearted women, with their incessant injunctions to 'eat a little more', 'take a little rest'. To be so indulged is to be patronized. Dreadful though the fate of Soviet women is, I would none the less prefer it to that of Soviet men.

Boris telephoned and asked me out to lunch. He was the engineer who had impressed me by the ingenuity with which he held down his job while simultaneously running his own book imprint, acting as a tour guide, and earning three times his salary writing cribs for rich chemistry students at the University. We met at a Georgian restaurant in the centre of town. Boris looked like a disciple in the Victorian oleographs in my childhood Bible. He had close-cropped dark hair, a trim beard and a mobile face. He was in a restless mood. His elaborately constructed life was threatened. 'I am going to have to leave my job,' he started to tell me almost at once. 'Ironically, it is all because of *glasnost*. I had started becoming less secretive about my publishing activities. My boss got to hear of them. He told me to stop, and for a while I did. Everyone has become very jumpy about the idea of cooperative publishing. But the job becomes unbearable if I can't even do what I enjoy on the side. But if I start again, he'll push me out. So I'm going to have to get out.'

My commiserations were unnecessary. Boris was looking forward to making a life in the private sector, although he had not yet decided what to do. As he considered his options he was like a gourmet studying a reliable menu: 'The last time I was in Batumi, I met a man who made his living by buying cars in Asia and driving them to Moscow to sell. It's a good living. If I did that, I could afford to drop the university work' (as he called his cribs). 'I might try a little speculating too. Then I've been asked to join a couple of cooperatives, one of them very lucrative, but I don't think I'll do that. It would be different if I were trying to become rich, but I don't want a full-time job. I just want to make a comfortable living so that I'm free to try my hand at writing.' Boris's idea of a comfortable living was much closer to a Western one than that of anyone else I knew here. He saw no intrinsic virtue in poverty. His approach to problems seemed different too. He seemed more detached than my other Russian friends. Since he was Jewish, I asked him if he had ever thought of leaving. 'Of course. I feel torn. Most of my friends have gone to New York and some of them are doing very well. The reason I'll stay is that I know the system here so well. I know how to make it work for me. Here, I am free. But it would take me a long time to get to that position in the West. The anti-Semitism I can deal with. It's something you either disregard or choose to take to heart. I have chosen not to take it seriously. Those who do become eaten up by it. I travel a lot and I never for one moment conceal the fact that I'm a Jew, although a lot of people do. People always want to know what I am, because I'm obviously not Russian, but I've never had any real difficulty.

'Of course I know it's there, the anti-Semitism, with Russians in particular. But I understand the reasons so well. People's lives are so hard. They've been brought up to believe that someone must be to blame. The difference between a Russian and, say, a Georgian or Armenian is that a Georgian will see how well his neighbour lives and will want to learn from that experience, so that he can do well too. The Russian seeing the same will simply envy the Georgian rather than learn from him. I suspect that this culture based on envy is far older than the Revolution here. But the Revolution reinforced the characteristic and developed it into a culture of denunciation. In the southern republics, Christian and Islamic, they never behaved quite like that. If someone denounced their neighbour down there, the family memory of it would go down the generations. It would never be forgotten.' Boris's opinion was confirmed for me again and again. But none the less, I feared for him in his move to the private sector. Even if he did count as 'one of us' while he was still working for the state, I had the feeling that once he became prosperous and self-employed, he might become 'a Jew' again.

After days spent in Olga's company in Stavropol', I could not help comparing the way in which the two of them used information. Olga listened to no news, read no newspapers and seemed to reject incoming information which could not be turned into a source of comfort. Boris, on the other hand, used information to fashion his life. For all the educational differences between them, Olga's passive stoicism seemed to me to be something which she shared with the culture around her. So many Russians whom I met, even among the educated, perceived themselves as victims of the volition of others. It was as if the 'I' had become so demoralized that people discounted their own interaction with the world in the way that they described it to themselves. This shrivelled self was all too vulnerable to the idea that the nearest 'other' in their midst, the Jews, articulate and active as they were, must be the 'enemy'.

One evening when I was last in Moscow, I had mentioned to a cultured woman whom I knew that I was interested in meeting a serious exponent of the views of the elusive Russian nationalist movement Pamyat'. It was unnerving to feel its influence every day and never to come face to face with it. I did not know the woman intimately, but we shared close friends in England and this connection had caused me to imagine that I knew more about her views than I did. 'I would too,' Galina had responded. Once she had started talking, her thoughts came tumbling out: 'Pamyat' was started more than ten years ago by a gifted poet for whom I have a lot of respect, Vladimir Soloukhin. It was started from the purest of motives – to rescue the trampled traditions of Russian culture, its Church and its philosophical and artistic roots. Soloukhin would never have been connected with anything disreputable. I really want to know what they have to say because all you ever hear about them is this stuff about anti-Semitism. There has to be more to it than that. And you know, these last few years I've begun to understand why this reaction against the Jews has set in. Frankly, in the past, I would never even have noticed whether someone was Jewish or not. But I do now. Let me give you an example. A Jew came to work for us a while ago. Every time he opens his mouth it is to say something belittling about the Russians; about the way we destroyed our churches, the ugliness of our women or our incapacity for work. Day in, day out, nothing but the same patronizing snipings. The first time I

222

took no notice. And the second . . . But the third time, something in me started to rise, something deeply Russian, which I didn't even know I had inside me. And another thing too. Once he'd got this job, suddenly they were all over the place in the office. And now they're all saying the same things. It's a terrible chorus. They're well organized. And it really does look as if someone is controlling them. That they're egging us on deliberately. The Russians, well, you know the Russians, we're an easygoing people, slow to take offence and, well, lazy. If there's anti-Semitism around it's because someone is stirring it up and it isn't the Russians.' After that, I gave up looking for exponents of the views of Pamyat'. I realized that there was no need. Pamyat' was not a clandestine group that existed somewhere else. It was here, in the heads and hearts of many of the people whom I knew. *Glasnost* had acted like paint remover on a wall. It had taken off one coat of paint, one layer of nasty rhetoric. But the wall itself, the way people had learned to think, remained. The real feature of the Jewish mind which so many Russians resented was their habit of questioning. Russia does not belong to the mainstream tradition of Judaeo-Christian thought, within which the ideas of change and development have evolved. While Western Europe was passing from its Renaissance and Reformation into the Enlightenment, Russia resolutely chose to stay behind. The Russian Church was finally emancipated from Constantinople in 1589, when the patriarchate of Moscow was created. But the country achieved spiritual independence only to opt for isolation. Every effort was made to expel foreign influence and the notion of change that attached to it. When Peter the Great finally breached this isolation and introduced the Enlightenment, he did so in such a despotic way as to set up a tension which is exhibited in the clearest way in the exaggerated fear the Russians have for the eternal foreigner in their midst, the questioning Jew.

Paradise Withheld

As I skirted Red Square that morning, the pavements around Aleksandrovsky Gardens were like a poppy-field. Little children were milling round by the bus-load in their red Pioneer scarves before paying their respects to Lenin. Today, 22 April, was his birthday. Although it was a Saturday, my friends were all working, or rather 'working', this being a *subbotnik*, a holiday when everyone was obliged to volunteer for socially useful work of some kind. In the relaxed atmosphere of Moscow, such days usually involved no more than a token gesture of work. But in the provinces, as a girl from the Urals had been telling me, *subbotniks* had not changed. 'You see doctors and lawyers sweeping the streets all day. It's a farce. Everything is still under deep snow. And what do I have to do? Wash the office windows. Can you imagine a more stupid time to fill the building with freezing air?'

Lenin's birthday seemed an appropriate day to visit the permanent Exhibition of Economic Achievements of the Soviet Union, or VDNKh, as it is called by its acronym. I had no idea what to expect. My Moscow friends had advised me, rather cryptically I thought, that it was an experience not to be missed. If Grisha could sneak off later, he would join me. Once through the barrage of turnstiles at the entrance to the VDNKh, I found myself standing on an almost empty stretch of tarmac as broad and long as a runway and fringed with flower-beds. The place, which occupied 300 hectares of the old Sheremetyev estate, had certainly been built to accommodate the masses. Some way off stood a vast white statue of Vladimir Ilich Lenin. Further off still, a series of grandiose architectural follies opened up a fantastical vision. I walked past monumental fountains, down an avenue of chestnuts, each planted by a different cosmonaut. From every lamp-post, a megaphone blared out a recording of Ilich's favourite song. As I approached the pavilions, they flowered before my eyes into an insane bouquet of kitsch styles. Yes, this was the pure expression of a dream conceived out of the experience of the industrial revolution. Here among these twentieth-century Taj Mahals built to celebrate the love between socialist man and production, it was intended that contented workers should spend their leisure hours contemplating the achievement of their own hands.

Surprisingly, the VDNKh had been opened only after Stalin's death, in 1954. The years of which it was the true expression were the heroic years of economic growth, 1929–32. Then, in a country that was only just recovering from war, civil war and revolution, a staggering growth rate of twenty per cent a year in gross industrial production had been achieved. Impressive though this was, it could not have lasted. Already the country's leaders had made the choice to put political control above economic achievement. Ten years later, the regime which had started by removing its opponents and gone on to destroy an entire class that stood in the way of its agricultural policy had cannibalized itself to the extent of finding wreckers even among the engineers, managers, technicians, statisticians, planners, foremen and Party cadres without whom no industrialized economy could function.

Many of the splendid pavilions of this people's paradise were closed and there were few people around. Of all the pavilions, the most magnificent was devoted to Soviet agriculture. It was covered in gilded scales and rejoiced in statues of muscular workers bearing sheaves of corn. A small crowd had gathered in front of it. But no one seemed to be going up the proud flight of steps, through the embossed doors. As I drew closer, I could see that the attraction lay elsewhere. Tucked behind a bushy conifer was a lorry from the back of which sunflower seeds were being sold. Suddenly, rising above the triumphal music, I heard the terrible screams of children. For a moment I was alarmed, but looking around, I caught sight of a big dipper through the trees. The sounds of pain and pleasure can be hard to tell apart.

The people were at the fun-fair. The pavilions stood empty, like the deserted shells of hermit crabs. Little stalls had been set up in front of them, selling Pepsi-Cola, chocolate bars and pairs of plastic shoes. The occasional person hurried by, carrying home-baked loaves of bread and small trees in their shopping-bags. Hours later, I found the entrepreneurs from whom they had been bought, tucked in sheds behind empty pavilions in the seedy outskirts of the park. Here, the confident stylistic effusion of the Stalinist pavilions had given way to flimsy later structures whose mean functionalism perfectly expressed the waning of the dream.

The sun had gone and a burst of rain drove me into the nearest pavilion, marked Health. I appeared to be the only visitor. The attendants were pleasingly attired in spotless white gowns. Behind glass, a life-sized plaster patient was being administered an anaesthetic by a life-sized plaster doctor. In this display, only the technology was real. I gazed at it full of wonder at this country where industrialization could coexist with primitive fetishism; where the products of the industrial process could end up being worshipped for their usefulness as an alternative to being used. Drugs of all kinds were well known to be in such desperately short supply that anaesthetics were simply not an option for minor operations.

Over the way, I was attracted by the splendid façade of a pavilion, entitled Fruits of the Cow, whose classical columns were topped by the noble heads of bulls. A party of sausage-makers from Tula were clustered round a gleaming machine.

226

Their guide was remarking briskly: 'There is no need for me to show you how it works because you are unlikely to use such a machine. There are only two in operation in the Soviet Union.' No one asked why the third was sitting here, behind glass. Meanwhile, my attention had been captured by a sumptuous display of plaster sausages: frankfurters, mortadella, coarse sausage, fine salami, liver sausage, black sausage . . . The sight filled me with carnivorous lust. There were marks on the glass where other visitors, shot through with desire, had pressed their mouths against its cool surface.

But perhaps I was misjudging the organizers. Perhaps this whole display of paradise withheld had been taken over by radicals, who were using it as an incitement to revolt? The thought died as I flicked through the Visitors' Book: 'Thank you heartily for an educationally nourishing display from which we all derived maximum profit. We come away very, very content with what we have seen.' After twenty-three pages of similar thank-you notes, I found one that simply said: 'I derived nothing from this exhibition.'

On my way back towards the statue of Lenin where Grisha and I had agreed we would meet if he could get away, I was side-tracked by the sight of a group of men standing on the steps of a pavilion whose doors were open wide. 'Good day. Where are you going?' asked one of them, barring my entrance. 'To have a look.' 'No, I am afraid this exhibition is closed.' 'But it's . . . 'Invitation only.' Ah yes, the exhibition is open in the same way that Lenin's birthday was a holiday. Except for ignorant foreigners, people chose not to go in, just as they chose to go to work.

Lenin's statue, with its familiar jutting chin and purposeful stride, had flowers piled at the foot of it. Standing among the deserted Soviet temples, I contemplated the irony that this man, of all men, should have fallen prey to idolatry. In his own lifetime he had inveighed against 'this completely un-Marxist emphasis on the individual'. But within a few years of his

227

death, people were being sentenced to ten years in camp for having used a piece of newspaper as lavatory paper which had Stalin's head on it. Now the idolatry was waning, but it died hard.

The last few days had given me a reminder of the continuing strength of Lenin's cult. I had been watching television when a leading theatre director called Mark Zakharov had suggested that the time had come to remove Lenin from his mausoleum. The press denunciation next day had been shrill and at least one person was sacked from the television programme because no one could believe that the editorial team had not been in on the plot. Just as the legitimacy of this Leninist regime was so closely bound up with the words of its founder, his body too seemed to have come to stand literally for the body of the state.

Although Gorbachev had stated his own hostility to this tradition of idolatry, aspects of it were still intact. Up until then, for instance, for all the new freedoms won by the press, it was not possible to criticize Gorbachev directly. That week *Pravda* had broken the taboo, publishing in full the speeches of Central Committee members whose disaffection was connected to their poor performance in the elections. Now the kind of people who never bothered to read *Pravda* were rushing round trying to get hold of copies of this historic document . . .

Grisha never came. But he more than made up for his absence when I next saw him by telling me a story that made me laugh so much that I had to concede that the old idolatry was good for something: 'A friend of mine was sent off by his newspaper to buy the obligatory bust of Lenin for the courtyard outside the office. They all cost far more than he had been led to expect – 1,000, 2,000 roubles. But he kept looking and eventually came across one, made of papier mâché, for 80 roubles. He couldn't believe his luck. He bought it, brought it back to the office and everyone was delighted. That is, until the problems began.

'First of all, the pigeons would settle on Lenin's head and my

228

friend, as the youngest of the editorial staff, was assigned to keep it clear. This he did. But soon, a crop of little mushrooms began to appear on it, sprouting in the damp cardboard. Horrors! It looked as if Lenin had a punk haircut. My friend had even learned to deal with this when one day there was an announcement that the paper was to receive a visit from an important official. Everything was spruced up and my friend went to do the usual job on Lenin. When he had cleared off the mushrooms, the whole top of Lenin's head fell in! Appalled, he thought of a cap. But none could be found that was large enough. Next he found a neat red cloth to drape over it, but his boss was furious: "The official will think he's meant to unveil it! You'll have to hide it."

'The entire office was turned upside-down by the day's adventures. They were just sorting themselves out when a horrendous cry ripped through the building. A woman's tragic shriek of pain. It turned out that in the general confusion, one of the clerical staff had shut her breasts in a drawer. Enormous breasts they were.' Grisha gestured graphically: 'The building was limp with laughter. Howls came from every office. But the woman, though unharmed, was inconsolable: "You've got to help me, comrades!" she wailed. People looked nonplussed, a little uncertain as to how to fulfil this request. She explained that if her husband saw the bruises he would think that it was another man. "He is desperately jealous. I don't suppose you could see your way to signing an official paper stating the real cause of the bruises?" The editorial staff cheerfully signed their names to this official testimony.'

The Train from Karaganda to Karaganda

On my way home that evening, I passed an excited knot of people standing by our local cinema, the Prague. I paid no attention. Whatever was going on, I did not want to know. I had been on my feet all day. I was carrying heavy shopping-bags; curiosity was dead. 'ONE NIGHT ONLY' screamed the flyer across the edge of a poster of a man's face. He looked like a conjuror at a children's party, with waxed black moustaches and a goatee beard. I paused to put down my bags. *Albert Ignatenko. Mind-Reader and BioEnergeticist of Incredible Memory.* The pause was fatal. People here talked a lot about 'bioenergetics', but what they said made no sense to me. My curiosity gave a feeble kick.

The show was sold out. But I had learned that there was rarely anything so sold out in Russia that there was no way in. Ignatenko kept us waiting in the thousand-seat cinema. Even full of people, it was a cheerless place, its high, concrete walls lit by a minimum number of watts. My neighbour, a portly woman in a blue nylon dress, was eating her way through a bag of sweets. It was an unsophisticated audience, much of it middle-aged.

Eventually, Ignatenko strutted on in his dinner jacket. With his white skin and slick black hair he gleamed like a limousine. Dimly, my mind stirred. He reminded me of someone, but I could not think who. With the speed and delivery of a card sharp, he tossed off dazzling tricks of mind-reading and memory before introducing the topic of hypnosis. 'The key to hypnosis is suggestibility,' he declared, 'the preparedness of the subject to be hypnotized.' He then proposed that the entire audience put themselves into a trance. He told us to relax, close our eyes and think that we were lying in a green forest. Within seconds, I was fast asleep.

I woke up, thoroughly refreshed, to find the stage crowded with volunteers. They were standing facing the audience, looking either vacant or asleep on their feet. Ignatenko, now in a glittering jacket, was twirling his moustaches and asking a young mathematician: 'What is 24 minus 24?' 'A fish,' answered the mathematician brightly. Ignatenko made as if to take off the mathematician's head and hand it to him. Reverently, the man held his 'head' in his hands and gazed at himself, stroking the hair back from his disembodied face in a gesture of fond recognition. Meanwhile, another young man was behaving as if he had drunk too much. My neighbour told me that he had just gulped back a glass of water which Ignatenko told him was brandy. Another group were gorging themselves with bananas from an invisible tree. With a wave of his hand Ignatenko removed the tree, leaving them looking cheated.

'In a moment,' he told a fresh group of volunteers who were not hypnotized, 'I am going to ask you to sit down on these chairs. You will tell me you can't because there is a chicken on your chair.' The volunteers giggled. One at a time, he passed his hand over their heads and asked them to sit down. They tried, some determined to sit straight down, others trying to defeat his purpose by edging their backsides on to the chair. 'Why don't you sit down? There's nothing wrong with your chair,' he asked a well-dressed matron. 'I can't. There's a chicken on it.' The woman sounded baffled. The audience collapsed in laughter.

Then I realized who it was Ignatenko reminded me of. He was a cosier version of the devil in Bulgakov's novel *Master and Margarita*, who staged a similar evening, on a grander scale. Acting the role of the magician Wolland, he 'dressed' his audience in luxurious clothes that vanished when they left the theatre, and filled their wallets with money that later dissolved into bees and bottle labels. The high point of that evening had been when M. Wolland had pulled off the compère's head. I wondered whether Ignatenko's pale imitation of this trick was intentional.

The act was over and we were putting on our coats when a young man leapt on to the stage, crying 'He's a quack! He's a quack! Watch!' He proceeded to demonstrate how he could do one of Ignatenko's tricks himself, without the help of hypnosis. He lay down, as Ignatenko's assistant had done, supported between two chairs, with his neck on the back of one and his heels on the back of the other. Ignatenko appeared from the wings, looking like a waiter, with his shiny jacket over his arm. Petulantly he said, 'If I had known that you had come to be destructive, I would have thrown you out.' He sounded deeply hurt. Gone was the air of confidence which had sustained him through his act.

By this time I had changed my mind about Ignatenko. At first I had been shocked by the petty humiliations to which this mountebank had subjected his victims. But as the show went on, I had begun to feel differently. For this simple Soviet audience to be roaring with laughter at their fellow countrymen who had volunteered to be made fools of by Ignatenko was, it seemed to me, a therapeutic experience. The night before, I had been sitting in the Film Union's cinema, watching documentary footage of the thirties which was being shown for the first time for decades. We had seen the twentieth-birthday celebrations of the KGB, then called the NKVD, in 1937. Around the dress circle of the packed Bolshoi Theatre ran a sign that read 'The NKVD is the Punitive Arm of the Soviet People'. Mikoyan, whose dark good looks were demonic in the Hollywood tradition, had been giving an impassioned speech to commemorate this 'holiday of the Soviet people'. 'The NKVD has saved thousands of lives from the Plot to Poison the People's Dining

232

Halls,' he declaimed to roars of applause. 'It has saved whole factories from destruction by the wreckers in our midst. And now the struggle against foreign spies has taken a new turn as we are forced to root out the agents of foreign powers in the ranks of our own people . . .' Slowly, the camera swept round the hysterically clapping, cheering audience, dwelling on familiar faces, like that of the young Khrushchev.

In the thirties, people had served ten-year sentences for having been the first to stop clapping after a speech such as Mikoyan's. Now, for the price of only 2 roubles 50 kopecks, Ignatenko was demonstrating to his audience the power of 'suggestibility'. In the West, we tend to dwell on the fear which kept people in a state of subjugation to the charismatic regime of Stalin. But living here had made me aware of the other element, without which the fear would not have worked. People had longed for the millennial dream to be realized. They were 'suggestible'. Combined with the ruthless control of information, this desire had been powerful enough to keep people in thrall long after the charismatic leader was dead. 'Each one of us felt that though, in our own lives, it might have gone wrong,' as Volodya from Kiev had put it to me, 'over there, elsewhere, the dream was even now beginning to come true.'

The spell had worked on a mass scale in Russia, as it had in Germany, in the crushing aftermath of the First World War. With the lines of their lives broken by war and civil war, people had reached for the millennial dream. I had seen the same phenomenon at work in my own generation, on an individual level, when the occasional friend had succumbed to a break in the thread of their emotional lives and joined some charismatic grouping which sheltered them from reality. What had surprised me was the discovery that, in Russia at least, the spell had been sustained among so many people, not all fools, until 1985. 'The first time as tragedy, the second as farce,' Marx had remarked of Hegel's perception that 'all great historical facts and personages occur, as it were, twice'. Traumatic as the transition between tragedy and farce might be, I thought as I was carried out of the cinema with the good-humoured audience, the qualities on display that evening had been such as to give me hope.

As Russia began the process of surrendering its colonies, as the empire based on rational principles collapsed to reveal its absurdities to the world, people were eager to explore inside themselves, into the virgin territory of the unconscious mind. In the Soviet Union the emphasis on the collective had resulted in a tendency to deal with dissent, or simply originality, as if it were a madness correctable by psychiatric means. But its converse, the use of psychiatry as a tool of self-discovery, had not, for understandable reasons, been encouraged. In the Soviet Union man had been required to hold together a pre-Freudian consciousness with a sophistication that was selectively post-industrial.

It was Bella, as might have been expected, who invited me a few weeks later to an evening at a House of Culture during which another hypnotist took a sample slice of the unconscious desires and fears of a group of young Muscovites. 'I've got a surprise for you,' she said on the morning when she rang to ask me along. If I had known that the surprise involved another hypnotist, I would probably not have agreed to go. I would have been the loser.

Shofiet was a generation younger than Ignatenko and the differences between the two men all stemmed from that. Their performances had many similarities, but unlike the old-fashioned showman with his bag of tricks, Shofiet was an early explorer of the Soviet unconscious. By training he was an engineer. The rest he had taught himself. As he said after the show, sitting in the bare room behind the stage, his face, still young, taut with exhaustion: 'It all began because I started to watch the way people sat. How tense they were. Look at the way you're sitting, for instance, and look at her.' I was sitting

234

back in my chair with my legs crossed, while Bella sat forward
with her head in her hands, vibrant with excited tension. 'And I
thought, that can't be right. I started to read. No, I didn't learn
off anyone, or I'd just be another of those magicians, or a
theoretician. I know that in the West you have to study for
years to become a psychotherapist. It's only here that someone
with no qualifications can put up a board and have people
flocking to him. I'm only just beginning. I don't have the right
to set up professionally. But with these little "sociodramas", I
just aim to give people a glimpse of their capabilities . . .'

Shofiet's audience were young and more educated than Ignatenko's. They looked like students. Unlike Ignatenko, he did
not cast himself as the star of the show, but as a facilitator for
those people in the audience who wanted to take a trip into
themselves. Even for this most intimate of journeys, large
numbers of people were happy to accept the mediation of a
Duce whose relationship to them was not personal.

The first crowd of young men and girls who flocked on to
the stage were, once hypnotized, told that they were reading
books. Then Shofiet went round asking them what their books
were about. First man: 'I am deeply excited. I am reading
Playboy. The pictures are awful . . . But . . . it's in Russian. Can
the revolution be happening so fast?' Girl: 'I am reading a
religious book. Mary Magdalen has a Negro baby . . .' Second
girl: 'I found these wonderful jeans, size 44 , , ,' 'I am reading
Novy Mir. A story about socialism in England.' 'Is it any
different there?' asked Shofiet. 'No, not one jot . . .' 'I am
reading a manual of kolkhoz farming in 1935. How to dig, how
to sow . . .' 'I am reading sugar-ration cards . . .' 'Stalin is with
us! Stalin is with us!' a woman kept repeating from the back of
the stage. A scared voice: 'I've got a medical handbook. It's
awful. It's about – breathing and how it works.' 'I had a book
about Brezhnev that turned into a crocodile . . .' Crocodiles.
Again and again in the course of the evening, the image kept
coming up. 'Father Christmas is having an interesting time.

There are no reindeer, so snails are dragging his sled . . .' The exercise collapsed in laughter when one girl said to Shofiet, her voice squeaky with indignation: 'We've all told you our books. Now I want to know what's in your book. You've said nothing about your book at all!'

Shofiet's next 'sociodrama', which he called his sex therapy, turned out to be not so much exploitative as revealing. A different group of young people were watching imaginary television sets: 'She's got nothing on but slippers, and epaulettes . . .' Plaintively: 'I can't see anything at all because I have no television . . .' A girl, shocked: 'Mine is very rude . . .' she paused, then went on boldly: 'There is a poster with the sexual organs on it!' A wildly excited young man: 'I can see it all, all! It's all happening on Red Square, at an official parade! Oh!' he clapped his hands: 'The goat!' A girl, cheated: 'I wanted to see, but it's all gone stripy . . .' Another, mesmerized: 'A Soviet delegation, carrying pistols, is undressing . . .'

Throughout this, the stage had been a pleasant spectacle. The hypnosis had sent some people to sleep. Others sat in circles, keeping up a gentle hum of hypnotized talk among themselves. What do the hypnotized say among themselves, I wondered? One boy and girl, who did not know each other, had started dancing and cavorting together, until the girl, a dynamic entertainer, decided that it was more important for her to act out to the audience, in a vividly expressive sign language of her own, everything that was being said on the stage. She kept this up for the rest of the evening.

A boy with the bluff face of a manual labourer was addressing the audience. Having been told by Shofiet that he was a famous poet, he was finishing the recitation of an improvised poem, whose scansion and rhythm had been impeccable in Russian. Its last couplet delighted the audience: 'What is it that smells so dire?/Is it shit, or is it the dog, money?' He went on to give a speech: 'I would like to say that, having travelled far and wide in this huge country of ours during *perestroika* . . .' He

236

paused, then went on in a different voice, that of the announcer: 'Ladies and gentlemen, the train to Tashkent is about to depart from platform six. Ladies and gentlemen, the person who has just lost 100 roubles – thank you. Ladies and gentlemen, the train from Karaganda to Karaganda is just about to depart . . .' Karaganda, in the wastes of Kazakhstan, had been the last stop for many people. It had been a famous site for labour camps. For all I knew, it still was.

A Keeper of the Old Faith

It would be Easter Day tomorrow and the May Day holiday the day after. In the course of the afternoon, the face of Moscow had changed from grey to red. All of a sudden, the buildings in town were draped in red cloth. Hoardings bearing slogans had appeared along the main roads. Even in our quiet, wooded street, clusters of red flags sprouted from every lamp-post. I was waiting from day to day to fly to Dagestan with Ira and Grisha, who were shooting a documentary high in the Caucasus. We should have left today, but, in the run-up to the holiday, it had proved impossible to get the six tickets we needed on the same flight.

Late that night, as the Christian year drew to a close, it had finally happened. The car which Grisha had kept going for so many years on love alone, had died. Together with their friend Pavel, the three of us had been driving through the deserted streets on our way to the all-night Easter service at the Cath-edral of the Old Believers. The noise that escaped from some-where under our feet was not mechanical. It was like a string breaking, like an escaping sigh. There was no need to ask what was wrong. There could be no doubt. It was the sound of death. Grisha had spent the last two days tracking that rare creature, a mechanic who was honest and knew his job. Before that, he had spent a long time looking for the spare part he needed. But the mechanical problems, though grave, were sec-ondary. This was a car whose continued functioning had long puzzled mechanics. The final breakdown could only be ex-

238

plained by a failure of will. But having responded to being treated like a human being, it died like one.

The man who gave us a lift had been excited by the idea of our celebrating Easter, although we had had to disabuse him of the idea that it was the occasion of Christ's birth. Seventy years of official atheism had left people without the most elementary grasp of Christian assumptions. The Church, for instance, had been obliged to ask the state to intervene recently to prevent the free sale of objects bearing religious motifs. This was because of the huge number of calendars that had appeared for sale depicting naked women and crosses in an over-enthusiastic display of previously forbidden imagery.

Pavel was Grisha's closest friend. He was an Old Believer, and it was by his invitation that we were attending their Easter service. Outsiders were not automatically welcome in this close, long-persecuted community. I had met Pavel at a talk on pre-revolutionary Moscow. Heavily bearded, with a mobile face and eyes that sparkled, he appeared to have difficulty keeping his gaiety from breaking out in the middle of the most serious conversations. On that first occasion, he had invited us back to share the family feast his wife had prepared to celebrate the beginning of Lent. As I had entered his modest flat, I had a feeling of stepping out of the Soviet Union altogether. It was not that the flat was opulent, quite the reverse. It was like the pleasure of coming across a medieval barn that had been built on monastery grounds in the English countryside. Because the builders had been inspired by a purpose higher than mere function, the stone would be dressed with the same attention to detail as the finest of monastic buildings. In Pavel and Nina's flat, everything was scrubbed and burnished. The Caucasian carpet on the living-room wall; the neat and dusted bookshelves full of Soviet translations of Hobbes, Berkeley and Hume; the smells of cooking, all suggested a world in which every object was cherished. I knew what it cost to make a home look like this. It cost not money, which some people had even if Pavel

239

did not, but time. For Nina, to cherish her family was a charge more important than any paid work could be.

That evening, as we ate Nina's Lenten feast of warm *blinis* and smoked fish, Pavel and Grisha had fallen into the familiar mode of their relationship, that of cheerful argument. They had become friends through arguing. At the time both had been employed as nightwatchmen, the job which had kept so many dissidents, *refuseniks* and poets alive in the years of stagnation. Though for Grisha it had merely been one of the part-time jobs with which he had supplemented his miserable income at weekends, for Pavel it was the only work he could get. The two men had argued for hours together as members of the philosophers' circle which met on the Saturday-night shift at the textile factory.

This evening the issue was the leading role of the Party in the country's renewal, an assumption which remained at the heart of Gorbachev's strategy for *perestroika*. 'It's an absurdity, a contradiction in terms.' Grisha, the Party member, voiced the opinion I heard everywhere. The Party was universally accepted to be a corrupt and moribund institution. But Pavel, the keeper of the old faith, was adamant: 'You lack any historical perspective, Grisha. If you look at the history of this country, you can see that it is only within the framework of strong power that radical reforms are possible. At this juncture, the only power that can serve that purpose is the Party. You may get your way, Grisha, and the Party may collapse. But I warn you now: if it does, the country will disintegrate.'

This was the note of pragmatism that I had been missing all these months. To sustain such an unfashionable point of view in Russia at that time took courage. Perhaps it was not surprising that the mood of the country after its first real election since 1917 was pre-political. But I had certainly not expected to find my fears for the political innocence of the Russians articulated by a man of God in a country where the monopoly of power was still in the hands of the Communist Party. Pavel's

240

viewpoint was a particular one. He did not belong to the main-stream of the Russian Orthodox Church. The Old Believers had broken away in the seventeenth century and been per-secuted ever since. It was this, according to Pavel, that explained the difference in his outlook: 'The Old Believers had to become students of power, in order to survive at all.'

Pavel's perspective on Russian history was illuminating. For him, the significant break in Russian history, between its real and its false traditions, had come with Peter the Great. It was the tireless Peter who had taken on himself the task of channel-ling the current of Western history so that it flowed through his country after its self-imposed isolation. He had chopped off the beards of his boyars and forced them into Western dress. He had built up an eponymous modern capital, a modern navy and an army. He had fought the ignorance and corruption of Church and government and introduced the idea of education and industry to his country. Peter had emancipated women and prevented the practice whereby deformed children were smothered at birth. But he had introduced these enlightened reforms using methods of coercion that were barbarous. The resulting paradox reverberates through Russian history. In Pavel's view, the ultimate responsibility for the Russian Revolu-tion belonged to Peter the Great.

The night air was sweet-smelling and warm as we walked through the wooden gate leading to the Cathedral for the Easter service. The song of a nightingale filled the air. Here at this gate, members of that youthful branch of the Party, the Komsomol, had stood as recently as 1987 to jostle the Old Believers every time they went into their church. Only children were actually prevented from entering. 'It is too late to save the grown-ups,' had been their attitude. 'But we don't want the children contaminated.'

The Old Believers had left the main body of the church in the seventeenth century rather than submit to changes which, to a secular mind, might seem trivial. They concerned small

241

inaccuracies which had crept into the liturgy and ritual since the tenth century, when Russia had adopted Greek Orthodoxy. With how many fingers should the true believer cross himself? How many times should you say 'Hallelujah' in the course of the service? How should Jesus's name be spelt? In Russia, the sanctity of the Word goes back beyond the ideological thrall of the twentieth century to the beginning of recorded history. On such questions hung the fate of the soul. For only if the ritual that a believer observed was correct would it guarantee eternal life. This preoccupation with ritual did not mean that the country's religious life was conducted on a superficial level. On the contrary, the rituals were the outward observance of a commitment that permeated people's lives.

Nor had it appeared to the Russians to be 'only' a religious question. Two centuries of Mongol rule had made the Church synonymous with Russian culture. When the Patriarch Nikon wished to amend the liturgy and details of religious observance to bring them into line with the Greek original, the fact that these amendments came from a 'foreign' Church had particular resonance. To a simple mind, the changes conjured up the notion of an invasion of the soul by a foreign culture. I was reminded how ancient was the voice of those who had warned me of the 'international Jewish conspiracy' against the Russians. It was as historically resonant as the panic inspired by the suggestion that the shrine of Soviet Communism, its central relic, Lenin's mausoleum, should be dismantled.

The church was packed with people, with middle-aged and elderly women in the majority. When Pavel had been converted, he had gone to the faith kept alive by his mother and grandmother. Looking down from the choir, I saw a field of headscarves through the flicker of candles that burned on the vast chandeliers in front of us. From time to time, a flutter ran through the congregation as everyone crossed themselves once, twice, thrice, with two fingers outstretched in the traditional gesture that stands for the half-human, half-divine figure of

Christ. In the name of this gesture, 20,000 Old Believers had voluntarily submitted themselves to death by burning in the 1680s, following the example of their leader, the Archpriest Avakuum. Patriarch Nikon had decreed that three fingers should be raised, as they were in the Greek Orthodox Church from which the church of the Russians sprang. The Old Believers who survived had turned their backs on society and founded communities in inhospitable tracts of virgin forest. Tenacious settlements, many had survived into the twentieth century. Only the year before, anthropologists in Siberia had found a family of Old Believers dressed in skins who had known nothing about the Revolution, about aeroplanes or world wars. Despite all precautions, the family had caught a virus and died, leaving only one young woman, who was now said to be thriving in a high-rise flat somewhere in Siberia.

Slowly, we followed the priests out and watched as the glittering cross was carried three times round the outside of the church. The night air was heavy with the scent of spring. The candle-lit faces of those who followed behind belonged to a simpler century. A strong man with red beard and piercing green eyes, who could have been a saintly nineteenth-century peasant, turned out to be a scholar of the Far East. There walked Pavel's seven-year-old son. All night he had been on his feet, this boy who seemed able to withstand it all, the cruel teasing at school, the lack of friends. His teenage brother and sister, who were not, I noticed, there that night, did not admit their parents' belief at school. The handsome, bearded young man in long dark vestments, passing now, had been an electrician before. While Pavel had still been working for a state publishing company, the young man had come to mend something in his office one day. A conversation had started, which had gone on and on. The young man's beautiful wife had fought against her rival, the Church, with all that she had. She had lost. There she stood, in a white headscarf by the porch.

Back inside the church again, the third part of the seven-and-

243

a-half-hour service began. Pavel, anxious not to test our endurance, had brought us only at midnight, in time for the second part. None the less, we had been there for three and a half hours. The singing had taken on a wild, syncopated lilt, as Christ began to rise from the dead. Yesterday, Good Friday, they sang the same music in the minor mode. No one knew how old this music was. It had no composer and its notation was different from that of the music of the main body of the Church. The voices were unaccompanied. Musical instruments had always been deemed to be of this earth, unlike the human voice, in which the divine strain could be heard. These voices produced a sound unlike any Western voice. The bass that filled the church had the density of the Russian forest. In the established Church, at Easter they hired singers from the state opera company. Here, Pavel told me proudly, no one was paid.

The schism between the two Russian Orthodox Churches was a searing one, as painful then as ever. The Old Believers felt themselves to be the repository of the country's spiritual values. After the schism, the established Church had become directly subordinated to the state, with the result that the Church had not, in the opinion of many, been in a position to provide a proper opposition to the power of the state in the course of the next two centuries. If the Russian Church had not been split and its spirit bowed, would her intelligentsia, whose disaffection had played such a formative part in the history of the last two centuries, have needed to act out the role that it did? Pavel believed the answer was no.

As the voices leapt higher and higher with excitement at the drama that was unfolding, the words 'Christ is risen' sounded through the cathedral. For the Old Believers, to be able to worship here at all was not something they could take for granted. Napoleon had stabled his horses here and the Old Believers had been barred from using the building for most of the nineteenth century. Now, they travelled here from all over Russia. I watched as the candle-light danced, like the voices, round the church. It flickered on the faces of the worshippers, each of whom carried a candle; on the icons which seemed to shine with a dull radiance of their own. In front of me hung the ancient icon of the Mother of God. As the light played on the painted wood, the stylized lines of her severe face became mobile. Privately, she smiled at the Child.

VII

DAGESTAN

The Code of Hadji Murat

By hot noon, in a vale of Daghestan
Lifeless, a bullet in my breast, I lay;
Smoke rose from a deep wound, and my blood ran
Out of me, drop by drop, and ebbed away . . .

Mikhail Lermontov, *The Dream*
(tr. Maurice Baring)

The first time I met Grisha, he had told me a story that belonged to another age. Nearly thirty years ago a shepherd in Dagestan had been punished for his insubordination by being thrown out of his house and off the collective farm. His crime had been honesty: he had not been prepared to keep his mouth shut about the corruption of his boss. As all the cultivable land in the area had belonged to the collective farm, he and his wife and five children had taken shelter in a cave on the bare mountainside. They had raised their family there. Now the shepherd's sons wanted to start a cooperative farm on the family land off which they had been driven. 'In the spring,' Grisha had said to me, 'we'll be going up there to make a film about them. You must join us.' Sitting in the Moscow flat, the story had sounded remote and the invitation like one of those which would be soon forgotten.

But here we were, Ira, Grisha and I. We had come with a film crew of three to spend the week doing a recce and some filming in preparation for the main shoot. In the company of two of the old man's sons, we were winding our way up the Caucasian foothills out of the ugly Caspian port of Makhachkala. The town lies on a spit of marshy land that runs along the Caspian. It is the only centre of any size in Dagestan and most of the shepherd's sons had built themselves houses there. They would bring their flocks down to Makhachkala in winter by lorry to graze on the pasture. But they did not like the place. These were highland people and their contempt for lowland life was undisguised.

Dagestan, flanked by Georgia to the West and Azerbaijan to the south, looks like part of Russia on the map. But it does not feel like Russia, and its conquest had been painful. Although notionally the north Caucasus had become a Russian province in the reign of Catherine the Great, it was not until 1859 that its military conquest was completed. For the thirty years before that, the Imams had been engaged in a Holy War against the imperial army. Through purely military means, the Russians would probably never have succeeded in breaking the independence of these mountain tribesmen. Like the Afghans, they proved too fanatical as warriors. Difficulties of supply made any victories over the strongholds of the mountaineers only temporary. The Russians owed their success ultimately to less glorious tactics: the destruction of villages, crops and stock.

My image of the country was romantic and literary. Lermontov, who had already served in the army in Georgia in punishment for the poem he wrote in honour of Pushkin's death, was later punished for his part in a duel by being sent to this part of the front to face the rebellious tribesmen. At first, he had shared the contemptuous attitude of his fellows towards his adversary, the warrior-prophet Shamyl. But the Imam Shamyl was formidable. It was he who had succeeded in uniting the feuding mountain tribes against the Russians. Lermontov, as brave a warrior as he was a poet, came to feel the futility of this mismanaged imperial exercise against a people whose struggle for independence was heroic.

Tolstoy had also been attracted to this part of the Caucasus. In *Hadji Murat*, the novel of his old age, he told the story of Shamyl's legendary lieutenant, who had surrendered to the Russians after a quarrel with Shamyl. The novel was to prove unexpectedly helpful to me, through its illumination of the complex and deadly code of honour of these mountain tribesmen. However much Hadji Murat had hated the Russians, whatever his allegiance to his own leader Shamyl, his first allegiance was a more personal one, to his own honour.

I had not expected to feel the shadow of this history on my visit. I imagined that the Autonomous Republic of Dagestan, one of sixteen homelands for substantial non-Russian populations that lie in Russia itself, would have become at least superficially Soviet. But this had not been the fate of the Gasanov family, at least. In front of me in the van sat one of the sons of the old man who had been thrown off the collective farm. Zakarya had a bushy black beard and watchful eyes. A beard on a young Avar is a sign of mourning and Zakarya was embarrassed by his handsome growth. He had taken a vow in his youth that he would cut it only when the injustice done to his father had been righted, and the man who had driven him off the farm and out of his home had been removed from power.

When the new law on cooperatives had been passed, it looked as if there would be no difficulty about the family returning to their land and being allowed to farm it. Makhachev, the head of the farm who had drummed Zakarya's father Nabi out, had finally lost his job. Until the Gasanov brothers proposed to start a cooperative there, the collective farm had been using the family's land only for grazing. But as with the attempt by Slava and the boys to build their own houses, the sons' initiative was only the beginning of the story. Irrespective of the law, the family had not been allowed to start their cooperative. Zakarya's beard remained uncut.

251

As Zakarya and his older brother Khiromagomed lobbed fragments of this story at me, the van made its way up the road that coiled up the lower slopes towards the high Andiyskiy range where we were bound. We would be travelling all day into these mountains where, for thirty years, Prometheus had suffered the punishment of Zeus for his trickery of the gods. The close-cropped pastures on either side were interrupted by outbreaks of rock. People lined the roads, begging for lifts. Everyone wanted to be back home in their own village in the mountains in time for the feast that marked the end of Ramadan. But transport was in short supply, as was petrol. It had taken the brothers all the previous day to find anyone with a van prepared to make the journey.

Presently, we stopped by a wood of hazel-trees and the brothers built a fire. Expertly, they stripped hazel twigs and cooked kebabs on the fire. The smoke rose straight in the air and the smell of charred meat tickled the appetite. People and traffic were left behind and the stillness of the mountains above us began to lift our mood.

Zakarya was the brother who had set off for Moscow in search of justice, as peasants throughout Russian history have done. When he arrived, he had gone to the Ministry and confirmed that they were free to start a family cooperative. But Zakarya did not assume that Moscow's support meant victory. Khotoda, the mountain town where we were going, is a long way away from the capital. He also visited the offices of *Pravda*: 'It was the most humiliating moment of my life,' Zakarya shuddered as he recalled it: 'As I told my story to the girl there, she talked on the telephone and read papers in front of me. I thought, well, she's like the young Lenin. She can do three things at the same time. But it turned out that she hadn't been listening at all. She was getting on with her own affairs.' Zakarya turned out to be right about the Ministry. For all their support, they had proved powerless to help. It turned out that their local representative was son-in-law to Makhachev, the man who had turned Father Nabi off the collective farm all those years ago. 'I sympathize. But what can I do?' he said.

Anticipating all this, Zakarya had then given up on the Establishment and gone to Pushkin's monument, to find himself a champion. He had spent day after day there, talking to anyone who would listen. Finally, some boys in the Popular Front had suggested he go to a lawyer, who in turn suggested that the press had more power to help him than the law. The lawyer gave Zakarya the number of a journalist whose crusading stories were beginning to bring him to prominence. That journalist was Grisha.

For Zakarya, this trip to the mountains with the film crew from Moscow was a final attempt to draw attention to his father's case. The timing of the visit had been long planned. Tomorrow Zakarya was going to take the law into his own hands and start to till the land which had been given to his family 150 years ago.

We climbed up serpentine roads until the mountains rose around us in starched brown pleats. Down below, grey waters hurled themselves against the rocks with a roar. The mountains looked barren of life. But as our eyes grew accustomed to this grand landscape, we glimpsed flocks of white goats on the scree, sprinkled like drops of milk. Here and there we saw high pastures that seemed inaccessible. On every part of these mountain ranges, the brothers told us, the grazing belonged to someone. I began to make out remote stone huts, barely distinguishable from the scree, that served as shelters for the shepherds. In the villages through which we passed the houses were large, with handsome verandas, glassed in like conservatories, whose wooden frames ran to elaborate designs. Walnut-, cherry- and pear-trees grew luxuriantly out of the mountainside in terraced clusters, the reward of tenacious husbandry.

In the morning I woke with the feeling that I was being watched. Two solemn girls with fair hair and earrings were chewing chunks of bread while they regarded me through the window leading on to the covered veranda. They were the daughters of our host Magomed, Zakarya's brother. The large room in which I was lying was simply furnished, with striped carpeting stretched in lengths along the floor. There were carpets on the walls and no other furniture apart from two iron bedsteads and a television. In the other bed, Ira still lay asleep.

I had no idea where we were, for it had been dark by the time we reached the village of Khotoda. The map told me that we were not far from the Georgian border. Near by was Vedeno, the town Tolstoy describes as Shamyl's headquarters. It was there that Hadji Murat's family had been held hostage when he defected to the Russians.

I got up to explore. The view from the covered veranda brought me up short. The house, which was set against a steep slope, looked out over hills in all directions. To the left, a town rose sharply, covering the rocky hillside. It looked as it must have done for centuries, its stone houses huddled together, connected by narrow alley-ways. The hillside ended in a point, where a sturdy tower jutted up. There was not a blade of grass to be seen. But to the right, a view opened up that was like the kind of visual cheat perpetrated by film-makers, who cut different landscapes together in a single scene. The green terraced hillside was dotted with fruit-trees. The dark lines of cypresses against the horizontal terraces gave the landscape a painterly, geometric finish. Beyond, the snow lay on the mountain peaks, as it would all summer long.

I had become so used to the paradox between the vastness of the Soviet Union and the cramped conditions in which most of its subjects lived that I found the space in the house exhilarating. These buildings were not Soviet. Up here, people built their own houses and they built them as they liked. The stone structure of this typical house was supported by long wooden legs built out from the mountainside. Animals and stores occupied the covered space below. The family lived in the strip of spacious rooms above, along the front of which ran the covered veranda, which served as the main living-room. Later in the day, I watched a group of young men filling a lorry with stones from the mountain stream for a house they were building. One house, they told me, needed 160 lorry-loads.

We breakfasted on flat bread made of flour and curd cheese, which we ate with mountain honey and *urech*. *Urech*, the quintessential mountain delicacy, is made of crushed apricot pips, linen oil and sugar. No one could tell me how these people had developed a taste for oil made from the seeds of flax, which grows in distant parts of Russia and commands exorbitant prices here. The mixture was extravagantly rich and delicate in taste.

We set off to visit the cave where the Gasanov family had been raised. After a drive along roads that seemed suspended on the mountainside, we left the car and started to climb up from the road. Where it was not held by prickly scrub, the surface was loose, making walking difficult. Zakarya and his brother Khiromagomed, though weighed down by camera equipment, bounded up like rabbits.

Half an hour later, we reached an enclosure of thorns, built to keep the goats in. Above it on the slope in front of us appeared a one-room stone hut that clung to the mountainside like a swallow's nest. What held it there was not clear. Next to it, the cave of which the brothers talked so lovingly turned out to be no more than a huge boulder, whose overhang afforded shelter. Father Nabi and his wife had brought their children here on the first night that they had been thrown off the collective farm. The hut had been added since. In front of it, on a terrace built like a shelf on the mountainside, grew a couple of pear-trees. Every handful of that earth had been carried up the mountain by Father Nabi. The couple lived here to this day.

From out of the hut stepped an old lady dressed in a black *jellaba*. She had the face of an eagle. But her smile brought out the sun. Her head was covered, and over her ears she wore silver earcovers, elaborately worked. Two baby goats had

255

escaped from their pen. They leapt from rock to rock, teasing us. Ignoring them, the old lady stood with her hand against the rock which had sheltered her family. Magomed, the second oldest brother, with whom we had stayed the night in Makhachkala, had talked of lying on top of that cave and reading *War and Peace*. 'Natasha Rostov's first ball, Prince Andrei, their spiritual searchings – all that is irrevocably linked in my mind with the cave,' he had said.

We went into the hut, as many of us as could cram in. A small iron bedstead, stove and chair was all its furnishing. The wall served the purpose of a cupboard. On it hung a few clothes, a cheese, a side of dried goat meat and some tools. While we ate a meal of bread and hard-boiled eggs, which Zakarya's sister had carried up the mountain, Zakarya talked about the eight years they had spent up here. 'Our youngest brother and sister were born here,' Zakarya explained. 'It was the nearest my father could get to our own land, which is up there.' He pointed straight up the mountain. His oldest brother Khiromagomed, who looked more like a shepherd than the lorry-driver he was, took over the story. To look at, he could not have been more different from Zakarya. His face, beneath a tonsure of silver hair, was as peaceful as his brother's was tumultuous: 'For us, the children, it was the happiest time of our lives. Father was working on the roads, while mother looked after the flocks. We looked after ourselves.' Now in her seventies, mother still spent her time cutting prickles for her goat. The alarm clock by the old couple's bed, which woke them each morning at dawn to take out the flock, was the only reminder of the twentieth century in the room.

'As for us, we would spend our days catching trout in the river,' Zakarya went on, 'collecting berries and tending the flock. Do you see that hole in the cliff?' Over on the far horizon, the sky showed blue through the rock. 'That's where I used to sit and watch the sun set . . .' '– after he had run up the mountain, which he did every day,' Khiromagomed added. From here, it looked like a sheer rock face.

The place had become a sacred memory for the children, and particularly for the three oldest brothers. This had been apparent that first night in Makhachkala, from the way Magomed had talked. Magomed was quite unlike either of his brothers. As a successful accountant, he did belong to the twentieth century. Until recently, he had been head of the big planning department of the state trading centre for fruit and vegetables. But he talked like a romantic too: 'It was a spiritual life. No radio, no television, no light. At night, we used to argue until dawn. We used to argue about how to change the world. I used to say, "You won't change the world, because you can't change people." For the sake of the argument, I'd be the conformist. But we were all of one mind: maybe it would prove impossible to change things for the better. But if we didn't fight against evil, things would get worse.'

He had paused, before adding: 'I really did end up becoming the conformist. Relatively speaking, of course. Zakarya despairs of us all.' All three men carried the same dream, the dream of independence that the mountain had taught them. But only Zakarya had devoted his life to its realization. 'He's our Shamyl,' as Khiromagomed put it.

We started on up the mountain again. Purple aubretia fell over the rocks. Among the flowering shrubs that held the loose surface of the mountain together, yellow berberis looked disturbingly familiar to the English eye, beneficiaries as we are of the great British horticultural travellers of the nineteenth century. Looking down on the Gasanov family home, I saw the figure of Father Nabi, who must have returned since we left, standing on the top of the cave, then prostrating himself towards the east in prayer. As we made our way on up the mountain we looked down more rarely at the glacial valley plunging below us, as the loose shale obliged us to concentrate on our feet. But we never lost the roar of the river below.

All of a sudden, a rock hurtled down the dried bed of a rivulet close by. Somewhere up there, Zakarya said, a boar was hidden among the stunted trees. Until recently, herds of boar were a common sight on the mountains. Now they were beginning to make themselves scarce. Although the Avars, being Muslim, did not eat boar, they hunted them because of the damage they did to the crops.

Without warning, a shower of icy rain swept over the mountains, drenching us and reminding us of the mountain's bleaker moods. We climbed for another hour and a half. I could understand why there was no rush to cultivate the Gasanovs' old land. Even to get there required some commitment. Finally, the ground started to level out and we reached the belt of pine-trees that stood on top of the mountain. As we came through the trees, the sun began to shine through again and a different landscape opened up.

It was hard to believe that this was the same mountain up which we had just climbed. In a valley, carpeted with short-cropped grass, stood the ruins of stone houses. We had arrived. Zakarya, forgetting his beard and his *gravitas*, sprang on to his hands and walked down the slope upside-down, as he used to as a boy. Among the ruins, kingcups caught the light like gold coins in the grass, marking the source of a stream. In the distance, the green hills were interrupted only by patches of pine and larch.

This was the land that had been granted to Nabi's forefather in the 1830s as a reward for the loyalty and courage with which he had fought for the Imam Kazi Magomed. Kazi Magomed had been the first of the warrior-prophets who tried to unite Dagestan's feuding tribes in the war against the Russians. Nabi's forefather had been rewarded not for defending the Imam against the Russians, but against the treachery of his own people. It was a story that echoed that of the rift a generation later between the Imam Shamyl and Hadji Murat. The individualistic notion of the blood feud frequently cut across the lowland notion of loyalty to one's own kind.

As we stood on the sunny bank, I could see how this high, rolling land could inspire mad plans in a man. Surely these sixteen hectares could be spared, out of the 500 hectares of cultivable land that lay fallow in the area? 'We could fatten up sheep straight away. Look, there's money right under our feet.' Zakarya picked up a pine-cone. 'A kilogram of pine nuts costs 30 roubles. I dream of growing wild strawberries here . . .' But quite how mad the plans were, I realized for the first time. It was no allotment the brothers were dreaming of, but a farm that would sustain the whole Gasanov tribe. There was no road that led up here, let alone electricity. Yet Magomed, the sober accountant, had talked of it as if it was all worked out: 'We'll make a road up the back. It'll mean lowering a bulldozer from a helicopter. Everything can be done if you have got the money. We'll be out of pocket for five years or so. But we're going in with our eyes open.' If anyone but Magomed had said it, I would not have believed a word of it.

Zakarya went off down the hill with a pickaxe in his hand, to claim with his own labour the land which the law said they could work, but which the community still withheld from them. There would be trouble by and by. As we walked through the village that morning, a woman had spat in Zakarya's face. There were those who were behind the Gasanov brothers, and those who were not.

A Mountain Warrior

To spend time in Khotoda was to understand that Father Nabi's quarrel with Makhachev was no private matter. The day after we arrived, our sound recordist Volodya had gone to the fields to do some recording. Volodya was a tough man, who had filmed for long periods in Afghanistan. He had come back looking discomfited. A man who had been training a pair of bullocks for the plough had stopped work, come over to him and said: 'If you show your face here once more, you'll be found in a ditch with your throat slit.' 'And do you know, I looked at him and I knew he was not joking,' Volodya had said.

The community was divided on the issue of the Gasanovs. It was not just the precedent of the cooperative that troubled them. The original action Makhachev had taken against Father Nabi had been triggered, it appeared, by a petty enough incident. Makhachev had stolen a sheep. The rest of the community had been prepared to go along with the boss's explanation that the 'wolves' had eaten it. But the shepherd had not been prepared to shut his mouth. The issue was power. 'Even now, no one has a voice in the village,' as Magomed had put it. 'Makhachev runs it like a khan. Can you really spend your whole life with your eyes trained on your feet, never raising your head?'

Years later, a corruption case had been started against Makhachev on quite other grounds. He had turned out to be involved, not just in the occasional theft, but in serious fraud.

But too many people in high places had been implicated and the case had eventually been hushed up. After thirty years as head of the collective farm and absolute ruler of the community, Makhachev had been pensioned off. But power like that does not just disappear. He had been made director of the new sewing workshop for which the village, long dogged by unemployment, had been waiting. Inevitably, the diktat had gone out: no one who sided with Father Nabi would be employed.

Makhachev was an evil man, and Father Nabi's moral case against him had never been in question. But over the next few days I caught an unnerving glimpse of the family's absolutism. I learned that seven years after Father Nabi's expulsion from the collective farm, his excommunication had been lifted. But without compensation and an apology from Makhachev, the shepherd would not go back. It took me much longer to find out that more recently the family had been given to understand that they would be allowed to start their cooperative on the family land. There had only been one condition: the past should be forgotten. This time it was Zakarya who would not agree. 'If we lose hold of the central point of our struggle, our fight for justice, we lose everything,' he pronounced.

Zakarya's justice involved an ancient and atavistic concept of honour, which I only began to understand as I listened to him talk about the past. 'I would give anything to be like the men of my grandfather's generation,' he said to me that evening, as we sat on the covered veranda after our meal. 'They were real men. We? Ah, we are nothing at all, excuses for men. We don't deserve the name.' It was the grand old men like Zakarya's great uncle, brother to his eagle-faced mother, who peopled his imagination: 'He was famous throughout the region for his bravery and sense of honour. He only died a few years ago. When they were young, he and my grandfather were robbed one time when they were in Georgia. Some time later, he saw the man who did it on the roof of a house. He sent word to him to meet him on top of the hill. The man was a

261

scoundrel, so he sent his friend up instead, all unawares. My great uncle looked at the man and said: "You're the wrong man. Fetch him for me." Eventually, the thief came. My great uncle took off his clothes, beat him, got on his horse and made the man walk on in front with a gun in his back all the way to the police. On the way they stopped at a house. He wanted the robber to be shaved for some reason. And somehow or other the robber got the old woman in the house to slip him a knife. When they were preparing to go my great uncle made to tie the robber's hands behind his back. The man stabbed him seven times around the heart. My great uncle should have died there and then, but somehow he managed to get his gun and shoot the man dead. They put him on trial for murder and when the judge asked him how many men he had killed in his life, my great uncle raised his hand to his head and started to say, "As many as the hairs on my head," but the judge interrupted him. He knew exactly what my uncle was going to say, and he knew it would be fatal for him. They don't come like that now.'

Twice this century, this land has dripped blood. The first time was the civil war. Dagestan's proximity to the Baku oil wells was vital. Futhermore, every conceivable power group had tried to enlist the legendary warrior skills of the mountain tribes to their cause. The fighting had destroyed not only people, but buildings and irrigation systems. Then had come collectivization, when, in a vast blood-letting, the spirit of the mountain people had been broken. Many of the bravest, like Zakarya's grandfather, had been killed: 'When they were taking my grandfather out to be shot, my mother tells me, his hands were tied behind his back. But he still managed to throw one man to his death down the mountainside. He was only twenty-five.'

From time to time, Zakarya would become aware of how his words must sound to me: 'I'm sure you think the old blood feud was barbarous. But it was a straightforward, open, honest way. The barbarous custom had its logic, there was a law

262

which you yourself, personally, could carry out. But what can we do now? How can you reach justice through all those courts, those complex, interlocking pieces of society! If only my hands were not tied. If only it were not for my wife and children! How could I have allowed myself to get married? It was the greatest mistake of my life!' Hadji Murat, I found myself thinking, must have said the same to himself as he chafed at his impotence in the Russian camp, knowing his freedom to be utterly compromised by his family whom Shamyl was holding hostage.

No wonder the community was divided by Zakarya's actions. It was not just that people slept more soundly at night, now that the blood feud was no longer pursued with the knife. The sight of abandoned fruit-trees and deserted terraces everywhere was a reminder that Zakarya represented a hard way of life to which few would be prepared to return.

Zakarya was a mountain warrior of the traditional kind, except that he had been disarmed of his sword, his knife and his gun. He was eaten up by his cause, obsessed in such a way that his perspective had gone: 'When I started the struggle against Makhachev, I had no idea that I was starting a struggle against the whole system.' But his brothers had known. They had watched him prepare himself, even as a child. 'He is a fanatic,' Magomed had said. 'He always was. When he was a child, he saw a man tormenting a dog, and he threw stones at him. Can you imagine? In a culture like ours? That a child should throw a stone at a grown man, his elder! They beat him up. All his life they have been beating him up for the same thing.'

Zakarya was engaged in a grand battle, but it had its petty moments. He was prepared to exploit the smallest opportunities to get at Makhachev; to report to the fraud police, for instance, the sheep that Makhachev was illegally fattening for private sale. For Zakarya, Makhachev had come to personify the hydra-headed corruption of the world and every bit of it was intolerable.

263

Makhachev had even come to be responsible for evils of which he was not the cause. It took me some time to discover, and then not from the brothers, that Makhachev was not to blame for Zakarya's father being forced off his own land.

In the course of one of his disastrous attempts at streamlining agriculture, Khrushchev had, in the early sixties, instituted a policy which obliged all the shepherd–farmers to abandon their isolated farmsteads and settle in the towns. If any conditions existed which were appropriate to this reform they were certainly not those of the mountain people, whom only the practice of generations had taught to coax a living from the rocks.

The only advance brought by Khrushchev's reforms up here had, as usual, been a political one. People had been brought under control and the power of men like Makhachev had been correspondingly enhanced. When he had made the mistake of wielding that power to protect himself, by throwing Father Nabi out of the collective farm, he could hardly have reckoned that, far from ridding himself of the troublesome shepherd, he was making sure that the spirit of the mountain warriors which Soviet power appeared to have broken was kept alive in the family of his enemy.

The Best of Us

Still in Khotoda, I lay in bed and listened to the chattering of a sparrow which had found its way into the glassed-in veranda. Overnight, the rain had come and gone, filling the buckets that Fatimah, our hostess, had put out yesterday. As I looked out at the town on the hill opposite, a double rainbow began to appear in the violet sky, embracing the hillside in its curve. Small figures were running up and down the narrow, un-metalled streets between the stone houses. Today was the feast that marked the end of the Muslim fast of Ramadan. Fatimah told me that it was the custom for boys and girls to go visiting at first light. Soon they started to arrive, carrying their plastic bags into each of which Fatimah put a handful of biscuits and sweets.

Fatimah was tall and dark with fair skin and the same large nose as Zakarya's mother. She wore a cotton flowered shift, black trousers, and a headscarf tied behind her head. Her daughters were still asleep, but her son gurgled in the wooden cot into which he was strapped. Although I had been surprised to see him swaddled, I soon understood why the custom had survived. Apart from keeping the baby safe and out of the way until his mother had time for him, a cunningly devised clay pipe did away with the need for nappies.

This morning, though the overnight downpour had spared Fatimah the task of fetching water from the tap in the town, she was already hard at work making flat bread for breakfast. Early morning was the only time of day when I really saw her.

265

The role of women appeared to be traditional. She prepared our food, but ate apart with the children. Ira and I, as foreign guests, were allowed to eat with the men. But I had noticed that some men we had met outside the Gasanov family were embarrassed at the idea of having to shake hands with women at all, even if they were visitors.

The separation of the sexes was carried on into the rigid division of physical labour. While the men herded the flocks, ploughed and built the houses, the women fetched water, dug the fields and cut fodder for the small flock that each family was allowed. Cutting fodder was time-consuming, as the nearby pastures were all assigned to the collective farm. The women might be forced to walk for three to four hours in the evening to get beyond reach of *kolkhoz* land, or at least to somewhere where no one would see them cutting the grass. They would cut through the night and return across the mountains with loads weighing up to forty kilos on their backs.

Apart from the children's visits, the feast day turned out to be distinguished more by the absence of work than by particular rituals. Father Nabi and his aquiline wife had come down from the mountain for the day. We paid them a visit in the house they shared with Zakarya. Father Nabi, with his grey beard and determined chin, sat with his best suit and hat on, his hands on his knees. His wife sat at his side. Their frail figures looked as indestructible as the trees that clung to the mountainside. Unlike their children, they had kept to the fast of Ramadan. For them, the goat that was being carried up the steps to be killed would be their first meat for a month. Except for the old men, few people went to the village mosque, which had only recently been reopened.

In the course of the feast day I had the chance to spend more time talking to Nabi's eldest son Khiromagomed. The circumstances which had marked all the brothers seemed to have made of him a utopian socialist, for whom the Kremlin had replaced Mecca. While his father prayed to the East,

266

Khiromagomed sent his prayers in the form of letters north, to the offices of *Pravda*, the newspaper whose name means Truth. The other brothers were inclined to laugh at Khiromagomed's graphomania. An innocent he might be, but he was a wise one. It was he who reflected on the irony of their family's prosperity: 'If they had not expelled us, we would probably have become like father. We would have tended the flocks. We would never have been beyond the local regional centre and we would never have started asking questions. We must be grateful to the man who injured us. Thanks to him, we are educated, we have homes in Makhachkala and work there. And how do people in Khotoda live? Our neighbours laugh and say: "Now it's your turn on top." It's our duty to save them from the yoke of Makhachev.'

I was beginning to see that, had it not been for Zakarya, the brothers would have had a far easier life. The quarrel with Makhachev would long ago have been resolved and they would now be farming their own land. As it was, they were carried along in the slipstream of Zakarya's intransigence. Was this a cause of resentment between them, I asked Khiromagomed? The gentle brother smiled and it was as if the rainbow had come out once more. He shook his head: 'He is the best of us. We will always stand by him.'

Meanwhile, the cameraman Seryozha was sitting at the other end of the table on the veranda, drinking tea with Zakarya. He was telling him the story of Orwell's *1984*, which was in the course of being serialized in the journal *Novy Mir*. I watched Zakarya's eyes grow wide. 'But how did he know more about us than we did ourselves? It couldn't have been written in 1948 . . .' Like children who have missed the end of a film, they came over and begged me to tell them how the novel ended. I looked at Zakarya, this man whose crusade was as absolute and as hopeless as Winston's and I did not want to tell him that Winston ended up loving Big Brother. Lamely, I said that I had forgotten. Seryozha went on to the story of *Animal Farm*. The idea of the revolt of the farm animals appealed to Zakarya. As the sun shone through on to the table, he sat there shaking his dark head and smiling to himself at the image of the fat Makhachev as a pig.

I revelled in Zakarya and Khiromagomed's company. They thought with the clarity of people who are accustomed to spend long periods of time on their own. But when the crew were around, our group was large and the conversation tended to be dominated by the Russians. Two of the crew were beginning to get on my nerves. The mood of Volodya, the sound man, had not been improved by the threat to cut his throat. With his clean-cut good looks he belonged to a type of journalist that is international. He was bright and pleased with himself. Having seen the world from Paris to Kabul he had concluded that it was all a whorehouse. In the company of these innocent people, his cynicism was wearing and unpleasant.

Tolik, the producer, was worse. A tall, gangling man with a pot belly, he looked like a Viking and seemed pleasant enough at first. But he was the kind of Viking they would have left behind when they set off in their curved boats. A day was enough to exhaust his vocabulary. 'Ooh, look at the *shashliks!*' he would shriek with pleasure every time he saw a sheep. In the mountains, we saw a lot of sheep. He had a binary mind. Everything was either 'a nightmare' or 'stunning'. All day he filled the air with noise, all evening he drank too much. He considered himself to be something of an authority on drink. He kept on telling me, for some reason, that the English did not drink gin, only liqueurs. His role as producer was unclear, but it seemed to involve making the travel arrangements and carrying equipment, both of which the brothers did for him, leaving him without a job'.

Bored by their primitive hosts, Volodya and Tolik had been conducting an idle campaign of destabilization against Grisha, as is the wont of film crews who sense uncertainty in their director. It was the first documentary that Grisha had directed. The quintessentially urban man, he had been an easy target as he struggled up the mountains, trying to avoid both the sheep droppings and the view of the valley below.

Because of this unpleasant undercurrent, it was a welcome distraction that evening when a policeman with a hooked nose walked into the veranda during supper and started telling stories. He had peasant shoulders and huge hands and he made the veranda seem like a doll's house. The energy bubbled up in him like water from an underground stream.

The policeman, whom nobody knew, had come from the regional centre Sovetskoye, further down the mountain. He had come to find the journalist from Moscow. He wanted to interest him in the story of his struggle to remain honest in a corrupt police force. But with the instinct of a performer he launched off not into the tale of his own grievances, but into an exotic story of how, for the good of all parties, he had aided and abetted a young man of his acquaintance to steal himself a second wife. He was a fine raconteur and he soon had Grisha's ear. As he kept the table amused, I watched Zakarya's face take on a shuttered look. 'Hm, he's full of fine words. But I never did meet an honest policeman,' he muttered afterwards.

This encounter may have helped to precipitate the argument that broke out between my two friends back in Makhachkala, just before we set off for the plane. Zakarya had gone all the way to Moscow to solicit the interest of a journalist in his cause. To watch that journalist, to whom he had opened up his heart, become interested in another story, casually encountered, reminded Zakarya that he fought his battle alone. Even those who were prepared to offer support, including his own brothers, did so not in Zakarya's way, by surrendering themselves totally to the cause, but conditionally, within limits of their own.

We were back in Magomed's flat when the argument began. Coming out of the shower, I could hear Zakarya's voice through the open doorway of the room next door. He sounded desperate. 'I had such high hopes of you and now I see that you are just like everyone else. You're afraid.' Grisha, I thought, poor Grisha, accused on all sides of cowardice. He might not be good on heights, but as a journalist, he was Zakarya's equal as a warrior. They just belonged to different centuries. 'I can tell your story in a film,' Grisha replied. 'But I am not in any position to take up your cause for you. If I go and talk to an official here, and another one takes him into the next room and has a word with him in your language, I haven't the slightest idea whether he is saying "Don't tell the man a thing", or "This is an honest journalist, give him all the help you can". I am completely at the mercy of what people tell me here.' Grisha went on to reproach Zakarya for the way he distracted himself with petty battles, away from what Grisha saw as his main aim of getting the cooperative going on his father's land. Zakarya shook his head. 'You don't understand anything, do you? You just don't understand that the battle is all one. The battle is against Injustice.'

It was painful to listen to this argument between these two champions of justice in a society in which there was no rule of law. There was no point in my intervening. There was nothing that would bridge the gap between them. For Grisha it was frustrating that neither he nor anyone else could help Zakarya, although the land was finally within reach of the Gasanov family. For his taste, Zakarya's atavistic notion of justice, that of the mountain warriors whom the Russians have always feared, was far too close to raw revenge. For Zakarya, Grisha's so-called civilized idea of justice had compromise at the heart of it.

In the voice of a man whose heart is breaking Zakarya went on: 'Everything has been proved, everything has been printed and nothing changes. The robbers go on as they always have and there is no justice in the world. What I should do is get a gun and finish off as many of them as I can before doing away with myself.'

VIII

MOSCOW

What Kind of God
Do They Worship, Then?

Since I had been away, summer had arrived in Moscow with an effusion of green. The earth's regenerative power after a winter under the snow was astonishing. A couple of weeks ago the naked ground, littered with a decomposing trail of last year's foliage, had seemed irremediably dead. Now, the well-trodden paths between the residential blocks in our district threaded their way through a tangle of green. Above, the etiolated saplings had won their struggle towards the light. Everywhere the lilac was in flower.

Ironically, in an empire starved of meat, I had been given nothing but meat to eat in Dagestan. Now I craved vegetables. On my first morning back I rushed to the market, no longer able to bear the constraints of an ordinary Russian diet. There I spent more than the average weekly wage on tomatoes, potatoes, apples and cherries. As I walked back carrying my fresh produce in trumpets of rolled newspaper, several people stopped me to ask how much the cherries cost. I was ashamed to say. Only crooks and foreigners bought cherries at the equivalent of £10 a kilo. Even more to the point, in this system where everything hinged on the illusion of poverty, no one but a crook or a foreigner would have been flaunting cherries in the street.

As I passed our local milk and meat shop on the corner, a consignment of frankfurters was being carried into the shop. From nowhere, a queue had formed before my eyes. An old woman was running through the traffic from the market stalls over the road. An old man was shouting at a broad-beamed housewife who had berthed in front of him in the queue. His face was contorted with anger. The famous patience of the Russian queue was beginning to run out.

What has happened to the food? In Dagestan, Magomed the accountant explained to me. It seemed that the economy simply followed the principle established by the hero–scoundrel of Gogol's novel, *Dead Souls*, back in the mid nineteenth century. Chichikov was a smart clerk who set about the business of remodelling himself as a landowner through an elegant accountant's dodge. He travelled round the countryside visiting landowners and buying up serfs who had died or run away since the last census had been taken. His plan was to mortgage his junk-bond serfs while they were still officially alive, and buy out an impoverished nobleman. Tragically, Gogol burnt Part Two of the novel and we shall never know how his plan to redeem Chichikov was realized. It might have been helpful at this juncture in Russia's history.

The Soviet economy was Chichikov's brain-child. 'Take Makhachev's sheep,' as Magomed put it. 'The state would pay him cost price for them, and expect him to sell them on at the highly subsidized rate set by the state. This he would do, but the transaction would occur only on paper. The mutton would not appear in the shop, but would be sold on at a far higher price privately. But that's not all. My father's original quarrel with Makhachev was over his own particular dodge. Makhachev was not declaring all the sheep that belonged to the collective farm. The ones he did not declare, he would sell for his own profit, after rearing them at the state's expense. A skilful operator like Makhachev could end up declaring so few sheep that he would even be entitled to a poverty payment as well.' This was a further elaboration of the Orwellian principle that poverty = wealth. The more serious the aspiration towards wealth, the greater the need to look poor.

As the *Dead Souls* economy moved into its final stage, the

artificial deficit became its essential adjunct. On our journey back to Makhachkala, I had seen a vivid example of this. The roadside had been littered with cars that had run out of petrol. A week earlier, on our journey up, there had been no abandoned cars. Our second journey had coincided with the end of the 'petrol month'. Stocks were so low that half the petrol stations were filling up cars only with petrol that could be paid for with petrol coupons. Nearly ten years ago, an experiment had been carried out in one area of Russia. Petrol had been made freely available. Consumption was lower than when stocks were controlled. The experiment had not been repeated and the findings had been hushed up. They had only recently been published. Where those in positions of authority at every level were cut in on the old system that depended on the limitation of supply, reform was in the interests of almost no one. It had taken me a long time to face that conclusion. The consequences were hideous.

The flat was empty when I arrived back in Moscow, as Elena had not yet returned from her long-planned holiday. Once more, I felt the luxury of being on my own after a week of enforced companionship. Seeking to prolong my solitude, I paid a visit to that best-known symbol of Moscow, the Cathedral of St Basil's in Red Square. Anyone who lives in Moscow can hardly avoid holding their own running conversation with this pugnacious building, which stands outside the Kremlin walls.

The baroque exuberance of its onion-domes, which compete with one another as they thrust towards the light, seems to take its inspiration rather from the world of plants than from architecture. The intricate, brightly painted interior beguiles, but I was in no mood to be seduced that day. I saw the tightly confined space as the expression of a profoundly Russian idea of how power works. The central chapel was cramped, like every other room, but the light flooded into it from above. When I raised my head, I found that it had no ceiling. As if

275

arrogating to itself sole access to heaven, it stretched on upwards and upwards to the top of the tall tower. All other rooms were low and dark. Leading off this main chapel and reconnecting with it again, down dark passages at oblique angles, the other chapels seemed to be trying to get away from the centre. In their failure, they were like a nest of foiled conspiracies.

Down one of these confining corridors, looking unnaturally tall and clean, a well-dressed American businessman was walking with his interpreter. 'What kind of a religion is this then?' he asked his interpreter loudly. 'Orthodox,' she answered. 'What kind of god do they worship, then?' Indeed this building hardly seemed like a place of worship for a Christian God.

They say that Ivan the Terrible had the eyes of the architect Posnik Yakovlev put out once the building was complete, to make sure that he could never create a church as splendid again. Legend it may be, but the story has a depressing ring of truth. The tradition of rewarding originality by punishment is an old one here. They did it to Chaadaev, to Radishchev, to Pushkin, Lermontov and Dostoevsky. This century, the principle had been democratically extended to include not just originality, but initiative of any kind. Hydra-headed, the tsars too had proliferated since the Revolution: every little boss had his own realm now, into which no higher authority seemed to penetrate.

Komkov, who ran the state farm in Konstantinovo, was one example. It looked as if the dream that Slava and the boys had had of building their own homes was at an end. We came back to find that, despite Grisha's television film and the article in *Izvestia* that had followed it, Komkov had managed to choke off the threat to his position by dint of mobilizing the serfs on his state farm. The telegram signed by 200 of them that had been sent to the television station had succeeded in stopping the programme's second transmission. Bizarrely, Komkov was now maintaining that Grisha's interview with him on camera

276

was an invention. As Grisha rang to tell me that morning: 'He says we have threaded together words which had been used in a different context.' 'But he's on camera, it's a technical impossibility. What can he gain by a charge as stupid as that?' There had been a sigh on the other end of the telephone. 'You still don't understand, do you? Of course it's impossible. That makes no difference. The point is that he said it and he is believed. The facts are beside the point.'

'You get used to being hated,' Zakarya had said to me in Dagestan. What chance did the economy have, as long as initiative needed to be fuelled by anything as consuming as Zakarya's vengeful pursuit of his family feud? I remembered how Valery, the farmer who had left his state farm in Konstantinovo to set up on his own, had expressed the fear that, unless he met with some glimmer of encouragement, he would relapse into torpor, or end up becoming that against which he was struggling. To resist the entire system was a burden so great as to make madmen of saints and drunkards of the finest.

On arriving back, I also learned from the newspaper that a case was being brought against Telman Dglyan. Dglyan was the prosecutor who had spent years trying to bring corrupt officials to justice. Although his efforts had brought Brezhnev's son-in-law to court, most of his targets had escaped because none of their subordinates had dared to testify. Dglyan had last month received the ultimate popular accolade of being voted a People's Deputy by a huge majority. Now he stood accused of beating those under interrogation, taking bribes and other serious charges. I had been there long enough to recognize the timing. It was inevitable that he would be brought to court.

As my Virgil, Grisha, had explained: 'It cannot have been hard to put the case together. Everyone in any position of authority breaks the law every hour of every day. Otherwise they can't get anything done. That's the tragedy. There are no irreproachable leaders. There are only those who, for one

277

reason or another, They have decided not to finger at the moment.'

On the bus on my way back home, I caught sight of a woman lying face down on the pavement as we passed the block of flats by the cinema. Her luxurious chestnut hair was spread wide around her. I assumed she was drunk. Then I saw the blood that was seeping from under her face. She could only just have jumped from one of the balconies above, with their high balustrades. A crowd had not even had time to collect.

The Old Hatred Will
Come Back

From time to time, I find myself getting left behind by the pace of change, hanging on to perceptions which were appropriate when I arrived in the autumn, but which have turned into something else. One such moment of realization occurred in Dagestan, on our last day in the mountains. After eating a picnic lunch in the orchard with the others, I had retired to my room, suddenly aware of being the only woman present in a society which does not expect women to participate in the same social life as the men. Ira had had to go back to Moscow early.

Half an hour later, there had been a knock on my door. Grisha had come in, looking upset. Tolik, the so-called producer, who had been making free with the potent home-brewed alcohol which the Gasanov brothers sipped so cautiously, had turned to Grisha and said: 'You're a Jew, aren't you Grisha?' In the West, such a question might be a neutral one. In the Soviet Union at that moment it was a provocation. 'No, Tolik, I'm not a Jew, I'm a Yid.' Grisha had answered the subtext of Tolik's question. In Russian, the word *zhid* is deeply racist.

There had been no more to the exchange. But Grisha, who was not usually thin-skinned, was shaken. As he paced up and down the room, I tried to articulate something contradictory that I had been feeling. It was impossible for me not to rejoice in the recovery of memory, of historical roots, I explained to Grisha, in a state which had aimed at total control over people's access to the past. But at the same time, I had found myself getting more and more alarmed in the presence of conversations about the past. Lately, they seemed so easily to take on nationalistic overtones. Grisha did not even allow me to finish what I was saying, before he interrupted me vehemently: 'No! No! You can't talk about historical roots now! Tree stumps have roots now, not people! There is no life to be found in roots any more? History has become a minefield! We have to turn our back on the past! Can't you see that it has become impossible even for a Russian to say "I don't like Gogol" any more? People look at you as if you have made an attempt on his life. Tolstoy, Dostoevsky, Gogol, Pushkin, Chekhov – you have to love them all equally. They are not landmarks any more, they're sacred idols.'

With the two little mountain girls gazing in at us from the doorway in astonishment, we had argued: 'Come on, Grisha, don't be ridiculous. You can't just declare the past a no-go area, after decades of people being denied access to their own past. The task of reconnecting people to their lost past is massively important. You're just . . .' 'No! No! You don't understand! Just as the search for the Jew has replaced the search for the Enemy, so those who now put their energies into the past are making a decisive move away from the issues that face our society today. The past, all of it, has become a distraction, a distraction from the present.'

I held out for a while. But Grisha was right. The time had gone for the distinction I was trying to make, between a proper and an improper use of the past. I was being logical in a situation which had gone beyond logic. Since I arrived in the autumn, something had changed. The return of historical memory had been overtaken by a process far more primitive. The victims of the old official lies were taking their revenge. They were doing so in a way that mirrored the cavalier attitude that Soviet historians had adopted to the facts. Meanwhile, as people battled to claim the past for themselves, the present was being lost.

280

In his own work as a journalist, Grisha was putting his argument into practice. He may not have been able to help Slava and the boys, but another recent article of his had had unexpected results. It was about Kudrin, a people's judge in Sverdlovsk, who had resigned his post in protest against political pressure.

Through Grisha's article, Kudrin had become a local hero. The Sverdlovsk Academy of Sciences had now adopted him as their candidate for election to the new Soviet parliament. Although there were a number of other candidates, the real fight in the city was between the supporters of the old, corrupt establishment, personified by an Academician called Mesyats, and Kudrin, the innocent. The city was in a state of excitement, as I kept hearing from Grisha's informants who brought regular news of developments. Sverdlovsk was closed to foreigners, or I would have gone there now. The result of the election would be known just before I left, the day before the Congress of People's Deputies opened for its first session.

The Monk without a Church

Every now and then, Kukobaka would come round and visit me. He had been described by a Russian friend of his as a coarse-mannered peasant, dressed in rags. But when he came to see me he was always immaculately dressed in the same clothes: freshly creased grey flannels, a short-sleeved green shirt, and a trilby. They were obviously presents from friends in the West and their pristine state suggested that he took them off as soon as he got home. With his newly grown reddish beard and shy good manners he looked more like a man auditioning for a job as Santa Claus at a department store than a notoriously intransigent Crimethinker.

I had met Kukobaka by chance back in December when I had been delivering something to a friend of a friend. 'Don't mind him,' the man had said: 'He only got out of camp three days ago.' Kukobaka had sat, with his shaven head, trying to make himself look inconspicuous in the corner of the room while we talked. The attempt was not successful. He looked like a naked man among the clothed.

In all, Kukobaka had spent seventeen years in camp. He was a dissident but not an intellectual. In 1968, just after the Soviet invasion of Czechoslovakia, when he was thirty, he had walked into the Czech consulate in Kiev and apologized for the occupation. He was not arrested immediately, but a conversation with his fellow workers soon provided the excuse they were looking for. The charge was Article 190/1, Thoughtcrime. After ten years in prison, he renounced his Soviet citizenship. Now that

Western pressure had finally secured his release, he had been told that he would be free to emigrate if only he would agree to leave Moscow, where he was an illegal resident, and return to the town where he was registered. He had refused. Having renounced his Soviet citizenship, he no longer considered himself bound by anything he was told to do by Soviet authorities.

Kukobaka had come again this morning. As usual he was sitting on the edge of a large armchair, with his trilby on his knee, and Elena's ragged furry slippers, which looked like toy animals, on his feet. As usual, he had refused all offers of food and drink. So downright was his refusal that I might have thought him rude if I had not begun to know him. His vehemence was the only sign of his struggle against himself. He would not allow himself to cadge off a Westerner. Only in the second hour, when he had finally set aside his trilby and was sitting further back in his chair, did he finally accept a cup of tea, 'since you are having one'.

'There are three categories of dissident,' he had said the first time he came. 'The first are the shouters. They lead normal lives until one day for some reason they forget themselves, do something unwary, sign a letter or something. And when they're arrested, they go utterly to pieces, ask to be forgiven. Then there are the run-of-the-mill dissidents. They behave all right in prison and they're not bad as people. But when they come out they start trying to make lives for themselves.' He pronounced these last words with a disdainful emphasis, as though talking about an activity which was patently absurd: 'They write articles for *Novy Mir* and try and establish themselves as writers. L is one of those,' he said bitterly of the man at whose flat we had met. 'That kind all think I'm crazy not to hang on to my Soviet citizenship, abide by the rules and emigrate. They simply don't understand that however much I may want to emigrate, I can't go against my conscience. I couldn't live with myself after that.

'Then there is the third group, my sort of people, people who

283

will make no compromise of any kind. Goodness knows that principle has cost me dear. It has cost me a home, a family, a job. It has cost me my country. I can't give it up now.'

For Kukobaka, this monk without a church, his integrity was his sole means of expression. His life had become his life's work, an act of symbolic resistance. Freedom and the changing political situation had left him in an uneasy position. Only history would be able to judge whether his language of total resistance remained relevant. 'About ten years ago in camp, I had quite a nice commandant. He was about the same age as me and he had some respect for me. He used to say, "If only you'd sign this paper, you'd be free to catch up on everything that you've gone without. You're not a bad bloke," he'd say. "You must marry and have a family. Give yourself a chance." That paper said something like: "I undertake not to take part in activities prejudicial to the interests of the state." Signing it would effectively have meant my saying, "Forgive me for my past actions." They all got out in the end by signing documents like that. L did, even P did.' P was a dedicated activist of our acquaintance who was one of the leaders of the Democratic Front. 'More recently, they used to ask me to sign every ten days or so. The minute I did, I would be freed. By that time it had been shortened so that it was nothing more than a simple request: "Please let me go free." But I wouldn't even sign that. I have never signed a single piece of paper of theirs and I never will. I know, I perfectly understand, what it has cost me. I have nothing and nobody; no work and nowhere to live. But every man chooses his fate and I have never for one moment regretted the one I chose. I remain simply an uneducated man who has lived by his principles to the end.'

Kukobaka spoke with the humility of a man for whom thoughts are not the games of a trained mind, but the work of solitary hours. The result of this painful process was often illuminating: 'You will be hard put to it to find many people who say that they are socialists here,' he was saying today. 'But

284

scratch a little deeper and you'll find they still are. I did an experiment on myself once when I was eight months in solitary. I used to write the word "Lenin" slowly on a piece of paper. Despite the fact that I actually think he's done infinitely more harm than Hitler, a feeling of warmth, affection and happiness would flood through me as I wrote out the letters. Next I would write out the word "Hitler", again very slowly. And I could feel myself getting angry and upset. That's how deeply imprinted we are. Even if our mind has arrived at a completely different conclusion, our emotions obey an earlier call. They are much more deeply rooted, much harder to eradicate than the conclusions we come to with our intellect.'

Kukobaka sat there tentatively, with his large working hands clasped between his knees, making a move now and then to leave, sure that he was boring me. What had inspired his absolutism, I asked him. 'I've thought about that a lot and I may be wrong but I think I know. My father died in the Finnish War and my mother, well . . .' He tailed off. Later, I learned that she had fought the Germans as a partisan and come back from the war crippled. She died young, having spent the rest of her life in one hospital after another.

'I started off living with my grandmother. She was a wonderful woman. Religious. But she had nothing, and she was ill and couldn't manage me. So she ended up putting me into a children's home.' Kukobaka talked without emotion, as if about someone else's life. 'We had a good teacher in the home, who taught us not to lie. She taught us about being a good citizen, about principles. Now if I'd been living at home with parents of my own, I'm sure I'd have learned something of the relativity of principles. Your mother behaves in a certain way at home and in another way when she's out. She tells you to do something this way at home, and they tell you to do it that way at school. You get used to living with double standards. But it wasn't until I came out of the children's home when I was seventeen and started to work that I came face to face with real

285

life. It was the opposite to everything we had been taught to value in the children's home. I had seen everything in pink tones in the home. Then straight away it all went to black and grey. I could see all the lies. It wasn't that life in the home was perfect by any means. It was full of *bezprizorniki*, orphans who'd been living wild. There were children who "told" on other ones. But they weren't at all popular. It was a different world from the one outside.'

When he talked about the past, Kukobaka was at home. His present life was not hard but it was clear that he hated it. He took casual work where no questions were asked in order to pay the exorbitant rent charged him by a drunkard with an extra room. 'Because I'm here illegally, I feel I have to avoid contact with my neighbours . . . Ah, you've got me complaining again.' He stopped himself short, not for the first time. 'Everything that I am, I have made for myself.'

It was not the conditions of his present life that were difficult. As a 'free' man, his life had lost its purpose. 'There, in camp, I had a code of principles. I lived by them, and they supported me. Every day I could measure my actions and those of the people around me against those principles.' Kukobaka had given his life to prove that not every man had a price. Finding himself in a world which seemed to attach little value to his moral absolutism, he still allowed himself no comfort: 'I've thought about religion a lot, but it makes so many people tolerate passively what they should not tolerate.' He paused. 'I don't want to be critical. I've got a great respect for religious people. But I think that for many people it is a kind of consolation.'

It was a Sunday morning and I was on my way to a service at Yelokhovsky Cathedral. The sun was shining and people were walking through the streets with armfuls of lilac and peonies from the market. Moscow had come into flower. Dandelions were growing in sheets on every patch of waste ground.

286

Wherever man had not covered the earth in asphalt or concrete, nature had invaded. In London, Washington or Paris, the summer greenery is tamed by man. Here summer seems to wash in on a tide from the countryside, bringing memories of a simpler rural life. I hear it too in the endearments that pass between men and women. 'My little swallow.' 'My little partridge,' whispers a man to his girl. 'My rabbit,' she replies tenderly.

I stood in the cathedral among the head-scarved women, feeling excluded from the ritual and only sporadically able to understand. The language of the church service is remote from that of everyday life. It has changed little since the Greek missionaries Cyril and Methodius coined it in the ninth century. They had grafted a largely Greek alphabet and syntax on to the unwritten Slavonic language which they found.

Language was not the real barrier, however. As I stood there, I felt out of tune with something deeper, the spiritual rhythm of the service. The priest's long blond hair was being untied like a wheatsheaf and laid across his back. They removed his tall hat and the stole around his shoulders. A lesser priest with a face the colour of a mackerel sky and a straggly undergrowth of hair on his face, led the singing in a commanding voice. Then he started to chant a prayer, in a bass so low that the boom was like that of a steamer leaving port. His voice slid up, quarter-tone by quarter-tone, and I found myself being drawn viscerally into the ritual, as I obeyed the impulse to resolve each moment of musical uncertainty by reaching towards the next whole note within myself. From that moment on, I was caught in every fluctuation in the mood of the service.

Two choirs were singing from galleries high to the right and left. They threw the drama back and forth from one side of the cathedral to the other. The main actors in the service were men and the congregation largely women. A secondary drama was being played out by black-robed women who were moving ceaselessly around the stage, replenishing candlesticks, shifting

287

sacred furniture from one ritual position to the next. They reminded me of the girl construction workers whose unexpectedly frail faces, framed in scarves, would look down every now and then from the scaffolding on the street, while their male boss paced the pavement below.

To my right, a middle-aged woman in a headscarf was restlessly rearranging the amber beeswax candles on the stand in front of her. Her officious busyness was embarrassing her pretty daughter, who backed away from her mother pretending to have nothing to do with her. Mother was now engaged in furious rubbing to remove a lipstick stain from the glass that covered the ancient icon of the Mother of God. The kiss had just been planted by a Grushenka who stood by the icon. She wore a low-cut black-rayon frilly blouse, long pink gloves over her plump white forearms and a G-string of a scarf balanced on her improbably blonde and undulating hair. In the West, her body would have been thought absurdly overweight. Here she was a beauty, her proud frame like that royal dish, roast swan stuffed with peacock, duck and lark. Her complexion served as a reminder why the words 'red' and 'beautiful' go back to the same root in Russian. Having hauled her frame into an upright position after the kiss, Grushenka stretched to her full height and gave the Mother of God a level gaze, woman to woman.

The blond priest tricking out his tresses on his gold vestments and the bass with the sliding voice seemed suddenly peripheral to the central power here, which was female. Though the baby Christ might be at the centre of the icon, all around was the Mother of God, whose embrace was oblivion.

Two old men shuffled their way through the free-standing crowd and, as coins fell into the plate, it was as if an evening breeze passing through the leaves had brought down fat drops of summer rain. The message of this drama was *sobornost'*, that particularly Russian word which means 'togetherness with the crowd'. My 'I' may be no more than the rustle of a leaf on a tree. But here in this cathedral, the rustle of that leaf had been given meaning in the seductive mystery that unfolded in front of me.

IX

NOVOSIBIRSK

The Essential Spirit
of the Russian People

I walked down the streets of Novosibirsk the morning after the eight-hour flight from Moscow and wondered where the people were. Could this capital of Siberia really have one and a half million inhabitants? The pavements were empty of pedestrians and there were few cars. The streets were so broad that they looked as if they had been designed for mass troop movements. The only building I saw which was not modern was the attractive yellow-and-white nineteenth-century barracks, which stood in the middle of town. Even now, it looked large. A century ago, it must have towered over the town and its low wooden buildings.

Now the city was dominated by the Opera House in the main square, in front of which stood the statutory figure of Lenin. He was flanked by a happy crowd of bronze workers and soldiers, waving excitedly. I suppose they were celebrating what I had been reading about on the plane: 'The full and final victory of socialism in the Soviet Union, (which) means that as a result of the self-sacrificing labour of the Soviet people and the activity of the Communist Party in the realm of theory and practice, mankind received socialist society in its concrete realization.' The words came not from a tract that was now being pulped, but from the latest edition of the tenth-grade school history textbook, of which I had been lent an advance copy.

That was when I saw him, socialist realist man. He was standing in the bus, with his heroic muscular arm in the air, not waving, but holding on to the strap. It was not just that he was

293

taller than I could have imagined possible. His build was that of no man I had ever seen. Strangely I seemed to be the only one who was staring at him. The small, plump, pale people in the bus behaved as if he was one of them. His huge, cropped blond head was bowed down low to hear what his normal-sized companion was saying. His heroic face wore that expression of gentleness which giants can afford. His shoulders dominated the bus. They described no curves. His craggy brow and the huge biceps which protruded from his short-sleeved shirt had been hewn out in facets. It was as if, with the grand design in ruins, one fragment had made its own concrete realization in this magnificent post-Cubist Golem and walked off to live out its life in the Siberian plains.

Feeling the need to ground myself in the past after this apparition, I set off in search of the historical museum. The city was impressively clean and solid. But it looked as if the memory of the place had been wiped. What had Siberians, as opposed to Russian political exiles, been like before the industrial age? I wanted an answer to my own question. 'Keep going in that direction. You'll see it on the left . . .' a woman said to me. I took a short cut behind some buildings and stopped short. There in front of me, standing on the rutted earth of the empty lot behind the tall building that faced the square, stood a group of Siberian trappers, waving cheerfully. As I approached they did not disappear, a figment of my imagination, but resolved themselves into a collection of ancient costumes, hanging on stands and waving in the breeze. Draped over the back steps was an array of intricately embroidered boots, hats and richly worked carpets. They looked like a warmer, richer kind of American Indian. I made my way to the front of the building and asked the woman behind the counter for a ticket. 'Where to?' 'The museum, of course.' 'But there is no museum here. You'll have to go down to the station, then walk up to the Central Universal . . .' 'But what about the costumes out there, behind the building?' 'Oh, those. Yes, we did have an exhibition of costumes here. But it had to be taken off. The moths got it . . .'

In Novosibirsk, I was the guest of a friend of Elena's called Irina. She was a distinguished art historian. Why she chose to live in Siberia, so far from the centre of the art world, I did not ask. There was something in the manner of this beautiful woman which kept questions at bay. She was tall and slim, with fine bones and a cap of sleek dark hair. She looked as wary and as highly strung as a thoroughbred racehorse.

Irina lived in a spacious, high-ceilinged two-room apartment. I was becoming so Soviet that I could not think what she did with all this space when she was on her own. At the moment, however, a friend with housing problems was staying with her. Katya was a journalist, a cheerful woman of the kind that is always asked to be a prefect at school.

That first evening, the conversation kept coming back to the subject of the nationalist movement Pamyat'. Its influence was strong in Novosibirsk and particularly in Akademgorod, the adjoining town which had been founded in 1958 to house academics. Irina had recently smuggled a tape-recorder into a meeting called by Pamyat' to discuss the local film society's refusal to show a film about the nineteenth-century poet Lermontov. The thesis of the film was that Lermontov, who had been killed in a duel, had been the victim of the 'dark forces' of the international Jewish conspiracy. It was ironic that Pamyat' of all groups should have appropriated the arrogant, gifted Lermontov as one of 'theirs'. Within the gilded circle of society's officer class, the quarrel that had ended with Lermontov's death had been provoked by the spite of a mediocre man called Martynov whose father's name had been Solomon, but who was not Jewish. Martynov, nicknamed 'the Monkey' by Lermontov's set, had become the butt of Lermontov's wit for his habit of dressing up like a Tatar. He had challenged Lermontov because he did not like being laughed at. The petty quarrel might have resolved itself, but it had become fatal when the poet refused to fire at Martynov in the duel, calling him a fool. Stung, the little man had aimed at Lermontov's heart and hit. It was a very Russian story.

The theme developed by the Pamyat' speakers had a mad simplicity: all the great turning-points of Russian history had fallen into the clutches of the dark forces, with the reign of Peter the Great as the darkest of them all. Through the heckling and the crackling on my hostess's tape, the same phrases came back again and again: 'Dark forces have stolen the flame of *glasnost*! They have led us to the edge of the precipice so that our culture will fall into the abyss.' 'It is not easy to catch them,' shouted another voice: 'You have to know their catch-words . . .' A woman interrupted: 'All these so-called spontaneous contributions from the floor seem a bit too well organized for my liking . . .' 'Of course we're organized,' someone retorted: 'Revolutionary struggle, as Lenin so rightly said, must always be organized.' Another dissenter broke in: 'I know what you're really saying – that the Revolution was the work of the dark forces; that we have to wipe them out. Come on, out with it! Say it! Or are you afraid?' The sudden silence on the noisy tape, which Irina had recorded from inside her pocket, had been long and sinister. Every time she had moved, the tape had recorded a sound like a giant turning in his sleep.

Some local pedant was saying, in a voice quavering with emotion, that the film about Lermontov 'reclaimed film as an art form from foreign hands'. One of the fixations of the Russian nationalists was that the Jews had appropriated this most persuasive of the mass media in order to poison the minds of the great Russian people. '*Lermontov* represents the crowning achievement of this medium. Burlaev has caught in it the essential spirit of the Russian people . . .' the man gushed. The film had not been released in public cinemas. 'You only have to compare it to *Andrei Rublyov*,' the pedant continued, 'where Tarkovsky depicts the Russian people as dirty and drunken. In

296

the end, he couldn't conceal his extreme bourgeois individualism . . .' Ah, to witness the cant of the left become the cant of the right! 'His flight to the West showed him up in his true colours, as a man who put his "I" before the general good. Not being Russian, he just could not give in to the *sobornost'*.'

Sobornost', that word again; togetherness with the people. I had only become aware of it recently. Now I heard it everywhere. As the Pamyat' speaker had put it earlier, you have to know their catch-phrase. Was that really the essential spirit of the Russian people? In its nationalist form now rather than its Communist one, the giant that was turning over in its sleep was the Russian chimera of belonging. It had no way of defining itself except in relation to those that stood out from the crowd.

The Maximalists

My friends from the Looking Glass Theatre group in Kiev were playing in Novosibirsk for one night at the end of a long Siberian tour. Though I was delighted, I was not surprised at this coincidence. In this country where intention seemed baffled at every turn, Chance, that healthy child of Confusion, had proved reliable in her interventions, as long as I did not presume to count on her.

I went to buy a ticket at the huge concrete House of Culture where the performance was being held that night. As I stood in the cavernous entrance hall wondering whether I should leave my friends a note, a young man walked past. 'You must be Susanna,' he said. I had never met him before. 'I've seen a photograph of you. Did you know you were in the show tonight?'

I had heard that they were working on a new show called *Arbat*, which had arisen out of their September visit to Moscow. The young man took me backstage, where one of the girls hugged me delightedly: 'Say something! Say something! All these months I've been trying to get your accent right!' Volodya looked so fraught that I hurried away accompanied by Misha, the producer, who was the only member of the company not involved in the evening's performance.

Misha looked tired but unnervingly smart in his suit and tie. 'I can't tell you. It's been a nightmare,' he said as we walked through the streets, trying to find somewhere for a cup of coffee. 'We've spent the last two weeks in the most dreadful places, with performances every night. That pace may be possible in the West, but here you can't keep it up. A couple of days ago the net on the set caught fire, burning Ira's hair. How on earth were we to find another net out here, thousands of miles from the sea, in time for the next show? We ended up making one.

'The real problem is Volodya, the way he keeps rehearsing them all day. They're on the point of collapse. Did you see Vitaly? He looks like a ghost.' Volodya's brother Vitaly was the company's irreplaceable singer. 'Last night his heart began to flutter. He's always had a bad heart. They'd been up late, drinking and talking as usual. We called an ambulance. It took an hour to arrive. If we'd been locals it probably would not have come at all. But they're obliged to turn up for people in hotels. They took him in, gave him an injection and the doctor said: "That's all I can do. You can go home now." Vitaly had to walk all the way back. He was feeling terrible, he had no money on him, and no idea where he was except that it was miles from the hotel. Now he's got to go on tonight.'

Having failed to find a café that was open we ended up in Misha's hotel room, where he heated up water with his electric element, mug by mug. He was tense and his eyes glittered behind his spectacles. 'You know why we're doing this tour through the sticks, don't you? We were thrown out of our premises in Kiev. When we got back from our Moscow tour, Volodya said something on television that they didn't like and they threw us out of our new premises. All winter we have had nowhere regular to perform. So we do these tours. They're hell. But lucrative. Oh Susanna, you've come at a bad time. It's not just that Volodya's been overworking them. The new production, *Arbat*, is a disaster. Night after night the timing just hasn't worked. But Volodya's put everything into this show. If something doesn't change soon, the company'll break up.'

It appeared that apart from Volodya's brother, his girl-friend and Misha, they had all joined the rebellion against Volodya. I was touched by the loyalty of the level-headed Misha, who was anyway a curious figure to find in this wandering troupe of players. He talked with distaste of Volodya's dissolute habits. But he remained loyal because he was clear about the reasons for his own commitment. Volodya, as he put it, 'aspires to be better than himself. In that desperate battle against himself, he carries us with him. I see that aspiration as something sacred, something that makes him capable of a *podvig*.' It was a surprising word for him to use. It means a heroic feat. 'And I see Russia too as capable of that, if roused.' Misha's words made their own kind of sense to me. I had found the problems facing Russia far more intractable than I had imagined they could be. Yet I could not feel depressed. Not all of the people I had met were capable of a *podvig*. But I had found in them the same regenerative power that had taken me by surprise this spring, as the devastated earth had come out in an abundance of green.

The quality Misha saw in Volodya, an attraction to the heights and the depths, had something in it of what Alyosha Karamazov recognized in his brother Dmitri. We were liable to read Dostoevsky in the West as though his characters were creatures of the mind who had little to do with real people. But here I had kept meeting people who were possessed, like Dostoevsky's characters, by dreams. That quality of 'maximalism' characterized Zakarya in Dagestan; Valery, the independent farmer; Kukobaka, who had given his life for an idea; and Slava, who had left Moscow for a dream of building his own house. At this moment of choice in the life of their country, all of them had, like Volodya, thrown their lives into the Tolstoyan question of how men should live.

Whether any of them could win the battles they set for themselves against their stagnant society remained in doubt. The odds were against them. But if they failed, it would be because they had started too soon. These were the people

300

whom the next generation would have to thank for the habits of freedom their maximalism would have helped secure.

I arrived at the theatre to find that my hostess Irina and her friend Olga were already there. This was a bad beginning. Rather than being put off by my evasive reference to a fringe theatre group from Kiev who were friends of mine, they had been intrigued. I had certainly not told them that I was a character in their play and that it had been dedicated to me. After four months of having lived as unobtrusively as possible, I was having difficulty adjusting to the fact that, though I thought I had been doing the observing, I had been as closely observed myself. The bizarre ordeal of watching a version of myself, as seen through Russian eyes, strutting around on a stage in Siberia completely out of my control was not one I wanted to share with anyone.

I was in no position to judge that evening's performance of *Arbat*. I saw not a show, but another point of view on incidents that I remembered well. There was the poor young policeman who had turned so pale when he realized that he had boasted about his treacherous grandfather in front of a foreigner. There was the Stalinist old lady who had shouted at Vitaly on the Arbat to get him to stop singing. The beautiful stage version of myself, speaking with an embarrassingly bad Russian accent, talked of the Arbat as 'half-dream, half-nightmare', and I recognized the words as my own. For months I had been fancying myself as having travelled unobtrusively. But I had been as unobtrusive as a unicorn.

The audience seemed to enjoy the play whose slightly frantic gaiety had given way in the second half to surreal blackness. At the end we all stood in silence for one minute to commemorate the thirty-two people killed in a Tbilisi demonstration forty days earlier. That occasion, when troops had hacked with shovels at unarmed, praying people and sprayed them with poisonous chemicals, had marked Volodya's final loss of innocence. 'We thought Soviet troops were there to protect us,' he said to me later: 'We saw it happening in Northern Ireland, but we never thought something like that could happen here.' Fifteen years ago, I remember being asked by bewildered Russians what was really behind the Northern Ireland conflict. 'It obviously can't be because of religion,' people had said. 'And here, they tell us it's a colonial situation, so we know that can't be true.'

Afterwards, the actors invited me to a party that was being thrown in their honour. On the way, Sasha the clown took my arm as we walked through the night: 'You know, we weren't just paying you a compliment when we dedicated the play to you. Without you there would have been a play called *Arbat*. But it was you who made us see it all with new eyes. All winter, while we rehearsed, we kept asking each other what you would have said about this or that character. Thank goodness you turned up tonight. You probably had no idea that tonight was decisive for us. We've done four performances of *Arbat* and each one has been a fiasco. The group was falling apart. I have to admit that I had lost faith in Volodya. Then you appear and the play comes together for the first time. You're our lucky talisman.'

She Had to be a Nut

We sat on the floor of a large room round a blanket where a feast had been laid out in honour of the Looking Glass Theatre group. A grey cat stepped disdainfully between us. Relief at the success of the performance took the actors in various ways. Misha keeled over and fell asleep in the middle of saying something. Volodya just sat and smiled. Vitaly poured out his feelings in song after song.

Next to me on the floor sat a woman who introduced herself as Marina. She had a thick bob of shoulder-length hair and a strong face with flaring nostrils. Every few seconds her slim body was shaken as she breathed out in a gust, as if to expel a feather from her nose. Each time this happened her face contorted. As she served a spoonful of meatballs across my lap she said to me: 'Don't worry, I won't drop it. I worked as a waitress for far too long. Over the last fifteen years I have done as many jobs as there have been years.' She was speaking in my ear: 'Now I've given up thinking I can do anything except write poetry. If I'd stayed here all the time I couldn't have gone on. I go and stay with friends in other towns. Then, when I come back, I know there's something for me to live for, because for them I'm a poet. I'm not Siberian.' She hurried on as if expecting to be cut off: 'I have no idea what I'm doing here except that my father was chief engineer at a huge plant here. I'm going to get out. We'll go to Chelyabinsk, I think.' If you start from Novosibirsk, Chelyabinsk is half-way to Moscow. Vitaly had just finished a song. Marina leaned over the blanket to take the guitar from him. The poem she sang was driven by a wild sadness so out of keeping with the mood of the evening that it silenced the room. While she sang, her face cleared and became beautiful. 'I will go mad if I stay here,' Marina continued, once the song was over. Her tic had returned and every time she breathed out, she snorted in my ear. She talked faster and faster, as though 'they' were coming to take her away. 'I did spend a week in a madhouse once, but I'm lucky that is all. I got married for the first time when I was nineteen, to a man who worked for the Fraud Police. I suppose I must have married him out of our infinite female capacity for self-torture. There isn't any other explanation. We were together for five years and throughout that time he was writing down all my eccentricities in a book. To what end I shall never know. Maybe it was just professional habit, but it nearly sent me mad. Luckily, that particular madhouse was not the kind that humiliates you by shaving your head and stripping you naked for inspection before driving you out to work. I was terribly lucky to get out in a week. It's unheard of for them to admit that they've made a mistake. My father did it. He moved heaven and earth, produced all my diplomas, dozens of testimonials, read them my poetry. I also went on hunger strike. They didn't like that one bit. What's so funny is that in the end they released me with a glowing testimonial to work in a literary institute!

'The reason I got there is the craziest thing. After my aunt hanged herself I really did slit my veins. I wanted to die then. She'd been like a mother to me. But it was a month later that they took me in. I'd practically recovered by then. I got this high, high temperature one night and they all got worried and took me to hospital. There was no room in the ordinary ward, so they put me in this luxurious empty ward reserved for crooks who can pay their way. Then, suddenly, one of Them was admitted and they needed the room. So they bunged me into the madhouse. A woman with no papers – because I'd been admitted in the middle of the night – who had slit her wrists, well, she had to be a nut.'

The party went on late. Night-time in Russia is the time when you do not even have to pretend to be working and people make the most of it. Under Stalin it had been another matter. Then the lights in the Ministries had burned through the night, compelled by the dictator's insomnia. My friends in the Looking Glass Theatre were leaving for Kiev at dawn. Although more and more of the actors had dropped out of the circle to fall asleep hunched against the wall, they had decided against going to bed.

It was past 3 a.m. when we all left. The streets were deserted and it took some time before we could flag down a rare car prepared to take me home. I was accompanied by a physicist from Akademgorod with a romantic face. All evening he had been fawning on Volodya, as the star of the evening. But now that he heard I was English and writing a book, he tried to make up for lost time by overwhelming me with attention. 'Why go home now? Why not come and see the beauty of dawn in the Gorodok?' The affectionate local name for Akademgorod means Little Town.

As he finally sped off in the car we had flagged down, leaving me at the foot of the staircase off which Irina's flat led, I felt pleased that he had agreed to leave in so gentlemanly a fashion. I walked slowly up the lighted stairs to the second floor, thinking over the long day. I put the key in the lock. It would not turn. Fool that I am, I thought, I must have the wrong staircase. The five-storey block in which Irina lived had about half a dozen staircases leading into it along the front of the building. Three flats opened off the staircase at each level. Cursing my carelessness, I walked along to the next staircase and went up to the second floor. The staircase was laid out identically, but somehow it felt wrong. The gloss paint on the walls was a slightly deeper shade of blue than I remembered, and there was a third lock on the door and an unfamiliar spyhole. None the less, I tried the lock. No luck. The third staircase was quite wrong. The trouble was that I had been so sure of the way that I had not even brought the address with me.

I retraced my footsteps to the first staircase, to the door that ought to have been Irina's. Maybe I had just been trying too hard. I tried less hard, with a detached casualness. The key did not move at all. By now a little dog had woken up in a flat on the same landing and started to bark. Perhaps its owners would appear at the door, I thought with hope. They did not. Why should they? I was reminded of a film called *The Irony of Fate* by Ryazanov. It was a comedy and I had thought it funny at the time. Its hero gets drunk and ends up walking into the life of a complete stranger with his own key, at his own address – but in the wrong city. At least I know this is Novosibirsk. And I know it is the right block.

Or do I? I had got to know the way by walking from the Metro. But tonight I arrived by car. There could be mile upon mile of similar blocks in Novosibirsk. I could be anywhere. Perhaps I had better make sure that the Metro was where I thought it was and work back from there. I set off through the trees. As I walked the story that kept coming back was Olga's account of her narrow escape from two drunken men with knives . . . The girls had been saying only last night that they never walked home alone at night. It was too risky. The matter-of-factness drained out of me. I stopped and gazed into the night. There was not a breath of wind. The still trees, benches, see-saw and swings in the distance were full of threat. A blonde foreign woman, lost in the Siberian night? How would you say in Russian, 'She was asking for it, guv'? I scuttled back to the first staircase and tried the floor above the flat that should have been Irina's. The scratches on the otherwise identical door looked alien. But how could I trust my memory now? I tried the door anyway. No luck.

At least I had Irina's number. I needed to find a telephone.

But that would involve another foray into the night, and in what direction? I strode off into the night, away from the Metro, and re-enacted my arrival from the airport by taxi. The place did seem familiar. But by now I had no confidence in my own power of recollection. I could be anywhere. I was anywhere. My mind had become an entire theatre group, moving wildly from role to role. I was purposeful. I was amused. I was coldly analytical. Anything in order not to have to face the fact that I was just scared, for the first time in many months in the Soviet Union. The irony was that no one was scaring me but myself. My awareness of the absurdity of the situation was no comfort. Cold and tired, I sat on the step outside the flat which still might be Irina's, planning to go to sleep until it was light. So much for being the Looking Glass Theatre's lucky talisman. I should not have given all the luck away.

There Will be No War, but ...

As the sun streamed in through the window next morning, I
was in no hurry to get up. It was a luxury simply to know
where I was. The explanation for last night's drama had been
predictably dull. Irina had absent-mindedly put up the latch
when she went to bed, so that the key would not turn. In the
end I had plucked up courage and rung the bell.

I was reading an extraordinary book which Katya's eight-
year-old nephew had taken out of his school library for me. It
was about a Soviet saint of about his age called Pavel Morozov.
The story was not a nice one. It exemplified the question
which, throughout the century, had underlain so many others,
like the smallest doll within a nest of Russian dolls: how could
a society that believed that the claims of the state overrode all
claims of the individual fail to make monsters of men? I had
been taken aback to find that even now public gardens and
institutions everywhere were still called after 'Pavlik' Morozov.

As a little boy growing up in the Urals, 'Pavlik' had read
about the glorious advent of Soviet power and wondered why
things had not changed in the village where his family lived.
Burning with zeal to realize Ilich's dream, 'Pavlik' had started a
Pioneer group in his school, although there were as yet neither
Party nor Komsomol members in his village. The year was
1931, and the country was in the throes of collectivizing its
agriculture, at a cost of about 14.5 million lives. 'Pavlik' had
discovered that his father, who was chairman of the village
Soviet, was accepting bribes in return for categorizing rich

peasants as poor ones. Ah, poverty equals wealth, the familiar scam again. 'Pavlik' denounces his father, who is sent into exile. His outraged grandfather then murders the little boy and his younger brother on their way home from collecting cranberries in the forest.

Katya relayed to me the conversation she had had with her nephew when he gave her the book: ' "Why was 'Pavlik' Morozov a hero?" Sergei asked me. "Because he betrayed his father," I told him. Behind his back, my sister was making these awful faces at me to shut up. She thinks it's better to say nothing than to tell the truth.' The story had revolted me when I read it years ago. Now it just made me sad. It contained a grotesque echo of the lives of those favourite Orthodox saints, the princely brothers Boris and Gleb. Their virtue had lain in their having offered no resistance when their older brother sent assassins to murder them. Revered for centuries for their meekness, they had become the patron saints of Russia. Although Pavel Morozov was not a passive figure, his age made him the innocent conduit of a ruthless ethic. But there were elements of his literalness, or innocence, in many of the finest adults I had met. Perhaps this was more than a matter of education? Was it not the other side of that dangerous and exciting quality of 'maximalism' which attracted the theatre's producer Misha in Volodya?

Towards midday, Irina, Katya and I set off to attend an important event in the life of the Siberian capital. An open-air meeting had been called to protest at the fate of the city's Alexander Nevsky cathedral. Whatever might have been going on under the surface, the life of Novosibirsk had been undisturbed by the breath of change until now. But judging by the flood of letters in the local newspaper, feeling was high about this issue. The cathedral had been confiscated in 1937 and used as an office ever since. It was now intended that it should be renovated and made into a cultural centre and home for the city's chamber choir. Popular feeling held that it should be given back to the Church.

309

The notion of making it into an arts centre was the perfect reformist solution from the point of view of the authorities. The building was being returned to a 'spiritual' purpose. I had been intrigued by the way the word 'spiritual' had been adapted for secular use in the Soviet vocabulary. In the 1988 history textbook for schools, for instance, the section entitled 'Spiritual Life of the Country' was all about libraries, museums and theatres. It contained not a word about religion.

The meeting had been jointly organized by the two far poles of the political spectrum, Pamyat' and the Western-orientated Democratic Union. Word had it that Pamyat' had been told to lie low and let the Democratic Union run the meeting. We turned up at the steps of the big modern building appointed for the occasion to find a crowd of respectable middle-aged men and women standing about uncertainly. There were plenty of policemen too, high-ranking ones. Near us stood a major and a colonel with a dog. Even they too looked unsure of themselves. No one seemed quite certain what should happen next. A woman with an inquisitive peasant face, who turned out to be a distant relation of Katya's, walked up and asked her in a stage whisper, 'Which side are you on, then?' It sounded as if we were playing a party game. 'The Church's, of course,' answered Katya. 'Well, that's all right then. That Müller who runs the chamber choir, he must be a Jew . . .' 'You're quite wrong. He's German,' tartly. 'Well,' said the woman magnanimously, as though side-stepping a quarrel, 'that's as maybe. But his deputy's certainly a *khokhol*.' *Khokhol* is an ugly word for a Ukrainian. 'What of that?' retorted Katya.

After we had listened to a few passionate and amateurish speeches from the microphone, a competent young man from the Democratic Union informed us that this was no longer a political meeting: 'We applied for a meeting, but we have been granted permission for a demonstration instead. So now we will march to the cathedral. Please do not bunch up when going over the foot-bridge as we have been warned that it might fall down.'

On receipt of this improbable instruction, we set off for the cathedral, banners high: 'You stole it, give it back.' 'The choir can have the Centre for Political Education.' This turned out to be the new building to our right. Vast and gleaming white, it had absorbed huge sums of money and now stood empty, a focus of local hatred. We were joined by a crowd of school-children who had come to support one of the schoolboy organizers of the demonstration. The bridge over which we had to pass turned out to be completely modern. No one took the slightest notice of the young man's warning, but our luck held and we passed safely over, colonel, dogs and all.

In high spirits, we arrived at the boarded-up cathedral. The atmosphere among these ill-assorted people was more like that of a wedding than a demonstration. Someone had been distribut-ing little flags, red, blue and white. 'It's the old Russian flag!' said a very old woman with a cry of recognition. 'I never thought I'd live to see that again.' 'What shall we do next?' asked a young man who was wheeling a pram and holding his flag like a wishbone. 'Let's have a hunger strike!' suggested a pretty girl with long chestnut hair gaily, in a tone that sounded more like a proposal to feast than to starve. I caught a glimpse of what looked like an Edwardian fop in a white suit and monocle. I looked again. He was gone. Was I seeing things?

A skinny young man climbed up on the fence: 'Before the Revolution, the Church employed 360,000 church workers and had 55,173 churches . . .' The colonel with the dog was standing by me. He sighed deeply, borrowed a loudspeaker from one of the Democratic Union organizers, and interrupted the young man: 'The demonstration is over. The crowd must disperse.' He paused and added doubtfully, 'Otherwise we will have to use force.' 'Why are you stopping us?' a venerable old man wagged his finger at the colonel: 'I'm a Communist myself, and surely you must agree that this is all most interesting and entirely healthy.' The colonel pushed his cap to the back of his head and blew out like a whale before muttering something

311

that sounded like 'I'm blowed if I know what to do'. 'In 1919, there were only 40,000 priests still alive . . .' With Democratic Union organizers tugging at both his legs, the skinny young man went on, balanced on a post high above the crowd: 'In 1927 there were 28,734 churches left. In 1941 . . .' He disappeared into the crowd, still shouting: 'There were 4,225 and in 1980, 7,500.' No, I had not imagined the fop. There he was again, a man who had spent seventy years in moth-balls. He was young, with pink cheeks and a straggling moustache. He wore a monocle. His white suit was exquisitely cut and he wore it complete with a white tie, wing collar and onyx tie-pin. The whole ensemble must have belonged to his great-grandfather.

It had not been a wedding but a christening, I thought, as the three of us made our way home armed with our little Russian pre-revolutionary flags. It had been the christening of political activity in the city. Never again would there be quite the feeling of innocence that there had been today. The seriousness of the cause had been drowned out simply by the celebration of freedom of expression. Next time the Democratic Union and Pamyat' would be on opposite sides. Next time the police would know what to do and the Communist might be more worried than he was interested. But today the three of us were giggling as if we had had too much champagne.

The telephone was ringing as we entered the flat. Katya picked it up. It was her nephew Sergei: 'Good to hear you . . . You've been watching a film in which they make those nice little round bombs in this Byelorussian village and wipe out the Whites with them?' She pulled a face. Her beloved nephew's militarism pained her. 'How interesting . . . No, we haven't been watching it . . . Have I seen a film called *Rambo*? About a chap in a red headscarf who wipes out hundreds of little gooks? No, but I know what you mean. Don't take those films too seriously, will you . . . Would an American horror film be any better? Well, not really. They all just fry the brains. You saw what in the road this afternoon? A car wheel? Very what? It's a bad line. Ah, wasteful. I quite agree. Like mother throwing out your bicycle wheel the other day, you mean? Absolutely. People should look after their things more carefully. By the way, Susan wanted to thank you for getting *Pavel Morozov* out for her. She found it very . . . helpful. What? Of course you should read it before taking it back to the library . . . Mother said not to? I think you are quite old enough. It's a difficult story, but it raises interesting questions . . .'

Until a few weeks ago, Katya had still been living in a two-room flat with her sister, brother-in-law and nephew. Now her parents were moving in with her sister, so that she could find a one-room flat on her own. She was the only one in the family with a higher education. 'For the child it has always been hard, because whatever his parents said, and his grandparents too, I said the opposite.' Later in the evening, he rang again for another chat. I got the feeling that Seryozha had already made his choice.

It was my last evening in Novosibirsk. 'I don't know what you have done to the city,' said Irina as we prepared a meal. 'But it's not normally like this at all. Nothing actually happens in Novosibirsk . . .' This afternoon, she had been happy. But now I watched as the sadness descended on her again. I would not presume to ask this beautiful, proud woman what had gone so wrong with her life that the most she could do was seek to distract herself from her unhappiness. Only once did she make any allusion to her sadness. I had invited her to visit me in London, thinking with pleasure how she would be appreciated there. 'I'm sorry, but I can't come,' she said with an unmistakable finality. She palmed me off with a number of unconvincing reasons. Finally she said, unwillingly: 'These last few years, I've had a . . . little depression. Nothing dramatic. Just a little depression. I don't think I could bear to see the West.' Perhaps it was the wine that made me insensitive. But at

313

that moment I did not accept her reason as good. She was forced to offer me some explanation. 'I have a close friend who went to London during the stagnant years. It was the first time she'd been to the West, and everyone was very nice to her. But because she had an interpreter with her, a charming girl, she was never able to be on her own. It became unbearable. In the end, the only place to which she could get away was Trafalgar Square. She stood there among the pigeons and she wept, wept openly for what they'd done to us.'

It was Katya who broke the silence, leaping up with the familiar words: 'Let's have a cup of tea. A cup of tea with jam.' And the words, spoken with conviction, acted as they did again and again in this country full of ghosts, to draw a circle round the people in that room and drive the shadows out. Strong tea with home-made jam. In it there was none of the oblivion of the vodka bottle. But there was comfort and a binding of friends.

'Now let me tell you one of my favourite jokes, from Armenia,' said Irina, laughing as she completed the act of exorcism: '"Will there be war?" "No, there will be no war. But there will be such a peace that not one stone will be left standing on another."'

X

MOSCOW

A Visit from the Pink Fairy

Bella came round this morning to say goodbye. She had news, and she had dressed up to deliver it. Her pink dress had a tight bodice and full flounced skirt, held out by stiff petticoats. In this monochrome city where even the oranges were grey, the sight of so much colour was almost pornographic. Balanced inexpertly on high-heeled shoes, her hands enveloped in pink gloves, she looked like the kind of vision that visits men after months at sea.

We sat in the sunshine on a bench near the flat. Since I last saw it the tatty corner had transformed itself into an enchanted garden. Wild strawberries, peonies and forget-me-nots were growing in careless exuberance round the lilac-trees. Bella was bubbling with excitement. 'Susanna, Susanna, you will never believe what I have to tell you,' she clasped her pink-gloved hands together, tears in her eyes. 'Today, Andrei set off to negotiate a million-rouble contract for his cooperative.'

'Cooperative? What cooperative?' Andrei, she told me, had just given up his job running the maintenance department of a state building-supplies firm, to become deputy chairman of a firm that specialized in building-maintenance. 'He couldn't sleep at night in the old job. He was the only one who really understood how dangerous the main boiler in the factory was. He said it was a miracle that it was still working at all. From minute to minute he feared that it would collapse. Oh, Susanna. Since he left, he's a new man.'

Eight months ago Andrei had still been dreaming of a career

317

as a full-time Party functionary. Until then he had succeeded in believing only what he had been taught to believe. Bella had feared for him then. 'I don't know what he will believe in next,' I remembered her saying to me at the baths in the autumn. But Andrei had proved resilient. In the spring, he had turned down the Party job for which he had waited so long. Now he had found a place in the new economy where he could provide well for his family and remain an honest man. 'If he pulls off this contract, he will get ten per cent of the deal for himself! And he's not cheating anyone!' said the pink fairy, as she hugged me and gave me the largest box of chocolates I had ever seen.

In Novosibirsk or Stavropol', history felt like something that happened elsewhere. In Moscow, on the other hand, every event in the Soviet Union seemed to pass into the bloodstream of the capital. Today, the day before the new Congress of People's Deputies was due to open, Sverdlovsk had elected Leonid Kudrin as its representative, by seventy per cent. The final round had, as anticipated, been between Kudrin, the lorry-driver, and Mesyats, the official candidate. Sverdlovsk's Party and state apparatus could not be accused of having underestimated the threat of this man Kudrin, whose appeal was nothing but his honesty. All means had been deployed to stop him. In one district, a woman reported that the ballot papers had been given out with all other candidates except Mesyats crossed out. When she had asked how she could vote when the choice had been made for her, she was told: 'If you do not want to vote, you don't have to.' In the local press, which I had been following, Kudrin had been accused of having raped a schoolgirl when he was a teacher and of having beaten his pupils. He was even accused of having refused to bury his own mother. This was an odd charge, as Kudrin had no idea who his mother was. She had abandoned him at a children's home when he was three.

The campaign had culminated in a live television interview set up by the Mesyats camp, who assumed that the experienced politician and academic would demolish Kudrin. 'But Mesyats was routed by Kudrin's simplicity,' Grisha had reported. 'For instance, they were both asked about their attitude to religion. Mesyats went on and on about his respect for the Church, his desire to protect it, and so on and so forth. Kudrin simply said: "Poor things, my heart goes out to them. I am not a believer myself. But if the Church had more power, we would not face the problems that we do."' Grisha smiled. 'Next day, the Church throughout the region, which had been under intense pressure to back Mesyats, had been saying prayers for Kudrin . . .'

The Car That Belonged to Kaganovich

'What Russian does not love fast driving? How could his soul, which is so eager to whirl round and round, to forget everything in a mad carouse, to exclaim sometimes, "To hell with it all!" – how could his soul not love it? . . . Oh you troika, you bird of a troika, who invented you? You could only have been born among a high-spirited people in a land that does not like doing things by halves, but has spread in a vast smooth plain over half the world . . . Russia, where are you flying to? Answer! She gives no answer . . . Everything on earth is flying past, and, looking askance, other nations and states draw aside and make way for her.'

Gogol, *Dead Souls*
(tr. David Magarshack)

My farewell party was to be held in the back of a car. It was no ordinary car, but one which had been owned by Kaganovich, one of Stalin's henchmen. It had just been bought by Masha, an ex-girl-friend of Grisha's, who had become an instantly successful businesswoman. If she had not happened to ring Grisha up just as Ira, Grisha and I were going out to a film, we would probably never have met: 'Grisha darling, tell me something worth listening to,' she had moaned. 'But you're a rich lady now. You're the one with the glamorous, high-powered life. What could I possibly tell you that would be of any interest . . .' 'Ah, but I'm so bored. Making money is so dull. Tell me something spiritual . . .' After the film, Grisha, Ira and I had gone round to see whether a bottle of Cinzano would cheer her up.

The door had been opened by an enormous woman who swamped Grisha in a bear-hug. Above Grisha's head, her face was creased into a smile so broad that her eyes had disappeared into slits. Her body was clad in a shapeless black skirt and jersey and old slippers. Masha did not look like the conventional idea of an entrepreneur, let alone one in the fashion business. But after only four months, she already employed 100 people. The only limitation on the size of her business seemed to be the difficulty of getting hold of material. Western businessmen had offered to back her. 'But do I really want Western capital?' she sighed. 'If I were doing any better, life would become unbearable.'

Although her flat showed no sign of money having been spent on it, this unusual woman had spent much of the evening complaining about the difficulties she was having giving her money away: 'I went to this hospital and asked them if I could give them anything. The problem was that they needed everything: dressing-gowns, sheets, towels, everything. So I said: "How about my adopting a ward and buying anything that they need?" But no, that turned out to be impossible too, because the other wards were ready to revolt.'

It was not that Masha was a saint. But she was untouched by the expectations that money breeds. It seemed natural to her to regard any money that she did not immediately need as available for some grand design. At the end of the evening, she had gone to the kitchen, opened the oven door and pulled out two tightly bound wads of roubles, the size of bricks, which she tossed in the air. 'These are the two back wheels of our new limousine,' she told me. 'It used to belong to Kaganovich. I'll have it before you leave. Then we'll do the town in it.' Tonight we were doing the town in Kaganovich's car.

Grisha, Ira, Elena and I arrived to find Masha and her husband, and the Old Believer Pavel already admiring the black Zil. Sinuously curved, gleaming, it stretched out along the road like a panther enjoying the evening sun. It was in perfect condition, having spent the last few decades sitting in a garage in the country. The seventy-two-year-old Kaganovich still had two years left in power in 1955 when he got his new car. Thirty-five years later, with the new Soviet parliament due to open tomorrow, the Zil was a potent vehicle for carnival celebration. Tonight, we would drive the old world out and usher in the new.

Blowing smoke rings from Stalin's own brand of tobacco, the seven of us sat back in the deep leather seats as Kaganovich's car rolled through the broad streets and down towards the river. As we gathered speed past the Kremlin, other cars drew aside, assuming at least that we represented the power of the mafia. The car seemed to gravitate naturally towards the centre of the road, not spluttering and hugging the kerb like Grisha's car before its demise. Now we were passing the vast open-air Swimming-Pool of Christ the Redeemer, as many people called it, after the cathedral of that name on whose site it had been built. It had been blown up with revolutionary zeal in 1934.

As we bowled along, I thought of Gogol's flying troika. His plans for its owner, Chichikov, had been overtaken by doubt and death and Chichikov remains for us the endearing villain who invented the Dead Souls scam. 'A villain?' Gogol anticipated the remarks of people like me: 'Why a villain? Why be so severe on people? It would be fairer to call him a business man, a money-maker.' Our Zil contained not only a less equivocal money-maker, but other characters of whose qualities Russia stood now in desperate need. But fine as they were, the question remained, carried as we were by Kaganovich's car: could they overcome the momentum of the past?

We drew up at a fine set of wrought-iron gates, behind which yellow-and-white eighteenth-century monastery buildings were clustered around a church. The wooded enclosure through which we carried our feast to Masha's office seemed a place out of time. In a city where premises had become prohibitively expensive for new businesses, Masha had been offered hers for a nominal rent by a state enterprise which liked the way she worked. Flinging open the doors with the glee of a child who has the run of her parents' house, she conducted us through room after room of newly decorated offices: 'I know it must look like an old boot-room to you,' she said to me, 'but to us it is paradise.' After a winter here, it looked like paradise to me too. The work had all been done free, in their spare time, by the husbands of the women who worked for her.

What was the secret of this huge, dimpled woman, that people gave her offices, did them up for her, and pleaded with her for work? Although she talked as if she were the beneficiary of a number of happy accidents, it was to her vision that people were attracted: 'I only take on people who would not otherwise be able to work. Either they've got small children, or they're not well. They work at home and come in once a week. They love coming in. It's cosy here.' Her employees could end up earning three times what they received working for the state. But for all this, her shirts, which were pretty and well sewn, cost half the price of those made by the state.

However effective Masha's vision was, at the point where her business depended on the Dead Souls economy, she remained powerless. She winced as Ira and I looked at the shirts: 'I know they look nice, but I'm ashamed to sell them. After a few washes, the material will be fit for the garbage. But what can we do? It's the best there is. The thread's rotten too. We can only make sure that the shirts are well cut and well sewn and not too expensive.' I looked round the bare shelves of her store-room. 'But where do you keep your material?' I asked. 'This is it. We only just keep ahead, from week to week. Even paying over the odds, it's impossible to find more.'

Masha and Grisha had been friends since their schoolays.

As we spread out our feast in one of the empty rooms, the two of them began to reminisce about an extraordinary teacher they had had: 'He was short and tubby, with fingers like plump little sausages. Grisha was his favourite pupil. But I was his favourite. Back in the early seventies, we were reading Solzhenitsyn at school. He would give us the formal lesson and then say to us, "Now, children, close your exercise books, and let's just talk." Then he would tell us about the camps, about Stalin's paranoia and Beria's lechery. He told us things our parents did not know. But he had a way of saying: "Let's keep this between ourselves, shall we?" After that, nothing in the world would have dragged the information out of us.'

As we listened, we sampled drinks whose names were familiar to them, but which they had never tasted: Bols, Martini, Gordons, Bordeaux, Vermouth. For me, they were just drinks. For them, they were staging posts on a fantastical journey. 'In the end,' Grisha went on, 'it was that way he had of sharing information with us that nearly got him the sack. One day, he started talking off the record and for some reason one of the girls wrote down what he was saying. That was completely against the rules. Why she did it I have no idea, but I'm sure it wasn't malicious. She probably just wanted to remember what he was saying. And of course, her parents got hold of the book, as parents will, and went to the headmaster. Next day he just wasn't there. Someone else took the class. When we found out what had happened, parents, children, everyone, we all went to the local Party offices and demanded that he be reinstated. And he was.' Grisha paused. 'The things we did to that poor girl. I hate to remember.'

We all changed drinks and Masha picked up the story: 'For a while, it was all right. But it was bound to end badly. He drank like a fish and the parents weren't usually so supportive.' 'Indeed, they weren't,' Grisha interrupted. 'My father was insanely jealous. I used to come home and say: "Alexei Dmitreevich said this" and "Alexei Dmitreevich said that . . ." He used to get all hot under the collar: "Well, I don't agree about this and that,"' Grisha huffed and puffed, imitating his father, ridiculous in his pain. 'He'd try being all wise and informative. But, unlike Alexei Dmitreevich, he didn't *know* anything . . .' 'He even proposed to me at one point,' Masha took over again. 'I adored him, but my parents said no and that was that. What was so touching was that the whole class was determined that I should "save" him by marrying him.'

Masha sighed. 'He was an odd one. He seemed to have no family, no background at all. Once we accompanied him to some block where he said he lived. At the door to the staircase, he said goodbye and disappeared inside. We hung around, as we were curious and suspected something funny. After about ten minutes, out he came again, settled on a bench and went fast asleep. I took his passport out of his pocket and looked at it. His registered address was somewhere out in the sticks. That was how we came to know that he was a BOMZH.' BOMZH was the acronym for a homeless person. 'We never told him, of course.' Masha sighed: 'He rings up from time to time. Last time was on my birthday, in February. He said: "I'm on my way. I'll be staying a week." That's what he used to do. Just turn up. But this time he didn't. I'm glad. He'd hate what we've become.'

What Alexei Dmitreevich had been to Grisha and Masha, Grisha had been for me. I looked at my Virgil as he sat with his arm around his wife, his plump face turning a strange shade of pink as we worked our way through the bottles. When Gorbachev had embarked on *glasnost'* five years before, he had set out to tap what he saw as the unused potential of the intelligentsia. But having got what they wanted, freedom of speech, most of them had dropped out of the struggle and returned to their role as armchair critics. Masha and Grisha were different. Until six months ago, Masha had been a journalist, and before that a teacher. It was only now that she had discovered that her real talent was for business. As for Grisha, without whom

Sverdlovsk would now have a different deputy, his writing was devoted to effecting change. Something had stayed alive in both of them, a quality of innocence which left them free to see the situation for what it was without being immobilized by what they saw.

'I had a wonderful teacher once . . .' Again and again I had heard those words from the people I had met who had emerged from the experience of totalitarianism unblinkered but with their will unbroken. Teachers were among the lowest-paid workers. For teachers, there were no special shops, no food parcels nor doctors in discreet private clinics. Yet the role of teacher, often by far the most educated person in a rural community, had for decades been an exposed one. A true word from a teacher, whose job it was to shape the minds of the next generation, could cost the applicant his, or more often her, career. Yet fine people had gone on joining this unrewarded profession, and they had gone on taking risks, in order to pass on to the next generation their obstinate faith in man. In drinks of many colours, we toasted the homeless teacher that night. It was a sight he would have enjoyed.

And the Fräulein Escaped

A Young Pioneer of seven was standing at the row of sinks in the Ladies at the Lenin Museum. She caught sight of her reflection in the mirror that extended along the wall on both sides of the room and smiled with pleasure. Reproduced an infinity of times in the double mirrors, she saw her trim figure in its fresh white shirt, blue skirt, and red Pioneer scarf. Her blonde hair was elaborately coiled and pinned and from the top of her head rose two enormous white bows like the ears of a startled rabbit. Through the doorway, her waiting friends called to her. Hundreds of fair-haired little girls raised their hands quite unnecessarily, to straighten their Pioneer scarves one last time, in order to enjoy for a moment longer this enchanting glimpse of unanimity.

On the first day of the new parliament, I had been unable to bear sitting at home any longer watching the proceedings on television. Restlessly I had dropped in to see how the founder was taking it. It was he who had closed the last Soviet parliamentary experiment by force in 1918 after only twenty-four hours. Lenin had been pleased with this 'complete and frank liquidation of the idea of democracy by the idea of dictatorship'. His tactics had been brilliant in the short term. They had allowed his minority group to seize power. But they had committed him to a political future which could only be sustained by force in that vast peasant country.

A man with a country complexion was making his way methodically round the rooms with his small son. Otherwise

327

the museum was almost empty today. 'I want to say this: yes, we have come a long way, particularly in self-knowledge.' The words, uttered in the jerky rhythm of Gorbachev's provincial accent, ricocheted off the high walls: 'How do we see ourselves . . . what is going on in the world around us . . . how must we transform both the internal political life of our country and our views of the outside world . . .' They came from a little transistor radio clamped to the ear of the elderly attendant who sat with her shoulders bowed, oblivious to her surroundings. In the next room sat another attendant, also listening, as were they all, in room after room throughout the museum.

Down the corridor I came across the Young Pioneers again, clustered round a glass case. In it hung the overcoat Lenin had been wearing when he was shot in August 1918 by a girl of proletarian parentage. She had felt betrayed by his brutal disbanding of that first Soviet parliament, the Constituent Assembly. But their lively tour guide did not mention why Fanya Kaplan did it. Her charges were being entranced with a heroic fantasy: 'The Social Revolutionary had bought South American poison and put it on the bullets to make sure that he would die, however lightly wounded he was.' 'Why did the poison not kill him?' asked the pretty girl, with a catch in her voice, throwing back her head. 'We will never know the reason. It is a miracle. Perhaps the traders who had sold it on the black market had cheated the SRs.' It was an inspired application of her own post-revolutionary experience of speculators. 'Perhaps the poison ceased to work once it was fired. Whatever the reason, he was spared for history and for us.'

That same summer, the Tsar and all his family had not been so lucky. They had been gunned down in a basement room in Ekaterinburg, now called Sverdlovsk, where Kudrin had just been elected People's Deputy. A Soviet journalist had recently claimed to have found the bodies. Wherever I had been in the last few months, everyone had been talking of the shooting of this unarmed group of men, women and children. They all talked as if it had just happened. 'If they could do that to unarmed women and children, including a haemophiliac little boy, they could do anything,' as Irina had said the other day. They talked not as monarchists, but as people freshly impressed by the value of life. In 1918, history had been moving in the opposite direction. It was after the attempt on Lenin's life that Zinoviev, as he mobilized Red Army soldiers to search out class enemies in the streets, had uttered the phrase: 'The bourgeois kill separate individuals. But we kill whole classes.'

Later that night, Grisha and I had gone to find Kudrin in the vast Rossiya Hotel. It had taken us some time to negotiate our way past the bulky security guards. When we got through to his room, he was sitting on his bed with his chin in his hands, looking as if he'd just been taken into custody. 'Oh, don't congratulate me. I sat there today and my back ached and my head ached and I thought, "What the hell am I doing here?" For the first time I found myself regretting that I ever allowed myself to be put forward. It's a farce.' Kudrin had the straightforward good looks that Hollywood buys in to represent its idea of good. 'The thing's sewn up from the start. Gorbachev's behaving appallingly. The only good thing about today is that you could see he was afraid. Afraid for the first time . . .'

The visit had not been a success. As Kudrin grumbled on about the new parliament, I had become alarmed. What did he expect from a totalitarian country enjoying its first day of democratically elected parliament for seventy years? And how would this innocent man survive the ordeal of power? It was only afterwards that I realized that Kudrin was in a state of shock. Eight months previously, he had unwittingly sparked off a chain of events which had carried him from total obscurity to national prominence, leaving him not a day to collect himself.

Ever since he had been a child, Leonid Kudrin had dreamed of being a people's judge. It was a strange ambition for a child, not exciting like being a pilot or an engine-driver, not even powerful like being a general. The boy simply wanted to dispense justice to other people, it seemed, as it had not been dispensed to him by the mother who had abandoned him in an orphanage. He had achieved his ambition only three years ago, at the age of thirty-five. Then, last September, just as I was arriving in Moscow, Kudrin had resigned his cherished job and returned his Party card. He had done so not to save a life or to spare a man from years of imprisonment. To have kept his job would have cost several young men a few days in gaol. 'I do not consider it possible to go on with my work as a people's judge, as my illusions about the independence of the people's judges to take their own decisions have finally been dispelled,' Kudrin had written in his letter of resignation. To many of his sympathizers, the reaction had seemed to be out of all proportion to the cause.

The case had concerned four young men who had applied for permission to hold a public meeting. The authorities had granted permission at first. Then they had changed their mind. Some sort of gathering had taken place, but without any speeches or banners. A national decree banning public meetings and demonstrations had just been announced, but it had not yet passed into law. But the local Party organization, who were getting worried by Sverdlovsk's increasingly lively political scene, had suggested to Kudrin that the men in charge should be warned off with a five-day sentence. It was not just that Kudrin had resented pressure from the Party organization. To charge the young men would also have been to anticipate the enactment of a law that was highly controversial in circumstances that were anything but clear. When is a meeting not a meeting? Does a group of people talking to one another in the street without any speeches constitute a meeting? There was no definition to be had.

'One day,' Kudrin explained, 'I was walking with my wife past the square where they used to meet, and I stopped to listen. Vitaly Suvorov, who was later brought before me in court, was talking, and I wondered to myself: why shouldn't people come together and talk about whatever they want without permission? As long as they're not in the way of the traffic or anything. I can't see what's so wrong with that. I'd read the decree that had just come out and I didn't like it. According to it, people who wanted to get together would have to say who they were, where they were going to meet, what they were going to discuss, how many of them there were going to be . . . But how can you tell with a live discussion? And what if the decree itself turned out to be unconstitutional? If it was, who was there to turn to, in the absence of a constitutional court?'

The night before the trial, Kudrin had been nervous: 'I said to my wife: "You know, Zhenya, I'm ashamed in front of these people. They're doomed. I've got to punish them, but I'm not sure that's right." I thought maybe I'd give them five days, as I'd been asked to, or a fine – in fact I didn't know what would happen next day.' Usually, such cases take a quarter of an hour. But Kudrin had decided that, rather than just listen to the witnesses and deliver his verdict, he would give the young men's lawyer the chance to defend them. The man had argued his case well, and Kudrin had been convinced. That was all there was to it.

In the West we have tended to know about the extreme cases of injustice in the Soviet Union, those that imprisoned men like Kukobaka for years on the basis of their thoughts alone. I had been interested to know what the experience of Soviet justice was at a mundane level. Wherever I had gone, I heard the same: the law was what the local Party leaders said it was. The law could be passed in Moscow and ignored, as it was by the heads of the state farms in Konstantinovo and Dagestan. It could be put into effect as and when it suited the local authorities, as Kudrin had found. Or it could be bought. In Stavropol', it cost 1,000 roubles per year to reduce a serious sentence to the minimum. In Baku, all minor charges at least were settled by a direct transaction with the judge. In Dagestan, no policeman was free to refuse bribes, because his boss would object to not receiving his cut.

Against this background, the minor legal infringement for which Kudrin had been prepared to sacrifice his career acquired a new significance. Kudrin had been not a martyr but a happily married middle-aged man, who at a particular moment had decided to prefer his own conscience to the instruction of the Party. It was for this precise act of principle that the voters of Sverdlovsk had made him their Deputy. They had voted for the part of themselves that was tired of saying one thing and doing another, that wanted to realize the connection between the intention of *perestroika* and the actual petty abuses which constituted the stuff of their everyday lives. The vote for Kudrin in Sverdlovsk had represented a public revaluation of the currency of honesty.

The following night was my last in Russia. Grisha was giving a party for Kudrin. I hardly recognized him. His wife Zhenya had flown in from Sverdlovsk, and as he sat with his arm around her, his face shone with happiness. Zhenya was plump, with peroxide hair and sharp features. As she talked, she laid her hand lightly on Kudrin's knee, as if to complete the circuit between them. Zhenya's grandmother had been 'Fräulein' to the Tsar's family. With them she had been exiled to Ekaterinburg, now Sverdlovsk, but she had escaped their violent death. 'To walk into Kudrin's flat', Grisha had told me, 'is to walk into a different world, full of this amazing furniture and photographs from the past. That contact with Russia in its continuity was Kudrin's real education.'

As well as Zhenya, the party had brought together the three other main agents in Kudrin's success. Across the table, strumming a guitar, with a dreamy look on his face, sat Vitaly, one of the four young men whom Kudrin had refused to convict. It was he who had alerted Grisha to the story which, through his article, had brought Kudrin fame. With his long hair and horn-rimmed spectacles, he did not look like the dynamic centre of Sverdlovsk's alternative political scene. His fastidious face suggested a young man from a golden background dabbling in politics. The truth was stranger. Until a few years ago, Vitaly had been an alcoholic, with a reputation for public brawling and a prison sentence behind him. Had Gorbachev come to power a few years later, it would have been too late for him. As it was, his pious mother, with whom he still lived, found one day that her son had taken Gorbachev's words literally. He had given up the bottle and taken to politics.

Next door to me, dressed in a three-piece suit, sat the lawyer who had defended Vitaly in court that day. Kotov, who was about the same age as Kudrin, had once been a Party functionary himself. Working for the first secretary, the district's top Party boss, his job had been to deal with all matters not important enough to be referred to his boss. In this capacity, he had defended someone who was in trouble with the Party. He had been sacked, both from his job and from the Party. With such a record, he was unemployable in any but a menial job. Even if he moved he could not get a job, and without a job he could not get a flat. To clear his name, he had challenged the Party, demanding reinstatement. Three times he took them on, and the third time he had won. Thereafter, he had become a defence lawyer. It had been Kotov whose defence of Vitaly had convinced Kudrin. An able man, he had been the natural choice to manage Kudrin's campaign.

A fierce argument was going on round the table. 'You don't know what you're talking about,' Kudrin was saying to Pavel the Old Believer, who had joined us: 'When he started *perestroika*, all he had in mind was a new way of cracking the whip behind the Party and the bureaucrats. But people took his words seriously!' 'I'm not going to argue with you about intentions. That will get us nowhere,' Pavel replied with characteristic precision. 'The reality is that Gorbachev is the only leader who can possibly carry through these reforms using the Party apparatus. I say this not because the Party apparatus is in any way ideal, but because it is there!' said this Old Believer, who would never have joined the Party, addressing Kudrin, Kotov and Grisha, three men who did. 'Of course Gorbachev belongs to the old world, but so do the people he has to bring with him if it is not to collapse. Haven't you had enough of conviction politics and revolution over the last seventy years? Everything that you've been fighting for depends on his pulling through.'

It was an argument rarely heard in Russia. It took courage to say something as unfashionable, courage of the kind this scholarly believer practised every day. In this culture where the practice of politics was only just beginning, there were few who could hold the ground between conformity and rebellion.

'I've been getting telegrams from Sverdlovsk ever since that first evening of the congress. They all say the same thing. They say it's a farce. They say it's all rigged . . . What do you expect me to do? Stand and applaud whenever his name is mentioned?' the elected Deputy from Sverdlovsk responded passionately. In his voice it was not so much conviction as desperation that I heard. It was integrity that had made Kudrin resign as a people's judge, and it was for this quality that he had been elected Deputy. Now, in his second day as a politician, this man of the Church was telling him that the language of integrity and that of politics were not the same. 'That's not what they voted me in for and that's not what I'm going to do!'

The argument went on, defeating Pavel by the weight of numbers. There it was, the central paradox: as this great, totalitarian country went through the motions of democracy for the first time, almost all those whose integrity I most admired were too much in love with the idea of change to understand the importance of Pavel's words. It would take time for Truth, which when threatened became a unified notion, to become merely truth, which in being less is so much more.

334

It was the Fräulein's granddaughter who reached for the guitar and asked her husband to sing. Diffidently, he began. As he grew more sure of himself, his voice became resonant, the voice of a natural musician. His handsome face, with its thatch of ash-blond hair, lit by one small lamp from the side, threw a shadow that filled the room. As we sat in the summer darkness, his voice held us, resolving in its beauty all our differences.

Epilogue

I MOSCOW

I returned to the Soviet Union in May 1990, a year after I had left, to find out what had happened to some of the people about whom I had written. Their contrasting fortunes indicate the complexity of the changes that were taking place as the empire unravelled.

None had thrived like Andrei, the Party member, and his beautiful wife Bella. Relaxed and confident, he looked like a different person from the beleaguered character I had met eighteen months before. When I left, Andrei had just taken up a job in a building cooperative, relinquishing with relief his duties as technical director for a state enterprise which manufactured building supplies. He had not lasted long in the private sector. 'They didn't think of me as much of a man, because I neither drank nor smoked nor swore. And they couldn't bear it that I still called myself a Communist.' He has recovered his ideological confidence and joined an organization run by the junior branch of the Party, the Komsomol. 'I'm the director of its free-enterprise department. That sounds grand, but I'm also its only employee. I'm free to operate as I like, but I'm not paid a salary. I just get a percentage of any deal I make. For instance, I might buy up a disused factory and set about doing it up, for the Komsomol to run.'

Andrei's move was significant. It illustrated the widely held view that the Party had seen its way forward and that it had

336

been busy rearranging its own economy to ensure its long-term survival. Indeed, there was abundant evidence that the principles of the free market had been successfully applied by the '*apparat*'. They were in a unique position to be able to use their capital to buy up the assets of the state, as well as to resell subsidized state goods at commercial market prices to 'the people', that is to say, those who were excluded from the benefits of this exercise of *perestroika* in miniature. With every month, the gap was widening between these two groups.

Andrei's wife Bella had produced another son and had been able to give up work. She was basking in the realization of her dreams. The family was moving to a larger flat and starting to talk about buying a *dacha*. Bella's anti-Semitic brother Arkady, the chess instructor from Stavropol' who aspired to become a psychic healer, had been similarly fortunate. His moment had come with the rise and fall of the healer Kashpirovsky. After practising his powers in a series of television seances which mesmerized a country hungry for miracles, Kashpirovsky was forced from the public eye after ugly attempts to discredit him. Arkady was among the hundreds of psychic healers from all over the countryside who had made their way to the capital to fill the vacuum left by Kashpirovsky's departure. He now had a flourishing practice of his own.

In the lottery of events, Bella's friend Olga, with whom I stayed in Stavropol', was the surprising winner. Against the odds she had been victorious in the court case over her flat. She had, Bella reported, transformed the simple rooms into a luxurious home that was a tribute to her determination: 'It's a dream, I can't tell you, she's done it up with such taste! There's this plaster moulding on the ceilings and columns on the walls . . . It's from a different world!' That was not all. Olga had discovered that, despite her Soviet passport, she was eligible to settle in Greece. Despite her mother's resistance, she planned to leave and run a café in Greece. She was part of a vast exodus.

Everywhere, Soviet citizens of all nationalities were looking for ways of getting out of the country.

When I first met Slava, I had had no doubts that his dream would come true. Inspired by Gorbachev's words, he had left his well-paid job in order to build his own house in the country and to work the land. It had been a bleak year. The boys were no closer to realizing their dream. The bricks still lay in piles on the site. Despite their skills, they were being employed on the lowest-paid jobs on the state farm, which had kept up its campaign of petty harassment. In order to repay their debts and avoid prosecution, they had been obliged to sell half their precious supply of building materials. They have finally concluded a formal agreement with the local authorities, but this had not helped, as Slava explained: 'The law is meaningless. We can't use it to resolve anything. Although we are in the right from a legal point of view, it turns out that Komkov is too!' Komkov, the director of the state farm, has also now been made a People's Deputy. 'So we're going to leave. A number of farms have offered us a place. The problem is how to choose? In a society where there is no rule of law, we will always be vulnerable. We have no backing but the personal commitment of the head of any state farm we choose. If he changes his mind, that's that. We will build our houses on land which to all intents and purposes is owned by the state farm in perpetuity.'

Slava and Natasha entertained me in one of their two sparsely furnished rooms in Moscow, where Natasha and her son were still living. In the corner stood a piano which had been in the other room before. The rooms seemed large after a long winter during which Natasha's parents, having been forced to abandon their home in Azerbaijan, had taken refuge there, joining Natasha's sister Valya and her three sons. Two months ago, all of them had been resettled in Krasnodar in the Caucasus. Slava looked thinner and paler. His confidence had been shaken, but there was a new tenacity about him: 'If I can only be patient and survive for long enough, I've got a chance. I may have started off with grand ideas about building a new world. But now the only hope I have is very personal: to be able to make a good life for my family so that my son can have a proper childhood. As for the rest, it won't happen. Even if we do manage to build our own house, and are free to raise our own livestock and farm our plots, we'll have to sell our products to the state – they offer you the same money or more than you'd get if you sold the produce privately. The old system has adapted itself and is moving from strength to strength. You know that the state farms are now notionally run on a profit-and-loss basis? But since they're still paid these ridiculous subsidies, there's no incentive for them to have two men who can work rather than ten drunkards who can't.'

Natasha was loving, but her loyalty had been under strain. Last winter had been bad enough, but she had no idea how the three of them were going to feed themselves this winter. To please me, she sat at the piano, which she had not played for a long time, and played the theme music from the film of *Romeo and Juliet*. Untuned, the lush chords had a disturbing edge. 'It broke my heart when Romeo died,' she concluded with unexpected feeling.

As Slava walked me to the bus-stop, he admitted how bad things had been: 'At times I've got terribly depressed. The most sensible thing for me to do would be to return to Moscow. I'd earn good money and it would be a huge relief for Natasha and the boy. But you know, I can't. I've changed. I've got used to making up my mind for myself.' Slava paused, then added resolutely: 'It can't get worse and this I can manage.' Even if it gets much worse, Slava, at least, has the character to survive without succumbing to racist or fascist lures. Of others, I cannot be quite so sure.

On the surface, Valery, who had left the same state farm to go independent two years before, was living much as he did a year ago. The local authorities had still not turned on his water supply again. Nor had anyone else in the area followed his example of leaving the state system for the life of an independent farmer.

But Valery's inner life continued on its turbulent way. After our meeting with the priest last year, he did start working for the local church. But something had gone wrong. Valery was reluctant to explain. 'I don't care what I say about the government. But the Church, that's something else. That's sacred . . .' In the end, after we had been collecting baskets of grass for his growing colony of rabbits, he said bitterly: 'It turns out that even the Church has been poisoned by that damned system of ours. I'm sure you know that the Orthodox Church is not independent of the state? I never used to think that that was important. Now I understand that it is. Its attitude to power is the same as that of the state. It's so sad that this revival of interest in the Church comes when it hasn't had time to undergo its own *perestroika*. Take the priest. He's a product of the Brezhnev years, a Pharisee. He'd ask me to get some lads to do a job for an agreed price. Then when it was done, he'd start backing off and trying to pay them less. He turned out to be very keen on money. He already owns a couple of houses in the village – all bought with Church money, of course. Now he's appropriating the house he's living in – you remember it – as his own property. If a man of God can't provide a model in his own behaviour, who is going to? I know I'm an exacting person. But I couldn't go on working for him after that . . .' Valery's disappointment with the Church had sent him back to the Bible for answers: 'I'm concentrating on the Ten Commandments now. They seem to make a lot more sense than anything people have come up with since.'

The picture of Marx had gone from Valery's wall, but Lenin was still there: 'Yes, I had a ceremonial burning of Marx last year. But I haven't finished with Lenin yet. This time last year I was still a Leninist. The others could go to hell. But Lenin was sacred. Then I went back to the texts, not the contemporary editions, but the 1930 one, edited by Kamenev. He hadn't been turned into an idol yet. Was that an eye-opener! I found he was just as much of a prostitute as the rest of them. I don't mean the little things, the bad language, even the violence. I mean that his ideas were no good. For instance, this edition includes a piece by Rosa Luxemburg in which she says that capitalism is very likely to adapt itself and survive, while Lenin was still saying it was doomed! So it turns out that some German woman knew better than the great Lenin!'

I sat there watching Valery as he read from the exercise-book in which he was collecting Lenin's sins. He may have nailed Lenin, but his craving for explanations made him vulnerable to any populist virus. Earlier in our conversation, he had sought to convince me that the right-wing society Pamyat' was 'an invention of the Jews to draw attention to themselves'. Since I had first arrived, popular myth had taken the place of ideology as the convenient shroud to throw over unpalatable realities.

After I had left the year before, Grisha and Ira had spent a month in Dagestan filming their documentary about the Gasanov family. I had been longing to hear whether Zakarya and his brothers had got their land back. But it was some time before I could coax the story out of my friends. In the end it was Ira who gave me an account of their trip. 'It was difficult from beginning to end. There were practical problems to start with: how on earth were we going to bring the story to life? The brothers would keep dragging out these ancient bits of paper and interminable justifications for their actions. There was nothing to shoot, no way of catching the drama of the story. So we decided that the best thing to do would be to try to get their land back for them. We spent a week working on the officials, pulling every trick imaginable. We threatened them with people that we know and people we don't. We told them that they would be the butt of every satirist in the country. In the end, we did get them to offer part of the land to the family – quite enough for them to make a living off. The officials said they would have been happy to give the lot back, but that the Gasanovs had made themselves so unpopular with their relentless denunciations and complaints that people wouldn't stand for it. Of course, we didn't believe them for a minute.

'But gradually we came to see how hated the family really was. All the same, the authorities agreed to give the family back a bit of land each year until they had it all. Well, the Gasanovs did not seem overjoyed at our triumph. They took a couple of days to consider the offer and then they turned it down!

'Throughout this time, we were having more and more difficulty with the family over the issue of what we could film. They wanted complete control over the material. This came to a head because of a quite unexpected element that had begun to emerge from the beginning of that second visit. It turned out that the entire village, all those mountain people in fact, were unreconstructed Stalinists. Stalinism had found a ready ground in the feudal, ascetic cast of their character. Night after night they would gather at the house and try and convince us that thirty million lives, the Terror, none of that mattered where the end result was order. Well, at one point we packed our bags. How could we go on with the film? Then, at the very last moment we decided to try and get this new element, the Stalinism, into the story. But the brothers soon smelt a rat and clammed up.' 'That wasn't all,' Grisha interrupted. 'They turned on us and accused us of having made a deal with the authorities to trap them into compromising themselves on film! Can you believe it? They were totally paranoid. In the end we realized that they really were professional complainers; that the last thing they wanted was a resolution to the whole affair.' 'It's not quite fair to say that they were all like that. Do you remember Magomed the accountant, the compromiser? He would have accepted the authorities' offer. Only the others wouldn't agree. We showed him the film. The others wouldn't come. He was shocked. But he admitted that our account was fair.'

'I have to admit that I shall be happy never to see any of them again,' Ira concluded. I did not need her to tell me how badly hurt she had been. Grisha was a journalist. He had always had his reservations about the brothers. But Ira, as a writer and a romantic, had given the Gasanovs her heart. She had been the absolute champion of their cause.

Although I was not entirely surprised that the brothers should have turned down the chance to return to their own land, I was as shocked as Ira to hear of their politics. It was not so much the fact that they were Stalinists, but the meticulous attempt they had made to conceal their views. Realizing how unreceptive progressive Muscovites like Ira and Grisha would be to their politics, the mountain people had simply tried to deceive them. If Ira and Grisha had been less serious in pursuit of their cause, the brothers might have got away with their bid to control the content of the film about them.

Ira's disillusionment with the Gasanov brothers stirred an echo in my mind. Among the parallels between the Russians and the Americans, the people of these two great cultures so closely attached to the European experience, one of the most striking is the innocence with which both nations tend to apprehend the world. Ira's adoption of the Gasanovs' cause had been innocent in this way. There was in her feeling of betrayal a certain naïvety which I also feared to find in the response of the American people to the painful unravelling of the Soviet empire. There was no 'happy ending' in sight in a Hollywood way. Much that had been revealed in the past few years was dark and little of it fitted familiar categories. I found myself fearing that, just as Ira did not want to talk about the Gasanov family any more, so the Americans would soon feel that they had had enough of Russian misfortunes. I feared that, with a sigh, they might turn over to another channel.

*

Ira's feeling of betrayal sounded a note which I was to catch again and again in the days that followed. For the most part this was a sentiment that was not overtly expressed. It could be heard like a ground bass under people's words. Her mother Elena, with whom I was staying, caught the mood when she told me of a recent dream: 'I have always dreamt about dogs. I love them. I have dogs all over me, licking me. Or I am being followed by this crowd of dogs wherever I go. But recently, I started having these terrible dreams. The dogs were there, but they were not real. These policemen dressed in black, with gold braid, would be walking down a long corridor. Each man had a dog. But they were all plastic. Their legs went this way and that, this way and that, like clockwork. They were terrible dogs. One of them, for instance, had a back that was rectangular, like a table top. As they went past, I ran my finger down their backs and it left a little path all the way along, the dogs were so dusty.'

II KIEV

'The Social Democrat wrote and drank, and drank as he wrote. And the peasant didn't read, he just drank, drank without reading. Have you read Marx? Universal. In other words, people were drinking more and more. The desperation of the Social Democrat grew accordingly, way beyond Lafite and Cliquot. All thinking Russia was legless, suffering for the peasant . . .'

Venedikt Yerofeev
From Moscow to Pyetushki

'How do you like our Soviet McDonalds then? Is the West ready for it?' Kotya, the speaker, was a young labourer. He was sitting beside a handsome woman, his wife, who looked as if she belonged to a minor branch of the House of Windsor.

They were dressed up in their Sunday best and seated on dilapidated wooden crates on a grassy slope. Everywhere, similar groups were sitting around among a litter of empty bottles, bones and paper plates. By the shabby hut below us, a tattered man was dragging his friend by the arms across the concrete towards a row of bodies in the grass. Though it was still early, there were three drunks lying there already. There was a gap in the line where a fourth had crawled away to lie crumpled under a hawthorn-tree.

The hut which was the focus of attention had a beleaguered look. Its doors and windows were bolted and, from one end, a zigzag queue stretched away. It led towards a single hatch, from which a large white hand was issuing paper plates of congealed meat accompanied by bottles of brandy and vodka. Unencumbered by glasses or cutlery, we drank from the bottle and wiped our fingers on the forgiving grass. 'I expect you're shocked,' said the young labourer. On the contrary, I was impressed. He and his proudly dressed wife sitting upright on her wooden box managed to confer dignity on the scene. 'I expect you think we get used to this,' he went on. 'Well, we don't. It's degrading. It's poverty. You don't get used to that. Sunday night is the only time Polya and I get to go out. I have no choice but to bring her here and to ask her to wait for two hours while I queue for this!'

I was sitting in this desolate spot waiting for a train. To travel from one city to another by any means had become a problem. There were no tickets for sale, even for foreigners, on any of the frequent overnight trains from Kiev to Moscow. Volodya, director of the Looking Glass Theatre company, had eventually secured some sort of ticket through the counter reserved for the military. With four hours to spare, we had checked in my luggage. But Volodya could think of nowhere that was open on a Sunday night for a meal, until he remembered this place, where Kotya was now chatting to us.

'My sister and her family went to America five years ago.

345

We're trying to get out, but I don't think we'll make it ...'
Kotya's wife had begun, before Kotya took over: 'If it were just
for us, we wouldn't bother. We're finished anyway.' To a
Western eye, they seemed young to be finished. They
were only in their twenties. 'It's the little ones we have to look
after. My daughter is the only important thing I have left. She's
six.' Kotya had come over to squat in the grass by me now that
the conversation had taken a personal turn. 'Every day she has
nosebleeds. My wife has to sleep with her instead of me now so
that she can stop the bleeding in time. What kind of marriage, is
that, I ask you? We take her to the hospital and they say there
is nothing wrong. Maybe they're right but how do we know?
They say that to everyone.' The fourth anniversary of Cher-
nobyl′ was a few weeks ago. Fifteen thousand people had
gathered at Lenin's statue to throw his collected works in a pile
at his feet. 'She gets these headaches too, splitting headaches.
All she can say is, "Mama, Mama, do something. My head,
it hurts so much." And there is nothing we can do. My heart
breaks, watching her. It has to be Chernobyl′. My father had
three sons and the other brothers have large families. There is
something wrong with every one of those children. My father is
a licensed hunter for the state and he has a gun. I dream of
taking that gun and finishing off every last one of them; every
doctor who has refused to help; every Party boss who's been
part of the cover up of Chernobyl′.'

Having eaten, Volodya and I walked past the ochre-walled
Vydubitsky Monastery with its gilded domes. According to
legend, when Vladimir, Prince of Kiev, adopted Christianity in
the ninth century, the pagan gods were cast into the waters of
the river that rushes down the hill to the Dnepr. One rose up
out of the water in a last assertion of his power and on this site
they built a church. Although many sacred buildings in Kiev
had already been given back to the Church, the monastery still
belonged to the state.

We slipped through the fence into the Botanical Gardens.

Kiev is the greenest city I know. Wooded hillsides rise up one after another from the town below like the coils of a sea snake. But here the green was broken with reaches of purple and white where the lilac was in flower. The air was heavy with scent.

Yesterday, the core of Chernobyl' had erupted once again, as it will periodically for a long time. When this happens, radio-activity rises to three times its normal post-Chernobyl' level. But today it was far higher than that because of yesterday's fire. The Brown Wood by the reactor, so called since it changed colour four years ago, had gone up in flames. The news had carried no mention of the incident, but word had got round. There had been an announcement that mothers with children should leave the city immediately and stay away for three months. Money, they said, would be provided. Volodya's girl-friend Eva would not allow me to be taken in by this apparently prompt response: 'It's a mockery. The amount of money they offer would last a month perhaps but not three. And how can women just leave their jobs? And where are they meant to go? Unless you have relations who live a long way away, there's nowhere to stay.' There had been a housing crisis before. But this had been so exacerbated by the need to house refugees from Azerbaijan that the issue had become the battle-line of racial conflict in many parts of the union.

It was on days like this when the radiation was high that they felt it. Eva, Volodya and his brother Vitaly were the three remaining actors in the company who had spent nine weeks out at Chernobyl' after the reactor had gone up. 'It's a sort of lethargy you can't shake off,' as Eva put it. 'You want to sleep all day. And there are the headaches . . .' To look at this girl with her doll's eyes and pouting lip, it was hard to imagine that she could have gone through so much, and voluntarily. She had been fifteen at the time. Vitaly's wife Oksana, who had been little older, had also gone. She had not known she was pregnant. 'When we got back, she went to the hospital for tests,' Eva went on. 'But the doctor tore up the paper she brought, which proved that she had been out there. "It's impossible," the doctor said. "These papers must belong to somebody else. No one as young as you would have been allowed in." Oksana had not gone back. What was the point? The child's normal. But we all know that it's not what happens now, but how our grandchildren turn out that's the problem. The radiation was three times higher than Hiroshima, you know.'

As Volodya and I enjoyed the poisoned beauty of the scene, we heard snatches of song further up the hill. A flock of Baptists were sitting among the lilacs singing psalms. Mostly women and children, they had the bedraggled look of people who expect persecution. Their pastor alone looked equal to the struggle. Broad-shouldered, he stood with his sandalled feet wide apart, braced for whatever was to come. 'We have a lot to thank God for today,' he smiled. 'This is the first year that the Baptists have been free to worship.' Last year I saw a girl in just such a group of singers being beaten up by the police in a Kiev street.

I had come to Kiev this time to see the first night of a special production by the Looking Glass Theatre group. A lot had happened since we last met in Novosibirsk. The felicitous performance of *Arbat* which I had seen them play that night had not, after all, saved the company. Most of the actors had left, finding Volodya too demanding. Only Volodya's girl-friend Eva, his brother Vitaly and the producer Misha remained. But Volodya had reconstituted the troupe and its spirit was the same.

When I had met them eighteeen months before, the theatre was still earning its living by performing song-and-dance routines in the park. At least then they had somewhere to act and some sort of regular wage, however mean. Now they were hiring theatres by the evening and living off their box-office takings. Every month, these were getting smaller. Partly this was because, as inflation bit, people were giving up going to

348

the theatre. But the theatre's present poverty was, in the view of many people, self-imposed.

It was little more than a year since Volodya had sat shocked in Yerofeev's Moscow room while the sick writer demolished Lenin and Volodya's political ideals. Now Volodya had produced his own adaptation of *From Moscow to Pyetushki*, Yerofeev's epic poem of a journey, his own and that of his country, into drunken oblivion. As a play, it represented everything that Ukrainians did not wish to see. To stage a play by a Russian against the background of rising nationalism was already to court unpopularity. But to choose one in which the characters were all drinking themselves to death was going too far. Volodya, playing the main character Yerofeev, had given an extraordinary performance, one into which he had put all that he knew of heaven and hell inside himself. But to offer this to a public conditioned to expect uplifting truths from art came over to the audience as a calculated insult. 'I'm not staying. It's disgusting,' a friend of Volodya's muttered in the interval. 'As if we didn't have enough of this every day. Why should I pay to sit through it again?'

When I had first met Volodya, he was an innocent, a very Soviet man. That quality had gone and with it all tolerance for the idea of pandering to an audience, as he had been obliged to pander to the crowds in the Kiev park. His confidence as a director had grown. But he came over as an increasingly lonely figure now. 'For the first time in my life, I can't think ahead any more. I can't make any plans. It all depends on what happens in the country. But I do know that whatever I will do, it will never be well received here.'

We were standing on top of the hill, looking down on the river Dnepr. 'There was a whole group in the audience last night who were class-mates of mine at school. I hadn't seen them since. I was unpopular at school. They were socialized children, brought up in the *detsky sad* (Soviet play-school, which looks after the children of working mothers during the

349

day). 'I'd been brought up at home. I was lost. They were always attacking me. They used to hunt in packs. Last night I looked at them and I was terrified. Nothing has happened in their lives. They've just grown old, knowing nothing, understanding nothing. Those little girls who had laughed at me were old women with iron teeth and arms bulging from years of carrying heavy shopping bags. If they look like that, I thought, then so must I . . .'

Volodya, so secular a year ago, had just been baptized. I was relieved to find him untouched by the rising mood of nationalism in the Ukraine. I remembered the conversation I had had last year about Volodya with his producer Misha, in Novosibirsk. He was right, there was a quality about Volodya which seemed to carry a portent of something larger. 'He's driven by demons and he drives all of us,' as Misha put it then. 'It was Chernobyl' that did it to him. He's a good example of what Napoleon came up against, and Hitler too, when they thought they could invade Russia. We look as if we will put up with things for ever and ever, passively. Then finally we are roused.

'I didn't know him before Chernobyl',' Misha had said. 'But they tell me he used to be much like everyone else, only more so: a desperate drinker, lazy as sin and not beyond fiddling things on the side. An ordinary *muzhik*, and a pretty coarse one at that. Even now, he could revert and become a drunk. It remains a possibility. But something happened to him out there that roused him out of his skin. He says so himself. He aspires to be better than himself. I see that aspiration as something sacred, something that makes him capable of things beyond his reach.' Misha was right. Volodya had it in him even now to revert and give in to the drink. But I was confident that he would not.

The open carriage of the train was meant to sleep fifty-four people, in triple layers. There were many more of us than that. All but three were men and as far as the eye could see they were drinking and playing cards. Each man had brought his own supply of *samogon*, home-brewed alcohol. Pure spirit hung on the fetid air. There was nowhere to sit, let alone to sleep.

After assessing the situation as the train stood in the station, Volodya had decided that I needed a protector. As most of the travellers had got off to buy refreshments, the choice fell on a young man with the face of a Crivelli angel called Bogdan. He had remarkable eyes, whose distended irises radiated out from the pupils in green and yellow stripes. They were the saddest eyes.

If I ended up knowing little about Bogdan, it was not for want of his trying to communicate. But, although he did not appear to be drunk at first, the alcohol had eaten so deeply into his brain that he could barely enunciate words. In the middle of a sentence, he would forget that he had been talking. Resting his tired gaze on some object, he would fall silent before continuing a train of thought that wandered like a stray dog. Only gradually did I realize that the emotion expressed in his poetic gaze reflected the afterglow of a consciousness that had long ago been switched off. Then I began to have doubts about the protector whom Volodya had chosen for me.

As far as Bogdan could hold on to intentions, they were good enough. But that was not far. He honoured his promise to Volodya by ensuring that I got a bunk to myself; he fetched me sheets and covered me with a blanket during the night. If I had to throw him off now and then when the carriage was asleep; if I needed to keep removing arms which attached themselves like ivy in the course of a conversation, it was because other means of communication between the two of us had failed. With the men, Bogdan made contact by treating them to a mug of spirit from his orange plastic container.

In the company of a woman and one who would not stop writing things down, Bogdan was confused. 'What if I order you to stop?' he said experimentally. I went on writing. Bogdan had received his fair share of orders. He had fought in Afghanistan for two years and sold his campaign medals for drink. After that, he had been sent to prison for three years 'because of a fight'. His story was confirmed when he removed his shirt and jacket to reveal a torso exquisitely tattooed with convict imagery which mated pornography and blasphemy to hellish effect.

For all his desire to communicate, alcohol had locked Bogdan into a solitude as complete as that of the monks of Kiev's ancient Pecherskaya Lavra who, walled into cells, had only a hole through which food and drink could be passed. In the course of the journey my sympathy for this man, who had received little training except in killing, became mixed with anxiety for my own safety. Bogdan's dogged questions revealed his intention of following me home once we arrived in Moscow. No one was meeting me and there would be no one at Elena's flat all day. In the packed compartment, I was all right. But the idea of coming face to face with Bogdan on a lonely street was frightening because I knew he had no control over his own actions.

When I reached home after shaking off Bogdan down the corridors of the Moscow Metro, I opened the paper and my eye was caught by a small announcement: Venedikt Yerofeev, the poet of the bottle, was to be buried in Vagankovskoye Cemetery the next day. He had died the day I was watching his play in Kiev.

III BAKU

The last time I had been in Baku, the air had been heavy with resentment and unacted desires. This time, I knew only that I was going to the city which had paid the final price for Gorbachev's persistent inability to formulate a policy on nationalities. What exactly had happened in January 1990, I did not know. Who and what had precipitated the pogrom of the remaining Armenian population in a city whose pride was its international community? What connection did the pogrom have to the fact that the Popular Front had virtually assumed control of the republic, at the expense of the Party and state authorities? Had the subsequent violent invasion of Soviet troops been justified? How was the fall of government after government in Eastern Europe at the end of 1989 connected to this bloody sequence of events? About Baku, I knew only this: nothing would be as it seemed.

I had been wrong to suppose that, in this period of comparative openness, events in the Soviet Union passed into the bloodstream of the capital. When I arrived in Moscow, I found that few Russians cared to know anything about events in Azerbaijan. They saw no possible connection between their own lives and the catastrophe that had overwhelmed Baku. Ira was an exception. She had taken the unusual step, for a Russian, of going down to Baku in January to circumvent the news blackout and find out what had happened. But even within her own family, she was alone in upholding the Azeri point of view.

Ira: 'The news black-out was total. No one in the rest of the country has the slightest idea of what happened, but in Russia they think they do. There was a pogrom of Christians. That's what they think.' (Two hundred thousand of Baku's original quarter of a million Armenians had still been living there in January.)

Elena: 'Well, there was . . .'

Ira: 'The barbarous Azeris had a pogrom of Armenians . . .'

Elena: 'You can't deny that that's what happened . . .'

Ira (passionately): 'You see, my own mother believes it. The news black-out worked. In fact nobody got killed in that pogrom. And the whole thing was provoked by the KGB in the first place. You know that it happened just before the election date was due to be fixed? You know what would have happened in that election? The Popular Front would have toppled Soviet power, that's what. The authorities provoked the pogrom.

353

Then they did nothing to stop it. There were enough Soviet troops permanently stationed in the city to have prevented it. But the troops did nothing. As for the police, they had their firearms taken away from them three hours before it all began. They were helpless throughout. They had to stand by and watch it happen. Of course the result was the indefinite postponement of the election. What a convenient way to tell the other republics: look what will happen to you if you get ideas. Azerbaijan has only learned one thing: never again to have any truck with Russian or Soviet power. Before that they were far less nationalistic than the Georgians, the Armenians or the Balts. They're an international lot, and simpler too. But they will never never forgive what was done to them. Three hundred killed by troops.' (Ira was referring to the invasion of the city by special troops armed with dumdum bullets a week after the pogrom. No one will ever know how many civilians were killed, as their bodies were taken out to sea by the boat-load and drowned. But her estimate was extremely conservative.) 'But in Russia, not to speak of the rest of the world, Europe and America, it's all put down to the Muslim element. Those little brown people. That "explains" everything. It's very convenient. But it could happen anywhere. Mark my words, it will.'

Elena (apologetically): 'But the Azeris did kill the Armenians . . .'

Grisha (diplomatically, not wanting to disagree with Ira): 'You see, we have nothing but versions. There's the version that Soviet troops moved in to stop a blood-bath. And there's the version that it was staged to nip independence in the bud. There's something in them both.'

Before I went to Baku, I was not inclined to take Ira's version of events seriously. But in the end it seemed to offer the best explanation for what happened.

I had been astonished to discover that Tatyana was still living in Baku. Her mother, whose nationality in her passport was Armenian, had had to flee to Moscow in January. As I set out for the flight to Baku, she and I travelled together in the bus to the airport.

'We knew exactly when the pogroms were going to happen. We just didn't believe it. The rumours had been quite precise. They began a month before the old Armenian New Year, which is on 13 January. We were celebrating with Rauf and other friends of Tatyana's.' Rauf was the handsome Azeri who had taken Tatyana and me to the discothèque last year. 'We were just about to start eating when my brother rang – you remember, he lived just down the road. "They're coming," he said. "A mob of them. They're in the house next door. We're going upstairs to our neighbours on the next floor," he said. The neighbours were Russian. "But I'm sending Seryozha round to you. Ring the police at once." My brother reckoned Seryozha would be safer with us because our surname isn't Armenian. I did ring the police and they said that help was on the way. A lorry-load of troops did turn up. But they just sat in the lorry opposite the house where my brother lived and did nothing at all.' Tatyana's mother sighed. 'The little boy arrived. He came all the way round the back, rather than along the street. Even then I still didn't really understand what was happening. I offered him some cake, which I'd just baked. He loves that cake. He sat there and said no to everything. I took a look at him. The boy was dead white. He was sitting utterly still, transfixed. Then I realized it had begun.

'My brother rang again, saying the mob had broken open the front door of one of their Armenian neighbours. Inside, they were waiting with an axe. The first man through the door was killed with one blow. That's what Seryozha had seen. Then all hell had broken loose. My brother could hear it all as it went on. They smashed the flat, beat them almost to death, killed one of them. The men had the housing list and they were picking out the Armenians by name. "You've got to get out," my brother said. "They're coming your way." My brain had seized up. But Tatyana and the boys kept their heads. One boy, we'd never even met him before, he worked with Rauf, had a car and he agreed to drive Rauf and Tatyana round to my brother's. It was pitch black outside. They'd put out all the street lights. Tatyana ran into the house, past the mob and slipped my brother and his wife out into the car. Later, they came back for us. Rauf's mother hid Tatyana and me for days. She'd never met either of us. She was wonderful.

'A week later, when the troops arrived, we thought, "It'll be all right now." Then the firing began, apparently indiscriminate; bullets spraying all over houses in which people were living! So many innocent victims.' Tatyana's mother was reliving the story as she talked. It was as if she still needed to appreciate that it had really happened. For this woman, nationalism could provide no comfort and no explanation. Her friends were Azeri and her home was Azerbaijan.

'Then the search for Armenians began in earnest. Word got round that they were after those in hiding, and that they would not spare those who had sheltered them. That was when I realized that I had to get out. Not for my own sake, but for theirs. Tatyana has a Russian passport, you know. But I had become the black sheep, the one who could bring disaster to them all.

'When you come back I want you to tell me honestly whether I can go back there to live,' she said as she kissed me goodbye. Even now she could not believe that the culture of this great Levantine city had been destroyed. Long after Cairo had succumbed under the weight of numbers and Beirut been torn apart by bullets, Baku had enjoyed its own kind of remission under a totalitarian regime.

The city was as beautiful as ever, clustered on the hillside, with its acacia-lined streets of European houses. Only if you looked closely at the walls and windscreens of the cars did you see the bullet holes. But it took no time to understand that something had broken. The exodus of Armenians had been followed by that of the Jews. Of the rest of the middle class, Azeri as well as Russian, anyone who had somewhere to go was making their arrangements.

'Never again will we be the international community that we were,' mourned Rauf, the elegant Azeri who had taken on the role of protecting Tatyana. 'We've swapped our own Armenians for these brutal louts, the refugees from Armenia. Everyone becomes like the culture in which they live. They may be Azeris but they're more like Armenians. They were the ones who joined the pogrom. They don't belong here and it's a catastrophe that they've come. Half the flats in this house, the ones in which Armenians used to live, are now occupied by refugees who were part of the mob that night.' We were sitting in Tatyana's drawing-room which had been my bedroom before. The flame in the boiler roared. Out of all Tatyana's cavaliers, Rauf had been the one who came forward to protect Tatyana and her mother with his life. Others, who had seemed closer to her a year ago, had sat in their homes and sympathized. Even now, Rauf did not leave her alone in the flat, but organized a relay of bodyguards. Although the city seemed quiet under martial law, these precautions were not exaggerated. Once when Tatyana was alone for forty minutes between watches, a neighbour whom she had known for years forced his way in and tried to rape her.

'It is the little things that you notice most,' as Tatyana observed: 'A girl-friend of mine was running to catch a bus the other day. She's pregnant, visibly, and not as nimble as usual. She tripped on the kerb and fell in the path of the bus. Now normally in Baku, people would have rushed to help her. It's a town in which, if you ask the way, people end up taking you to the place. That's gone. There were people all around, but no one moved. As she was struggling to get up unaided, she held out her hand to the man in front of her who took it, then let go of her, so that she fell once more.'

What had broken was the trust that holds people together.

357

There was no such thing as a 'Bakunite' now. There was only a collection of people, who feared each other but who were obliged to live too close together. No one had even pretended to do any work since January. Even now, supplies were more than usually scarce because of the long interruption to rail traffic. Days were spent foraging and trying to find ways round the absence of doctors (the good ones were Jewish and had left), teachers, cobblers and television repair men (who had mostly been Armenian).

In this atmosphere fraught with petty difficulty and real danger, Tatyana, whose abilities had been rusting last year, was visibly more relaxed. But she could not remain for long in a city where all her movements had to be shadowed. She had applied for a prestigious design course in Moscow. She had the talent. But everyone knew that talent and knowledge were no criteria for entry. The question was, had she got the contacts? A few weeks later, when I was back in England, the answer reached me. Tatyana had failed to get in. She had no way out of Baku now.

Tatyana had just had a spell removed. She was making the most of this diversion: 'You must understand that I tell this story not as a believer, but as a story-teller. Some years ago, my mother went to consult an old woman about my health. She didn't believe in that kind of thing any more than I did, but she was at her wit's end about me. For reasons the doctors could not explain, the skin and flesh were peeling off my fingers. In places, it was down to the bone. I couldn't work, of course. In fact I couldn't do anything. I could hardly think for the pain. Anyway, the old woman told my mother that I had had the evil eye put on me by two people. One she named as Anya, whom I knew. She was a jealous woman. The other she did not name. The old hag just got up, straightened herself up and gave a perfect imitation of this woman's distinctive walk.' Tatyana stood up, stuck out her chest and her behind and lurched across the room, in an imitation of the imitation. 'She also said

358

that someone had put a spell on me. It would be in the house somewhere, she said, but I would have to find the right person to locate it. She gave my mother a name. After that it was all very strange. In the course of the next five days, my fingers completely healed, leaving not so much as a scar. And my friendships with those women somehow came to an end. I quarrelled with them, which is most unlike me.

'A long time passed and I did nothing about finding the woman who locates spells. Then Rauf's mother, who has become like another mother to me now, started looking for her on behalf of Rauf and me. It took her a long time. But a couple of weeks ago, the woman finally came. She undressed down to her underwear so that we could see that she didn't have anywhere to hide anything and went round the flat with a needle and thread between her teeth. If there was a spell anywhere, she said, the needle would fall. For a long time she insisted that there was no spell in the house. Then, when she was just about to give up, the needle fell while she was going over the floor under which the cellar lies. She didn't know the cellar was there, as it's hidden under the linoleum. We lifted the floor and she brought out a little bag which was hidden behind some pine-cones in a corner. I'd been meaning to clear those cones out. I couldn't think what they were doing there. She couldn't possibly have hidden the bag, as she was wearing so little. And it was covered in dust. It must have been there for ages. We opened it up. There was a whole bunch of things sewn into it: a pumpkin seed; a pin through a scrap of paper from the Koran; a sparrow's left leg; a sparrow's eye; a piece of jackal fat. Each item was part of a recipe specially prepared for me. She said it was a deadly spell. I can't remember it all, but I do know what the sparrow's left foot was for; I'd been having trouble with my left foot for ages. And I remember that the pin in the Koran was to make sure that nothing would go right in my sexual life. Well, that had worked too. The jackal fat had something to do with death.'

The way Tatyana told the story did not suggest that she was as detached as she claimed to be. When the trust between men who live side by side has gone and when explanations no longer seem to explain, there comes a time when ancient recipes of female spite seem to provide clues to some small aspects of the question, 'Why me?'

The doves were cooing on the window vent as Tatyana told the story. Out in the bay, a big ship boomed. It seemed years ago that I had sat in this spellbound room talking about Borges and the plays of Peter Brook. Soon, there would be Azeris living here. The only question was, would the new occupants keep up the pretence that what was happening was normality and pay for the transfer of property? Or, following another upheaval, would the refugees from Armenia simply chase Tatyana out? And where could she go?

IV MOSCOW

Surprised to see no queue at the shop, I wandered in. The shelves that stretched from one end to the other were empty. On the counter, beside a dusty pyramid of tinned fish which even now no one would buy, sprawled a young man with blunted features. Pushing his dirty white hat to the back of his head, he yawned. The door behind opened just enough for someone, clearly his boss, to direct a string of obscenities at the boy. These days everyone needed someone less important than themselves upon whom to vent their disappointment.

The little privileges which used to distinguish life in the capital had vanished as the regions had begun to hold back supplies of food. The verb 'to buy' was rarely heard. It had been replaced by the word *dostat*, 'to procure'. For this, money, contacts and a thick skin were needed. Everyone was talking about the coming hunger. There had been a scramble to 'procure' safe jobs and to earn large sums of money by hook or by crook.

Elena had none of the qualities to survive the catastrophe she saw moving slowly towards her. Soon she would also be a pensioner. I was walking through the Moscow streets to try to shake off the gloom I felt before going back to her at the flat. It was Victory Day today, but even that had not cheered her up. 'I always used to look forward to it. Of all these Days of this and Days of that, it's the one which represents a real achievement. But it's lost its meaning for me now. Was it really such an achievement, I find myself asking, that victory won at so high a price? All those millions of men who served as cannon fodder; Russia left shattered. We don't know how to run the country. We don't know how to work. We don't know anything any more. Perhaps it would have been better if the Germans had won it.' So said this woman whose parents had been shot by the Germans for being Communists.

'Civil war', 'bloody dictatorship', 'the end of history' . . . Apocalyptic conversations abounded. They told me not how things were but how they felt. 'Two Russias are facing each other eye to eye. And the contact is unbearable,' as one friend expressed it. The element of hysteria made it hard to distinguish the false fears from the real. Like the racism, this hysteria represented the projection of anxieties which twentieth-century people denied psychological tools were more than usually unable to deal with. I tried unsuccessfully to reach for the good news which I knew was hidden somewhere in the folds of this confusion. Freud was just beginning to be published. People were learning to live with politicians who were not idols. Politicians were learning how to live with uncertainty. For the rest of the world, this country was becoming not Them, but part of us . . . I gave up trying. It was all true. But as long as I was here, it seemed like cold comfort.

I hurried home in time for supper. We were expecting Pavel, the Old Believer who had taken me to the Easter service last year. He bounded through the front door, radiating energy: 'I want to know how my ally is, our representative from Foggy

Albion. I trust you haven't all started losing faith in Gorbachev as well?' 'Well . . .' 'Even his most enlightened critics here know nothing about power. These democrats of ours who shout so loud about "freedom" are only feeding the really dangerous element in our politics, the right. Without the radicals, the right have no excuse. The two extremes have become interdependent. It has been ever thus in Russia. Tell me what you think? Has much changed?' 'People seem to have lost hope . . .' 'Ah, not another one. You are all so faint-hearted! I seem to be the only one who really understands Hegel's dialectic here! I am more hopeful than ever! We are coming to the end of the darkest period of our history, the Age of Decree. It began three hundred years ago . . . If you're really interested, I'll read you a bit of the article I've just published. I just happen to have it on me . . .'

Pavel was off, leaving his soup untouched. His beard was longer than ever and he was pale. But his mood was one of feverish excitement: 'It started with the schism in the Church, when Nikon said . . .' and, reading from his article, he began to quote the words of the Patriarch's decree of 1653 which split the Russian Orthodox Church in two: ' "From tomorrow onwards, everyone must . . ." They must, moreover, do that which they have never done before and renounce customs that reach back into antiquity. Even now, when we have understood the fatal nature of this approach, that of brute force, we are still trying to escape from this period by dint of the same method, that of decrees. We announce: "From tomorrow onwards *perestroika*, democratization, *glasnost'*, will begin!" and by this means we fall prey to a contradiction. It is the very same contradiction which has led the historical life of our country into a dead end. It would be frivolous of me to attempt . . . trum, trum.' Growing impatient with his own verbose written style, Pavel began to skim through the text, reading aloud the plums, paraphrasing his argument. A sweat had broken out on his pale face as he developed the idea that Peter

362

the Great, by attempting to reach noble ends by ignoble means, those of violence, had set in train a chain of events which had culminated in the Terror and the camps that had claimed thirty million lives.

It was hard to believe that this radiant man had been struck by misfortune since we had met a year ago. His 'little earthquake' as he referred to it dismissively in the course of the evening, had begun some months ago. His oldest son, who had a job in a petrol-station, had gone to his father one day when he came home from work. 'I need your help, father,' he had said. 'I've never asked you for anything before. But this is different. My future depends on it.' He had been offered a quick way of making a lot of money. If he could raise 13,000 roubles to buy a car, he would be able to resell it within a few days for 20,000 roubles. Pavel was torn. He had wanted nothing to do with the business. But he felt that he had never given the boy a chance.

In the end, he had agreed to try to raise the sum by borrowing off his friends. Like most of the Russians that I knew his own savings amounted to little. But his friends rallied round. The boy bought the car and sold it again. He was paid in vast wads of notes. When he came to count the money, he found that he had been given a *kukla*, a bundle of fakes made from newspaper, with genuine money at either end. The *kukla* was a speciality of the Russian mafia. It was a beautiful piece of work. The boy was advised that if he breathed a word of the affair, 'they' would come for him.

While I was in Kiev, 'they' did. The boy was out at the family's *dacha*, with a friend. They smashed everything in the house, beat him up and strung him up to the ceiling by his heels. 'If you breathe another word, you won't get off so lightly again,' they said as they left. The boy had been unwise enough to mutter, among his friends, that he would get even some day. Nobody knows how Pavel will ever pay back the money he owes.

Pavel was still reading out his defence of *perestroika*: ' "The grounds for hope consist in the following circumstance: the present revolution is proceeding not by means of force . . ." Of course, you radicals are going to chant "Baku! Tbilisi!" at me – and those episodes deserve a separate conversation. Yes, they were violent, but they were still the exceptions. They do not destroy my main thesis. Of course it's going to be a rough ride, but . . . Listen, listen, this bit is good: "In the atmosphere of demystification and deutopianization, in the impetus towards repentance and recollection, we break with a tradition of utopian thinking which has held us in thrall for 300 years." That's it in a nutshell! Again and again we have seized on a political idea emanating from the West and lived it through to the bitter end, to the point where it reaches its highest realization in its own terms and falls victim to its own internal weaknesses . . .' Entranced by the beauty of the idea he was expounding, Pavel had forgotten not only supper now, but even his article: 'You must agree that this was true of the Russian monarchy?' Someone nodded. 'And that the Bolsheviks were entirely successful in achieving the status of a world power? Well, now it is Russia's turn to take hold of the idea of democracy and to realize it within an ecological and moral framework! Just you wait a couple of generations,' said this man who, though he owed a fortune, had lived to see the death of an age of tyranny. 'You'll see, this will be a country of millionaires and millionairesses!

'How can I not be hopeful when everywhere around I see echoes of the movement that has been apparent in my own life? I went to technical college to learn how to become an electrician because I longed to understand the mystery of light. But when I discovered that there was nothing to it, no mystery, that you just had to put this bit together with that, I left and joined the philosophical faculty of the university. The more I studied, the clearer it became that philosophy without religion was a nonsense. I was drawn to the established Church and came up

364

against all kinds of anomalies and frailties. So I ended up with the Old Believers, the Church that did not substitute the meek Christ of old Russia for the Grand Inquisitor. All around us, I watch that happening now! People are drawn to religion but the established Church is not up to the challenge they put to it, so they come to us!'

A week later, I was on a plane from London, bound for America. A weary, middle-aged couple over the aisle from me in club class were accepting champagne from a plump, genial air hostess. 'Boy, do I need this!' They all laughed. The air hostess dropped a napkin. 'Dropsies today, lady!' said the man. 'Don't even *say* that, it may get worse!' The heavily made-up hostess was quick to respond. 'How long have you been over?' 'Twelve days, but it seems like a month!' 'I'd also like to give you two wonderful people today's dinner menu and a catalogue of duty-free goods. Just so we can take a little more money off of you!' 'You've come too late!' 'Did you spend that much?' 'We spent everything. I don't even have any small change left. I've licked that problem at last. Here's how: the last thing we bought we tipped out our pockets first and paid what was left by card!' 'Great idea!' The hostess sailed off brimming with pleasure to deploy her charms elsewhere and the couple, revived by this exchange, toasted each other playfully in champagne.

I listened with incredulity. So adjusted had I become to the principle of limitation upon which the Soviet economy was based that I was taken unawares by the assumption behind the conversation, the assumption of abundance. The couple had spent all their money, the man had said. But he did not really mean that. He meant that they had spent all that they could afford to spend just now. Wistfully I thought of the lifetime of debt to which Pavel was condemned.

The same assumption had infused the brief relationship between the tourists and the air hostess. They had actually been flirting. I was astonished that they had the energy for it. I found myself thinking of the blank faces I had met on Kalinin Prospect on the first day that I had arrived in Moscow. At that stage, I had not understood what it was that made Soviet people keep up their masks in public. It was no longer fear. Nor was it just that life was exhausting and that the best of oneself was something to be kept back for one's friends. In a world in which material pleasures were scarce, the gift of self, of friendship, was the ultimate gift, not to be lightly squandered. There was the charm of simplicity about a world in which the public and the private were so clearly divided. Here, in giving a top-spin of coquetry to an exchange about duty-free goods and lunch, the hostess had just been doing her job well. The couple had paid extra for their tickets and they were entitled to such treatment. It left everyone feeling good. Yet it all meant nothing.

I had gone to Russia to try to understand a strange culture. I came back experiencing my own as if for the first time. I was more alarmed than impressed. Abundance seemed in so many ways harder to cope with than scarcity. Surrounded by a superfluity of trivial choices, it was hard to keep one's bearings. How would my Soviet friends survive in this world of pleasant surfaces and hard underlying realities? I found myself fearing lest contact with the West should undermine the qualities in them that I had come to appreciate most.

The other side of the same question also kept returning to me. How might our culture be affected by contact with this other world? Having experienced the generosity of people who had nothing, I had arrived back thinking how little our prosperous society knew about giving. What chance was there that we would have the humility to learn from these people who lived in the wreckage of a dream that had failed?

366